THE WATKINS BOYS

August Courtauld
Martin Lindsay
Quintin Riley
John Rymill
Jimmy Scott
Freddy Spencer Chapman
Gino Watkins

For Julia & Robert—

with love

THE WATKINS BOYS

Simon Courtauld

MICHAEL RUSSELL

© Simon Courtauld 2010

The right of Simon Courtauld to be identified
as the author of this book has been asserted by him
in accordance with the Copyright, Designs
and Patents Act, 1988

First published in Great Britain 2010
by Michael Russell (Publishing) Ltd
Wilby Hall, Wilby, Norwich NR16 2JP

Page makeup in Sabon by Waveney Typesetters
Wymondham, Norfolk
Printed in Great Britain by the MPG Books Group,
Bodmin and King's Lynn

ISBN 978-0-85955-318-6

Contents

Acknowledgements

All members of the British Arctic Air Route Expedition (BAARE), 1930–31, died in the twentieth century. Gino Watkins died in 1932, but one person who knew him and the others lived until 2009. That was Mollie Butler (Lady Butler of Saffron Walden), who married my uncle, August Courtauld. At the age of 101, she still had clear memories of several members of the expedition and of her own trip to east Greenland in 1935.

I met four of the men who went with Gino, but only briefly and long before I had the idea of writing this book. In 1975, however, I did talk to Quintin Riley at some length about the expedition and recorded the conversation, which provided much useful information and anecdote. It made me realise that the innate modesty of the expedition members, the playing down of their achievements and of the hardships and dangers they faced, concealed a remarkable physical and mental toughness. None of them underwent any special Arctic training before the expedition; none of them had any form of communication when they were away from the base camp. How different they were from some of today's 'explorers' who make televised polar treks with all the most modern equipment, clothing, high-calorie foods and technology and then ring up a doctor at the first sign of frostbite.

I am very grateful to several people who gave freely of their time to talk about their fathers, who are the subject of this book: Christopher Courtauld and Julien Courtauld (sons of August Courtauld); Nick Spencer Chapman (son of Freddy Spencer Chapman); Noel Owen (daughter of Quintin Riley); Jacynth Fitzalan Howard (daughter of Martin Lindsay); Peter Rymill (son of John Rymill); Jeremy Scott (son of Jimmy Scott). I also wish to thank Jeremy Scott, whose mother was Gino's sister, and Anne Edwardes-Jones (daughter-in-law of Gino's fiancée, Margy Graham) for their insights into the Watkins family.

My thanks are also due to Paul Caffyn, of the Kiwi Association of Sea Kayakers, who has paddled down the south-east coast of Greenland

and sent me his photographs of the BAARE base site and of the Watkins memorial cross at Lake Fjord; to the Scott Polar Research Institute and the Royal Geographical Society for their assistance in tracing letters and other documents; and to Jennie who, when I was in need of encouragement and constructive criticism, was always there to provide it.

The indigenous Greenland people were known as Eskimos in the 1930s, and that is how I refer to them. I have used the term Inuit, which is now more generally acceptable, when writing of them in more recent times. Where appropriate I have added in brackets in the index the modern versions of place names in use in 1930.

Throughout the book I have referred to Gino Watkins by his first name, and to the others by their surnames. This is principally because several of them called one another by surname on the expedition, while they all addressed their leader as 'Gino'.

A Summary of the Expeditions

This book looks at seven individuals and their relationships with one another when brought together in a context of precarious adventure. It may be helpful to have to hand a concise record of how it worked out.

THE PLANS

First expedition (July 1930 to October 1931): to facilitate a transatlantic air route over Greenland; record the weather, at the coast and up on the ice cap, over a twelve-month period, establish an ice-cap station and survey the east coast and mountain ranges.

Second expedition (July 1932 to September 1933): to continue survey and meteorological work on the east coast 100 miles north of Angmagssalik.

THE PEOPLE
(* involved in both expeditions)

Gino Watkins (expedition leader)*
August Courtauld
Martin Lindsay
Quintin Riley*
John Rymill*
Jimmy Scott
Freddy Spencer Chapman*

Surgeon-Lieutenant Ted Bingham (doctor)
Flight-Lieutenant Iliffe Cozens (second
pilot and aerial photographer)
Flight-Lieutenant Narbrough 'Jimmy' D'Aeth (pilot)
Wilfred Hampton (aircraft engineer)
Captain Percy Lemon (wireless operator)
Arthur Stephenson (chief surveyor)
Lawrence Wager (geologist and mountaineer)

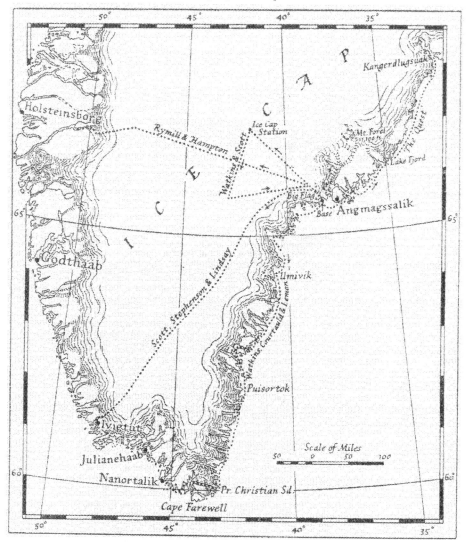

Greenland, showing the major journeys of the expedition

1930

Expedition arrives at east coast of Greenland last week of July. Coastal base established. In mid-August, Chapman, Courtauld, Stephenson and Wager sail up coast for survey work as far north as Kangerdlugsuak.

Watkins and D'Aeth, making flights inland in a Gypsy Moth, spot hitherto unknown mountain range with Greenland's highest mountain.

First journey into the interior by Scott, Rymill, Lindsay, Riley and Bingham to set up ice-cap station. Lindsay and Riley left at station at end of August, relieved five weeks later by Bingham and D'Aeth, who are escorted to the station by Chapman and Rymill.

Watkins and Scott arrive at ice-cap station at same time as Chapman and Rymill, then start a southerly journey over the ice cap, returning to base mid-November.

Chapman, having got back to base in mid-October, sets off again for ice-cap station less than two weeks later, accompanied by Courtauld, Hampton, Lemon, Stephenson and Wager. Because of dreadful weather and painfully slow progress on the ice cap, Hampton, Lemon and Stephenson sent back to base after two weeks. The wireless which Lemon was to install at the ice-cap station is dumped.

Chapman, Courtauld and Wager finally reach ice-cap station at beginning of December, but have insufficient rations to leave two men there safely for the rest of the winter (relief could not be expected at least until March). Against the advice of his companions Courtauld volunteers to stay there on his own. Chapman reluctantly agrees and leaves for base on 6 December with Bingham, D'Aeth and Wager.

1931

Relief party led by Scott, with Lindsay and Riley, leaves base for ice-cap station in first week of March but is hampered by blizzards and severe cold. They fail to find Courtauld – ice-cap station now buried by snow – and return to base six weeks after originally setting out.

Watkins leaves base with Chapman and Rymill three days later (21 April). They find ice-cap station and dig out Courtauld (seemingly none the worse) on 5 May.

Three more journeys made during the summer, two across ice cap to west coast (Scott, Lindsay and Stephenson to Ivigtut, Rymill and Hampton to Holsteinsborg) and one by open boat (Watkins, Courtauld and Lemon) down south-east coast, through Prince Christian Sound, then up south-west coast to Julianehaab.

The following summer Watkins takes Rymill, Riley and Chapman back to Greenland to continue survey and meteorological work on east coast.

Ten days after arriving at their new base at Lake Fjord, Watkins disappears, presumed drowned: his kayak is found but his body is never recovered. The others, under Rymill's leadership, stay on for a further year 'sledging on the pack ice, hunting with Eskimos for seals and bears, taking perilous boat journeys to survey the coast, keeping up weather observations'.

Introduction

By almost all accounts the story of Greenland begins with Erik the
Red. A red-haired Norseman who, according to his Saga, had killed
several people (one of them his neighbour in an argument over a
shovel), Erik fled from Iceland in the late tenth century and reached the
south-west coast of a country which he decided to call Greenland.
There were trees and pasture, and he thought that by giving the place
such a name he would encourage others to follow him from the Land of
Ice. (His son Leif was almost certainly the first European to reach
North America, landing in Newfoundland or Nova Scotia 500 years
before Columbus's voyage to the New World.) There had been a few
earlier attempts by Norsemen to colonise Greenland before Erik, but he
was the first permanent settler. About four centuries before him, St
Brendan and other intrepid Irish monks had been sailing or drifting in
these seas in their sturdy coracles, but there is no evidence that they
came to Greenland's shore.

The first Bishop of Greenland, an Icelander, was appointed in 1112,
and the Norse settlement increased and multiplied with the help of the
indigenous Eskimos; but by the fifteenth century the population was
starting to dwindle. Due in part to climate change (500 years ago it was
cooling, not warming), to disease and to increasing hostility from the
Eskimos, the Norse Greenlander communities went into terminal
decline. Fishermen from Bristol and Hull were also responsible, coming
ashore to force any able-bodied men (and often children) into what was
in effect slavery – working either in English boats off the Newfoundland cod banks or in the markets of Europe. By 1500 they were all
gone, their homesteads abandoned or burned.

A Yorkshire mariner, Martin Frobisher, sighted the west Greenland
coast while searching for the North-West Passage in 1576. He landed
a couple of years later, found the natives to be unfriendly, shot a
number of them and named the place West England. John Davis, who
gave his name to the strait between Greenland and Baffin Island, was

there a few years later and called it 'the Land of Desolation'. So desolate was it that Edward Pellham, who had himself been stranded on Spitzbergen (now Svalbard) in the seventeenth century for most of a year, recounted that a group of English malefactors who had been condemned to death were offered a pardon if they would spend a year in the Arctic as crew of a whaling ship. Having reached the inhospitable coast of Greenland, they decided they would rather be taken back to England to face execution.

The landings and settlements in Greenland were all in the southwest; eastern Greenland, beset by coastal pack ice for most of the year, was a *terra nullius*. (Part of it was claimed as such by Norway as recently as 1931. The International Court of Justice rejected the claim, and Denmark continued its sovereignty over the country, granting internal autonomy to Greenland in 1979.) Nineteenth-century explorers found musk oxen grazing summer pasture in parts of north-east Greenland; but south of Scoresby Sound (named after a whaling captain from Whitby), as far as the southern tip of Greenland, the mountains and glaciers fall sheer from the ice cap to the often frozen sea, with occasional wild flowers and berries providing the only summer vegetation. The first European face seen by the Eskimos of this glacial south-east coast was a Swedish baron's, Adolf Nordenskjöld, who came ashore in 1883, five years before Fridtjof Nansen crossed the Greenland ice cap from the east to the west coast. James Wordie, who had been south with Shackleton on the *Endurance* expedition in 1914–16, took two expeditions in the 1920s to the east Greenland coast, landing some 300 miles north of Scoresby Sound. But Gino Watkins, leading the British Arctic Air Route Expedition, was the first Englishman to take a party to that most inhospitable stretch of the coast just south of the Arctic Circle.

After three days of nudging slowly through the closely packed ice floes as the ship neared the rocky shore, landfall was made at Angmagssalik in the last week of July 1930. It was the only settlement on the east coast with a Danish presence, apart from Scoresby Sound which had been recently colonised by taking Eskimo families from the Angmagssalik district. As their ship, the *Quest*, which had taken Shackleton to the Antarctic on his last voyage, steamed into the fjord, Gino and his companions gazed in wonder at the beauty of this natural harbour enclosed by mountains which, in the limpid early-morning light, were reflected in the calm ice-scattered waters of the bay. The people of Angmagssalik, numbering no more than a hundred, came from their painted wooden shacks roofed with corrugated iron, or their peat and stone houses, climbed into their kayaks and umiaks* and paddled out to greet these alien visitors. In addition to the Eskimos, Angmagssalik in 1930 had a Danish wireless operator, an administrator who also acted as storekeeper and a missionary who looked after the Protestant church standing among the little houses on the slope of the hill overlooking the harbour. A Danish government ship called with supplies once a year.

Today the annual supply ship from Copenhagen reaches Ammassalik (as it is now called, when it is not called Tasiilaq) about three weeks earlier than it used to. The pack ice now begins to break up and disperse in June, due apparently to a rise in water temperature or to what is widely referred to as global warming. The Arctic ice is thinning, in winter as well as summer, to such an extent that the North-West Passage has recently become navigable. There is evidence, too, to suggest that the melting permafrost is releasing vast amounts of methane gas which may result in increasing global temperatures. This is all very alarming, but one should also consider that it may be a cyclical phenomenon rather than an irreversible trend for which man is responsible. Polar ice has been increasing and receding for thousands of years. It is worth recording that at the turn of the twentieth century the east Greenland coast was never free of ice in summer. Then, for about twenty years until 1933 there was virtually no pack ice off the coast between August and November. In 1934 and subsequent years the pack ice returned to block the Angmagssalik fjord in late summer, sometimes at the beginning of September.

The Greenland ice cap, covering more than 80 per cent of the land mass of what is described as the largest island in the world that is not a continent, may be up to 10,000 feet thick. It is surrounded by a coastal ring of mountains which hold the ice back. But the melting ice, and the pressure of its weight, force it through the valleys between the mountains in the form of glaciers which, when they reach the coast, may calve and send huge floating icebergs into the sea. Much of the ice also

---

* Umiaks are larger boats traditionally rowed by women and used to move a family to new hunting grounds.

comes from close to the North Pole and is borne south in the East Greenland current.

As the daily flight from Iceland's airport at Reykjavik approaches the east Greenland coastal airstrip at Kulusuk, a scattered array of broken white plates becomes visible on the blue water below. Among these ice floes a giant L-shaped block of ice with vertical walls can be seen; my son and I gasp in wonder at the sight. The black-and-white mountain coastline now appears out of the haze and beyond it the beginnings of the featureless ice plateau where the Eskimos would never venture, believing it to be a place of evil spirits.

Arriving at Ammassalik after a ten-minute helicopter flight over rocks and fjords still covered with ice floes in mid-June, the claims of some scientists that the Arctic will be ice-free in summer by 2015 seemed highly improbable. We spotted the old church, now a museum and one of very few buildings still standing eighty years after the Watkins expedition. In 1930 there were about 900 people living along the 3,000 miles of the east coast, from a total Greenland population of 17,000. Today the proportion is similar, at about 5 per cent: 3,000 inhabitants of east Greenland out of a total of 58,000. Ammassalik's population has gone from 100 in 1930 to 1,800 today, but it is still an isolated settlement, with access from the sea blocked by ice for more than half the year and the one helicopter often grounded by bad weather. A few vehicles are driven on the road and tracks round Ammassalik, but there is nowhere else for them to go. The little houses, mostly built of wood these days and dotted around the hill overlooking the bay, are painted in the colours – blue, green and red – often used on the façades of town houses in northern Scandinavia.

One old peat and stone house remains, as a museum piece. The seal gut used for making the windows has been replaced by polythene, and wooden beams now shore up the original roof. But the layout of the house clearly shows the tiny compartments in which each family huddled together, the communal cooking pot and stove fuelled by blubber, the walls covered with sealskins and the raised benches provided for guests. Until the 1970s Inuit families would take their kayaks and umiaks up or down the coast, where the hunting was better, and they might be away for a month or more. Old hut sites can be found in many fjords along the coast, but they were all abandoned years ago; the nomadic life is over.

The sealskin kayak is also a thing of the past. Modern Inuit hunters – there are few left in Ammassalik, though hunting is still a way of life in the five outlying settlements – use outboard motor boats and rifles. (When a seal is shot, its skin is sent for tanning to south-west Greenland, though the market is limited in these politically correct times.) A kayak, with a harpoon as well as a rifle, may be used against narwhal whales, but it is made of plastic or fibreglass these days and is not capable of being rolled. This skill, which the Eskimos passed on to the Watkins boys, and at which Gino excelled, is now redundant. The kayaks which are seen today along the coast are more likely to belong to adventurous Europeans or Australasians. When one of the latter was passed in his kayak in 2007 by an Inuit family in a motor-boat, he saw the father hold up his young son and point out the white man in his strange craft.

Of the quadrupeds, only the polar bear is seen and shot in this part of Greenland. Despite gloomy predictions that polar bears are now an endangered species due to global warming and the thinning of the ice, licences are issued for the killing of around thirty animals every year in the Ammassalik district. There is very little commercial fishing on the east coast: the one fish processing plant is ice-bound for much of the year, and salmon rivers are mostly inaccessible. But fishing helps to sustain the Inuit family: most houses have rows of cod and capelin* drying on lines attached to the roofs, while the fish heads and guts are fed to the dogs. Though motorised skidoos have become popular, Greenland huskies are still generally used for sledging in winter; and the howling of a hungry pack is a familiar daily noise. There is a strict ban on the importing of dogs, so the strain has remained pure.

Though ice-bound for many months and frequently cut off by winter storms, Ammassalik is not out of touch with the twenty-first century. There is a ski lift, street lighting, access to the internet, a bookshop, tourist office and a couple of hotels. Inuit children play on trampolines, and the popular football pitch is still in use after midnight in summer. The small outlying settlements are provided with electricity generators and about 20 per cent of their population have a telephone. They also have a church, community hall, school, nursing station, service house

* Capelin is a slim fish about six inches long, in the local Inuit language known as *ammassat*, which has given the settlement its name.

(with washing facilities, kitchen and a room where sledges are built or repaired and carvings are made, often from whale or walrus tusks), fuel depot, post office and shop. While the people of these tiny village communities still eat seal meat, also eider ducks and fish, as their staple diet, they have the opportunity to buy – one assumes there must be a demand – such foods as pot noodles, packet cereals, soya milk and tins of pineapple chunks. Hunting rifles and ammunition can be bought in the same shop, also flat-screen televisions and electric irons. A supply ship reaches these settlements with provisions and supplies at the end of June – to much rejoicing. The inhabitants will not have seen the ship since the previous October; for eight months they will have been cut off, except for the one helicopter, based at Kulusuk, which can land in an emergency.

How the lives and lifestyles of the Inuit have changed in little more than a generation. Before the Second World War Denmark did its best to protect the indigenous people from outside influences. (Before Gino's expedition set out, he had to agree to indemnify the Danish government against the possibility of any births resulting from their stay in Greenland, and all fourteen members of the party had to submit to an examination for venereal disease when they landed.) A paternalistic policy was pursued of limiting not only foreign visitors but imports and exports. Then war came, the United States assumed the defence of Greenland in 1941 and the following year built a runway close to Ammassalik.

Gino's two Greenland expeditions had identified two large lakes as suitable for landing commercial aircraft on their route to and from North America, but nothing came of it. By the time transatlantic air routes had become a reality, aviation technology had developed to the point that bases were no longer necessary on either the east or west Greenland coasts. The Arctic air route which Gino plotted, however – from London via Iceland, Greenland, Baffin Island, Edmonton to Vancouver – was the one adopted by commercial airlines flying to the Pacific coast. The first solo flight across Greenland was made by a British aviator, John Grierson, in 1933 on his way to Ottawa. Other small planes were crossing the ice cap in the 1930s, but it was not until the war that large numbers of aircraft, many of them Hudson bombers, were being flown over Greenland by RAF Ferry Command, on their way from North America to Britain. Several crashed on the ice cap, others made emergency landings at the airstrip on the east coast. Here the US servicemen who manned the base introduced the locals to imported goods, and thereafter it would only be a matter of time before the westernising of the Inuit was under way and the east coast opened up to civilian flights.

The US runway near Ammassalik was abandoned in 1951; six years later a radar base and airstrip were constructed at Kulusuk. Commercial flights from Iceland and west Greenland began in the 1960s, and Ammassalik underwent a process of modernisation – with an increased Danish presence, more houses built, and medical, social and educational services provided. By 1970 umiaks, the traditional Inuit boats for transporting families, had ceased to be used, people stayed in their village settlements and were no longer dependent on seal hunting for their livelihoods.

Cui bono? It has all been a great cultural shock for the Inuit, who are likely these days to wear jeans and forage caps and buy packs of Red Bull. They are a resilient and enterprising people who have survived for centuries in this hostile climate. And while their lives are much changed and they are no longer required to be self-sufficient, they have mostly retained their open and straightforward character. But what has been called their 'compulsory civilisation' over the past fifty years has brought alcoholism, sexually transmitted and other diseases, crimes of violence, suicides. Unemployment is evident in Ammassalik today, as is the proliferation of litter and graffiti. The mostly imported food eaten by the Inuit, with high levels of sugar and starch, led twenty years ago to a major dental health problem, with many young people becoming almost toothless.

To the foreign visitor the prices of food in the shops are prohibitive. The Inuit could not possibly afford to pay them without the subsidy they receive by way of family allowances and welfare benefits. The annual grant to Greenland from Denmark is equivalent to almost £7,000 per head of the population. Greenland was granted home rule in 1979 and opted out of the European Economic Community in 1985; but it still remains under the sovereignty of Denmark. Greenland took another step towards complete independence in 2009, when Denmark for the first time recognised Greenlanders as a separate people with their own language, and acknowledged their right to benefit from the proceeds of future gas, oil and mineral exploration off the coast. If the polar ice continues to melt, there may be large reserves waiting to be discovered and exploited. Greenland and Denmark would share the proceeds equally and Denmark's 50 per cent would be deducted from its annual grant to Greenland. Financial independence from the mother country may yet be some years away.

Eighty years ago, such possibilities would not have been in the minds of Gino and his companions during their twelve months on the east coast. They did provide some of the data – the meteorological readings, the surveys of coast and mountain ranges – which would lead indirectly to the modernising of east Greenland and the 'civilising' of the Inuit population in the second half of the twentieth century. However, they went to the Arctic not as pioneering scientists, much less as missionaries, but as enthusiastic young amateurs imbued with the spirit of adventure. They made a contribution to knowledge – of the topography of east Greenland and of the potential for transatlantic air travel – and to future development. But they left no enduring marks of their time in Greenland, except for a few rusty relics at the site of the base camp which was built thirty miles west of Ammassalik.

Here, in summer, it is possible to identify on a flat promontory a rectangle of low rocks marking the outside walls of the expedition's sizeable hut. A few empty cartridge cases, pieces of coal and broken glass still remain, and in 2007 two New Zealanders found part of the hut's chimney flue. The site was chosen for its proximity to the ice cap, a good anchorage for the *Quest* to unload equipment and building materials, and a bay for flying the two seaplanes. At the end of July it seemed an idyllic spot. But in the darkness of winter, when they were cut off from the sea by an impenetrable armour of ice, when the wind blew at more than 100 mph and they had to haul sledges up over glaciers and crevasses to the bleakness of the seemingly limitless ice cap, this extraordinary adventure would test the mettle of Gino Watkins and his boys.

I
Augustine Courtauld (1904–59)

The Norwegian Fridtjof Nansen, probably the greatest polar explorer of all, landed on the eastern seaboard of Greenland in 1888 with five companions and skied across the ice cap to the west coast. Later he made his memorable voyage in the *Fram* (the ship which took Amundsen to the Antarctic in 1910) to reach farthest north. His attempt to ski as far as the North Pole was unsuccessful, but he was able to establish beyond doubt that the Pole was an ice-covered sea. He and his companion were entirely alone for more than a year.

Exploring was by no means his whole life: when he made the first-ever crossing of Greenland he had just received his doctorate for research into the structure of brain cells. And he was not only a scientist but a diplomat and humanitarian. In his subsequent career he was Norway's ambassador to London during the reign of Edward VII, and was awarded the Nobel Peace Prize for organising the repatriation of prisoners and the relief of famine on behalf of the League of Nations after the end of the First World War.

It was forty years after Nansen's Greenland crossing that a young Cambridge undergraduate, Gino Watkins, was learning the art of sledging with dogs in Labrador and thinking about a commercial air route over Iceland, Greenland and Canada to the Pacific coast of north America. In those early years of flying, very little thought had been given to the idea of regular flights across the Atlantic. The Great Circle route had two considerable advantages: a shorter distance and the relative safety of few long sea crossings. But hardly anything was known about the ice-covered mass of Greenland, the configuration of the east coast and the mountain ranges which aircraft would have to fly over. Nor had anyone recorded the weather conditions on the ice cap at different times of year. Gino decided to take an expedition there, stay for a year and maintain a weather station throughout that time in the middle of the Greenland ice cap.

He put his plans to the Royal Geographical Society which approved them and gave a small amount of financial support; but the bulk of the money required to fund the expedition, estimated at about £12,000 (£550,000 today), would have to come from private sources. It was now the summer of 1929 and the New York stock market was about to crash. However, the economic crisis and the world depression which followed seemed to have little effect on the fortunes of one man, who was persuaded without too much difficulty to sponsor this youthful enterprise.

Stephen Courtauld was a modest, quietly laconic man in his mid-forties who would become something of a modern Maecenas. The youngest brother of Sam, who founded the Courtauld Institute of Art, Stephen used his inherited wealth for a number of philanthropic purposes – from the building of an Art Deco house adjoining the medieval Great Hall of Eltham Palace in south London to the endowment of an art gallery and a multi-racial theatre in Southern Rhodesia. Stephen enjoyed giving his patronage to developing talent: at Eltham Palace he would employ the young architectural firm of Seely and Paget, and he liked the idea of an Arctic adventure led by a 23-year-old from his old university. He was himself an enthusiastic mountaineer – he made the first ascent of a difficult face of Mont Blanc – and when he learnt that his young cousin August Courtauld would be joining the expedition, his support was assured. He stumped up nearly all the money for which Gino had budgeted; he was made chairman of the committee of what was now called the British Arctic Air Route Expedition, and August was appointed treasurer, to look after the family funds.

The three Services each lent two men, and Gino chose seven others. Six of them, like him, had just come down from Cambridge; the seventh was an Australian, John Rymill, who had been working at the RGS. The average age of the party was twenty-five, and only three of the fourteen – Gino, J. M. (Jimmy) Scott and Courtauld – had previous Arctic experience. In addition to all the equipment and the provisions which were needed (and in many cases supplied free by various companies), Gino took two De Havilland Gipsy Moth aeroplanes for aerial survey and photography. The vessel which would take them to Greenland was a wooden Norwegian sealing ship, renamed the *Quest*, which had been to the Antarctic with Shackleton on his last expedition (he died on board). She had also taken part in the search for Umberto Nobile and his airship off Spitzbergen in 1928, when Amundsen was killed in his seaplane.

The *Quest* had already had an interesting history, therefore, when she left St Katherine's Dock in London, flying the expedition flag which depicted a polar bear with wings, and steamed down the Thames on 6 July 1930. August Courtauld leant over the side and shouted to the cheering crowd of wellwishers: 'If anyone wants a car there's one over there – help yourself!' It was an old banger, but it worked and he had left the keys in it. Stephen Courtauld had given a farewell party at the dockside on the previous evening: it was attended by Lord Thomson, Secretary of State for Air, and Sir Sefton Brancker, Director of Civil Aviation (both of whom died three months later in the R101 airship disaster), and George Robey entertained the guests. The following day Stephen Courtauld was at Gravesend to meet the *Quest* and give the Watkins boys a last lunch on board his motor yacht *Virginia*.*

The *Quest* followed the proposed air route, via the Faroe Islands and Iceland, then through the pack ice to the east coast of Greenland at Angmagssalik, which at the time had a settled population of just over a hundred people, of whom three were Danish. Eskimo men and women, paddling their kayaks and umiaks alongside, greeted the ship's arrival with noisy enthusiasm, and the welcome party which followed was not dissimilar to John Davis's experience when he had arrived there more than three centuries before Gino.

A contemporary account records that Davis 'caused our Musicians to play, ourselves dancing and making many signes of friendship'. One Eskimo beat his breast repeatedly and pointed to the sun, and so the Englishmen copied him. In 1930 the music was provided by a wind-up gramophone which Gino had brought. A reasonably flat piece of the shore was chosen, the excited Eskimo girls in their ornamented red sealskin boots and seal-fur trousers started dancing a frenetic double time to the music of Irving Berlin and Jerome Kern, and the young explorers did their best to keep up. Then the songs of Tin Pan Alley –

---

* *Virginia* was named after Stephen Courtauld's wife, an Italian divorcee whom he had married in the free state of Fiume (now Rijeka in Croatia) in 1923. She had a snake tattooed on her leg which curled upwards at least as far as her knee. No one dared ask the chairman of the expedition committee how much further it went.

'Ain't She Sweet?'and 'Happy Days Are Here Again' – rang out across the icy water, the white men tried to teach the natives the Charleston, and the party came to an end with much laughter and good humour. A relationship with the locals had been successfully initiated. With some of the girls it would get much closer as time went on.

The men, wrote Freddy Spencer Chapman, one of the expedition's surveyors, were 'of small stature with copper-coloured faces, dark lank hair, high cheekbones and amazingly dirty teeth. They seemed to be extremely friendly, and inordinately fond of tobacco. It rather took my breath away to see them knock the hot ashes out of their pipes into their mouths, and then chew them with evident gusto.' The young men did not adopt that particular local practice, but they did learn from the Eskimos how to survive in this alien environment – the art of kayaking, the shooting of seals and the cooking of their choicest parts. The Eskimos learnt, as far as they were able to imitate it, the form of greeting used by their new guests when they met. In this age of formality it was not 'Hi' or 'Hello' but 'How do you do?' which were the first words an Eskimo heard as Courtauld or Gino or any of the others introduced themselves. In the local language of the east coast the words came to be rendered as '*adudadu*', used as a collective noun to refer to their courteous British visitors. Fifty years later, young British explorers landing at Angmagssalik were still being called *adudadu*.

The programme for the next twelve months was started as soon as a suitable base had been found, about thirty miles west of Angmagssalik, and a wooden house erected. Gino planned a number of inland sledge journeys, the setting up of a weather station in the middle of the Greenland ice cap, to be manned throughout the year, and the mapping of the coast for several hundred miles north and south of their base. The two Gipsy Moths would support their work, providing aerial photographs, dropping supplies to the ice-cap station and landing there if possible. During the winter the intention was to fly both aeroplanes along the air route as far as Winnipeg and back.

Almost all the photographic work was successfully completed, but the Moths were never able to find the ice-cap station and the planned flights to Canada had to be abandoned. The problem was the winter weather: the Meteorological Office in London had failed to warn of the large number of gales, with wind speeds of more than 100 mph, which roared down from the ice cap. (The forecast, from the meteorological station at Angmagssalik, was for about one gale a month.) Not only was flying impossible in these conditions, but both Moths were badly damaged on the ground during the winter months.

It was Gino's bad luck that the place he chose for their base had to endure the worst of these very local winter storms. Thirty miles away at Angmagssalik there were fewer gales recorded and of lesser force. Thus the meteorological observations so conscientiously taken every day at the base were of limited value. The records of weather and wind speeds on the ice cap, 130 miles inland and at a height of 8,500 feet, were of greater importance for a future air route, but they were made over a period of little more than six months. However, the BAARE did identify two potential air bases – at Angmagssalik and in a fjord, known as Lake Fjord, a hundred miles farther north – where conditions should be suitable for landings. In Lake Fjord the wind strength in winter never exceeded 40 mph.

There was plenty of meteorological activity in Greenland during the first years of the 1930s, resulting in a broader and more comprehensive picture of Arctic weather. The University of Michigan sent a series of expeditions to Greenland around this time, with their base on the west coast and weather stations inland. During the same year that the Watkins boys were travelling on the ice cap, a German expedition, scientifically more productive and technologically more advanced than the BAARE, established a winter weather station also in the middle of Greenland but farther north, measuring not only wind speeds but ice thickness. (Its leader, a fifty-year-old Professor Alfred Wegener, died on his way back to the coast.) The year after Gino's expedition ended, 1932, was declared the Second International Polar Year, during which there were almost 100 manned meteorological stations in the Arctic.

It was to Gino's credit that he was in the forefront of those who recognised the importance of meteorological observation in Greenland. But he was not as scientifically motivated. For him, and for most of his boys, the expedition was an adventure, something to test them physically and mentally, a few months of hardship but also of strenuous fun.

For all that, this was hardly a venture lightly undertaken. It was the biggest British polar expedition since Scott and Shackleton. If the weather readings brought back by the BAARE provided little more than confirmation of evidence being gathered elsewhere in Greenland at the same time, the expedition did achieve a notable, indeed unique, success in its detailed survey of the east coast and the discovery of a hitherto unknown range of mountains which turned out to be the highest in Greenland. Mount Forel, at 11,000 feet, was thought to be the highest, and three members of the expedition climbed to within 200 feet of the summit in the spring of 1931. But the previous summer, while surveying by air inland from Kangerdlugsuak, Gino had seen a mountain range whose existence had never before been suspected. He described it as of Himalayan grandeur and believed it might rise to over 15,000 feet. In fact the highest mountain in the range (now called the Watkins Mountains) was found to be 12,250 feet, and the first ascent of it was made by August Courtauld in 1935. With the era of flights over Greenland already beginning, the discovery was of real importance. Nansen was founder and first president of an international society for the exploration of the Arctic by air; he died in 1930 as he was planning a flight in the airship *Graf Zeppelin*. And Charles Lindbergh was not the only one to fly across Greenland two years later in a single-engine, fixed-wing aircraft.

Courtauld was the one member of the expedition to take part in the whole coastal survey – north to Kangerdlugsuak (where a glacier and a fjord were later named after him) and, the following summer, south of Angmagssalik by boat as far as Cape Farewell (Kap Farvel) at the southern tip of Greenland. His was an important contribution to an expedition which, if it had continued with its various journeys and the relief of the ice-cap station at planned intervals throughout the year, would have come home to an RGS lecture, an expedition book and a couple of articles in *The Times*. But the expedition became big news as a result of something else which Courtauld did. He volunteered to stay at the ice-cap station in midwinter, alone and without radio communication, and was not rescued until five months later, by which time many thought he must be dead.

Among the members of the expedition, Courtauld was unique in three respects: he had been to Greenland before, he was engaged to be married, and he came from a wealthy family. No one would accuse him of conspicuous extravagance, but he didn't need to work – in fact he only ever had one paid job, with a City stockbroking firm, which lasted barely a year. He declined to follow his father into the family textile business; that was left to his younger brother, who was sent to work after leaving school and without benefit of university education.* Courtauld was indulged by his parents: he went to Trinity College, Cambridge and read engineering, he bought his first yacht, and by the time he came down he had decided that his foreseeable future would be in the Arctic.

The man who inspired him was James Wordie, a fellow of St John's College and a veteran of Shackleton's *Endurance* expedition who now led groups of young would-be explorers to the Arctic. Courtauld went twice with him to Greenland – to learn how to survey a stretch of the east coastline, and to climb one of the highest mountains, Petermann Peak, which had then been identified. (Among the climbing party with Courtauld was Vivian Fuchs.) After two expeditions, and living with him at close quarters, Wordie was well qualified to assess Courtauld's character. He found him to be a delightful companion, equable, introspective, mentally tough without being ambitious. He was also absentminded, stubborn and perverse – qualities which would acquire particular significance on the ice cap in the winter of 1930–31. It was his natural rebelliousness at school (Charterhouse, where he shared an intense dislike of authority with a contemporary called Orde Wingate) which helped form his attitudes to those who presumed to know better than he. Wordie used to say that if you wanted to get Courtauld to do something, your best chance was to ask him not to do it.

Between his two trips to Greenland, Courtauld went on a camel trek in the Sahara with two brothers, Francis and Peter Rodd (who later married Nancy Mitford); and he started going out with Mollie Montgomerie. They had met as children in Essex; on one of their first dates they went to hear *Die Meistersinger* at Covent Garden. She introduced him to Chopin and Bach, also the duets from *The Beggar's Opera* which they sang together, though only to one another – and he took her sailing in his yacht. She was his first girl friend, and he never had another. At the third time of asking, towards the end of 1929, Mollie agreed to marry him.†

---

* My father Peter (1910–89), who became deputy chairman of Courtaulds Ltd.

† She had her own family link with Greenland, through her sister who married the stepson of Ejnar Mikkelsen, a Danish polar explorer who spent much of his life in east Greenland.

Although they were at Cambridge at the same time, and both were protégés of Wordie, Courtauld and Gino did not meet until a year before the expedition was launched. They had several things in common, apart from a longing to go back to the Arctic. Both had disliked organised games and were contemptuous of authority at school. Both had applied to join the Navy and been turned down. But whereas Gino's idea of relaxation was to go to parties and dance, Courtauld cared nothing for the social scenes in Cambridge and London and felt awkward in female company. Gino, sharply dressed and with his hair always carefully parted and smoothly brushed, was strikingly good-looking. He appealed to young women; and he enjoyed sex. To Courtauld outward appearance was irrelevant, and sex non-existent. While at Cambridge, 'I had no use for girls and thought them a nuisance. I never really saw one at close quarters until I became engaged.' He would rather be walking up grouse in Scotland, wildfowling on the Essex marshes, or sailing his yacht.

Courtauld liked and admired Gino, but found him a bit disconcertingly 'keen'. In the psychology of the public school amateur, to be seen to be trying too hard was unacceptable. Success was, of course, applauded but should be achieved through affected indolence rather than conspicuous effort. When he was not partying, Gino was serious, determined, ambitious, and possessed of an iron will – qualities which were less evident in Courtauld and which he may have considered to be not quite those of a gentleman. However, he had no doubt that Gino was a born leader whom he would happily follow to Greenland for a year. And he may even have become infected with some of Gino's ambition, having told Mollie he wanted 'the chance of doing something really big'.

Courtauld gave Gino to understand that his father might be persuaded to help fund the expedition. A meeting was arranged but, to Courtauld's disgust, nothing came of it. It was his cousin Stephen who stepped in and provided most of the finance, though Courtauld himself chartered the *Quest*. Two months before he left for Greenland, he and Mollie announced their engagement, and a few days before the expedition sailed, they laid the clues together for a treasure hunt which took place in old sports cars round central London. As the *Quest* headed north to the Faroe Islands, Mollie did not need reminding – though there were plenty to commiserate with her – that she would have a long and anxious wait before her wedding.

Courtauld's first, late-summer surveying journey up Greenland's east coast was arduous but for the most part enjoyable. He and three companions did much of their mapping from a small boat, returning to the *Quest* at weekly intervals. Instruments and other equipment were lost overboard, they were constantly at risk from calving glaciers and polar bears, but food was plentiful. On Courtauld's twenty-sixth birthday the dinner to celebrate it consisted of bear's tongue soup, sea trout, seal's kidneys and stewed crowberries.

Back at base, he became somewhat disenchanted with the expedition, thinking that the very idea of having a base was misconceived. 'One should travel on and always on, never coming back to the same point.' He expressed his feelings in a letter to Mollie, characterising himself as 'lazy, selfish, crabbed. Likes annoying other people and is most unpopular member of the expedition.' There was very little truth in that self-assessment, but it indicated his mood at the time. He longed to get going again, to travel inland on to the ice cap and, as he wrote to Mollie, 'If I get the chance to do anything worthwhile it will be for you.'

That chance came in the last week of October, when Courtauld set forth, with Freddy Spencer Chapman and four others, to cover the 130 miles to the central weather station in order to relieve the two men who had already been there for almost a month. This journey is recounted in the chapter on Chapman – the appalling weather, reducing their progress to fifteen miles in the first fifteen days, and the extraordinary chance encounter with Gino and Jimmy Scott. Courtauld recorded some of their experiences:

> Towards evening the wind increased in violence and as darkness fell the tent was thundering and shaking as if it would be torn in pieces at any moment. Had to shout to make Hampton hear, although he was only a foot away.... Sleeping bags wet. We slept in our clothes and prayed that the tent would stay up.... Inside of tent covered with hoar frost which drops on to us.... Sledges, dogs and traces were in horrible mess after the gale.

It was the day after the meeting with Gino and Scott that Chapman decided to send three men back to base and continue with Courtauld and Lawrence Wager, a geologist, who would man the ice-cap station

during the winter. On the same day Courtauld volunteered to stay at
the ice-cap station alone. It was becoming clear to all of them that there
might not be enough rations to leave two people there for what would
probably be a long winter. The journey was taking much more time
than anticipated and, in view of the severity of the weather which might
continue until March, it might be impossible for a relief party to reach
the station until then. The possibility that one of the Gypsy Moths
could resupply the station during the winter was too remote to be
seriously considered. The only realistic option, other than closing the
place down, was to leave one man there on his own.

Chapman was reluctant to take the decision; Wager thought it a
bad idea to leave one man there; so did the two men who had been at
the ice-cap station for nine weeks when they were finally relieved. One
was a doctor who gave 'a very decided opinion against it'. But they
did not know, as Wordie could have told them, that if you advised
Courtauld not to do something, it would make him the more determined to do it.

If the station were to be abandoned, the expedition would have
failed in one of its principal objectives – to record the weather conditions in the middle of Greenland throughout the winter. By staying
there himself, Courtauld saw his opportunity to do something worthwhile for the BAARE – and for Mollie, as he had put it in his letter. And
there were other reasons, in his mind, for him to be left on his own.
Wager had been getting on his nerves, and he certainly didn't want to be
confined with him for the whole winter. He had frostbite in his fingers
and toes and didn't fancy the arduous journey back to base. Nor did he
relish the thought of living cheek by jowl in the base hut with his
companions for the next three months. He preferred his own company,
he had plenty of food, books and tobacco, and he would sit out the
winter by himself, doing his bit for meteorology and the Arctic air route
and dreaming of Mollie.

And so it was reluctantly agreed that Courtauld would stay alone.
After an early Christmas dinner cooked by Chapman – sardines, ptarmigan, plum pudding with rum sauce, 'angels on sledges' and 'no pemmican' – the others left him, on the morning of 6 December, to his lonely
vigil. One might imagine that, in opting for solitude in the middle of
Greenland in the depths of winter, which no man had done before,
Courtauld was consciously putting himself to the test, undertaking a

rigorous exercise in self-discovery. It is highly unlikely that any such thoughts occurred to him. He was happy to be on his own, he had plenty to occupy his mind, he was not of a nervous disposition, and he was confident that he would be relieved in about three months. He was taciturn by nature and preferred to do things without fuss or outside interference. He had made his choice, and would never have considered that someone, some day (David Howarth in his book *Heroes of Nowadays*, published in 1957), would describe his exploit as 'the greatest in modern exploration'.

Unlike those who have been held prisoner for long periods, Courtauld had no sounds to listen for, other than the elements, and nothing to observe outside his tent except for the meteorological instruments and the unrelieved whiteness. For the first six weeks, however, the sun never rose above the horizon and he was in almost unrelieved darkness. There were two or three hours of semi-daylight or dusk, but in midwinter it would be dark by two o'clock in the afternoon. 'Outside the tent, when the wind wasn't blowing, it was amazingly still. The only thing you could hear was the blood pounding in your ears.... . In every direction snow stretched to the horizon like the sea. There was no life on the ice-cap; I never saw a bird or even a fly.'

Many men would have suffered from claustrophobia while in the tent and digging themselves out after a blizzard, then from agoraphobia when they got outside and were confronted by the limitless snowscape. There was also the risk that in a blizzard and in darkness he might become disoriented and fail to get back to the tent. But Courtauld seemed quite content, except for the frostbite which continued to trouble him, causing some of his toenails to fall off. The other problem was lice, which migrated from his sleeping bag – he blamed an Eskimo girl to whom he had lent it – into his clothes. Two days outside were not enough to kill them off; he had to leave the clothes out for a fortnight in temperatures of 50 below zero before the pestilential creatures finally froze to death. These were the only living things he saw in five months.

Six times a day he would dress up and go outside to read the weather instruments; having dug himself out of the tunnel, it would become blocked again after half an hour of gale-force winds. In the first week of January the entrance to the tunnel became completely blocked and he had to cut a hole in the roof of one of the adjacent snow-houses, using a ration box as a door. This served well enough as an exit for the next two and a half months, though the igloo itself would sometimes fill with snow. Finally, on 19 March, it became completely inaccessible, and he cut a hole in the roof of the other snow-house. But the shaft to the surface was too long and three days later the weight of drifting, frozen snow on the ration box hatch became so heavy that he couldn't move it. He was buried, imprisoned, and wouldn't be able to get out again.

Of course he could have dug himself out, according to his friend Quintin Riley, if he hadn't left his spade outside. 'Typical of August,' he said affectionately. 'The last piece of advice to him was, "Whatever you do, for God's sake remember to keep your spade inside the tent because you'll have to dig yourself out." But he forgot.' Fortunately, Courtauld was as cool in a crisis as he was absent-minded. Now that he was buried he had three anxieties: that the accumulation of snow on the roof would crush the tent; that the ventilator pipe on top of the tent would become blocked and deprive him of air; and that the relief party would never find the station. On the first two points he was soon reassured. The tent was bulging and sagging but it didn't collapse, and the air inside remained fresh.

In the last week of March Scott, Riley and Lindsay were in the vicinity of the ice-cap station, having left base at the beginning of the month (see the chapter on Scott). They had got as close as their latitude calculations would allow, and they searched the area for two weeks. But due to the continuing blizzards, the snowdrifts and the probability that the Union Jack on Courtauld's tent was now buried or torn to shreds, they failed to find him and returned to base to give another relief party, with a surveyor and instruments for measuring longitude, a better chance to pinpoint the position of his ice tomb.

Courtauld was enviably phlegmatic in adversity. 'It was clearly futile to get anxious, when by no possible endeavour on my part could I make any difference to the course of events.' But he had been hoping and expecting to be relieved by mid-March, if only because his rations and fuel were running low. Again his absent-mindedness was partly responsible. The two men whom he had relieved at the beginning of December had warned him there was a leak in one of the paraffin tins and that he should therefore use that one first. But he left it until last and found it empty. Most of the paraffin and the food boxes had been left outside for lack of space in the tent and the snow-houses.

Courtauld did not mark them before they became buried by snow, and he spent many anxious hours probing for them and then digging them out. Scott made a telling point years later when he wrote of Courtauld: 'A temperament that accepts – welcomes – a winter alone in inimical surroundings is not a temperament for meticulously disciplined care.'

At the end of February he had only four gallons of paraffin left; he spent half the day in darkness and used the primus for cooking only to give himself hot porridge in the mornings. He described the food situation as 'becoming interesting', but after he was trapped in his tent, unable to reach the open air, 'the food problem solved itself, since one's appetite becomes very small if one takes no exercise'. With little fuel left and candles running out, he had to spend most of the time in the dark, and the cold. Frozen condensed moisture covered the inside of the tent, and icicles hanging from the roof would drip or drop on his face.

By the middle of April he had finished his last pipeful of tobacco and was reduced to smoking tea-leaves. He had only one candle left, hardly any paraffin and lay in the dark all day. The lamp, when he could light it, smoked and blackened everything around it. Food consisted of a little oatmeal warmed up for breakfast, and thereafter uncooked pemmican, biscuit, margarine and anti-scorbutic lemon juice. 'There is now precious little left to live for… . Left foot swelling up, hope it isn't scurvy.' He was now reduced to living in squalor and could not dispose of his own waste.

When he had light, much of his time was spent reading, from a library of about thirty books left by previous occupants of the ice-cap station. Among his favourites, some of which he read more than once, were *Jane Eyre*, *The Forsyte Saga*, *Vanity Fair* and *Guy Mannering*. He also enjoyed dipping into *Whitaker's Almanack*, and 'there were times when the Bible made very good reading'. The books available to him by more modern novelists – Charles Morgan, H. W. Freeman, Beverley Nichols – did not have as much appeal.

At other times he would design his ideal yacht*, and he resolved to buy a house in Suffolk 'near the sea, preferably Pin Mill. No land

* He found it at Burnham-on-Crouch when he returned to England. She was a yawl, fifty feet long, built in 1912 and named *Gaviota* (sea-gull in Spanish), which he renamed *Duet* at the time of his marriage. She was still sailing in her ninety-eighth year.

except a garden and fewest possible servants. No waiting at table.' He compiled a wish list of his particular pleasures, which included getting into a hot bath and then into bed with clean sheets and pyjamas. On a summer morning he imagined being 'at the helm of a small boat, a fresh breeze blowing, all sail set, with Mollie and a smell of breakfast coming up to say good morning'. Breakfast often occupied his thoughts: he dreamed of eating an apple in the garden on a bright autumn morning, followed by an enormous breakfast of kippers, poached eggs, kidneys, mushrooms and cold partridge. On another occasion he longed to be at sea and eating a beef and onion pudding. (Suet was one of his favourite foods. Soon after arriving in Greenland he had sent a message back to England for some suet, but unfortunately it was interpreted as a request for a suit.)

His mostly factual and laconic diary record of his months of isolation occasionally gave way to a few philosophical musings:

> Why is it men come to these places? ... Is it curiosity? A yearning to look behind the veil onto the mysteries and desolations of nature in her forlorn places? ... Do we in fact morally bury ourselves in fleeing from this world? Do we simply rot or grow rank like some plant thrown over the garden wall, or do we rather come nearer to reality, see more clearly the Great Purpose behind it all in stripping our souls of the protection of our friends and in putting from us the pleasures of the body? ... In leaving behind the transitory hopes and fears of pathetic humanity, does one perhaps come closer to the things that abide, to the forces which endure?

While he was able to go out and take the weather readings, Courtauld had the satisfaction of knowing that, however long it took to burrow himself out of his tent and back again in a blizzard, he was doing an important job for the expedition. But once he became snowed in and short of fuel, he could not continue to keep his spirits up while lying in the dark and wondering whether he was also morally burying himself, or coming closer to reality and the things that abide. There were only two things to sustain him: the prospect of getting back to Mollie, and his belief in God. He spoke directly to Mollie through his diary: 'If it were not for having you to think about, life would be intolerable. I wonder what you are doing. If I could be sure you were happy

I wouldn't mind. But I trust in God absolutely. I am sure He doesn't mean me to die alone here.'

What was remarkable, and of course enormously helpful to his state of mind, was that as each month passed he became more, not less, certain that he would be rescued. By the time he was snowed in, he had no doubts at all, which was an immeasurable comfort to him. 'I will not attempt any explanation of this, but leave it as a fact, which was very clear to me during that time, that while powerless to help myself, some outer Force was in action on my side, and that I was not fated to leave my bones on the Greenland ice cap.' In an intriguingly similar way, Shackleton and his two companions, as they struggled over the mountains of South Georgia on the last stage of their epic journey from Elephant Island, had felt that there was a 'fourth presence' with them. (T. S. Eliot wrote about this phenomenon in *The Waste Land*.)

Relief, in the shape of Gino, John Rymill and Chapman, arrived just in time. It was 5 May, 150 days since Courtauld had said goodbye to his companions as they headed for the coast. The primus gave its last gasp as he was melting water for his morning porridge. He had just decided that he would soon have to start walking back to base, if he could get out,

> when suddenly there was an appalling noise like a bus going by, followed by a confused yelling noise. I nearly jumped out of my skin. Was it the house falling in at last? A second later I realised the truth. It was somebody, some real human voice calling down the ventilator. It was a wonderful moment. I could not think what to do or say. I yelled back some stuttering remarks that seemed quite futile for the occasion. 'Hooray,' they shouted. 'Are you all right?' 'Yes, thank God you've come; I'm perfectly fit.' 'Thank God,' they said.

He was not only alive but, after six weeks imprisoned in his cell under the snow, he was still perfectly sane, bolstered by his faith in God and by an enviable inner calm. Amazingly, once he had been pulled out through the roof of the tent, looking 'as if he had stepped straight from Oberammergau', Courtauld was able to walk and even to ski slowly for a few hundred yards. He rode on a sledge the whole way back to base, writing his diary and reading *The Count of Monte Cristo*. The journey took a little less than a week in glorious spring weather. The four men reached the coastal base at four o'clock in the morning, to 'great rejoicing', as Percy Lemon described it in a wireless despatch to *The Times* which was published the next day. 'All in the hut turned out in pyjamas to photograph August Courtauld in his prophet's beard and locks.... He is now having his first proper wash for seven months.' Eskimos from the nearest settlement arrived to congratulate him, and after greetings had been exchanged and stories told, Courtauld breakfasted on bread and marmalade before going off with Scott to clamber up the rocks and shoot ptarmigan.

In a leading article, *The Times* congratulated Courtauld 'for the calm determination with which, in the interests of the expedition's aims, he deliberately took the risks of remaining alone for so long a period in circumstances where any failure of nerve, any bodily weakness, might well have proved fatal'. He could hardly have objected to this pat on the back from the newspaper which had the press rights for the expedition, but he was horrified to learn that his plight had become big news back in England. There were newspaper reports, most of them exaggerated and inaccurate, to the effect that he was lost and in danger of starvation, and there were air rescue attempts, of which Courtauld was fortunately oblivious. When he heard what had been going on he described 'this absurd hysteria' as 'really too ridiculous'. To Mollie he sent a message: 'Take no notice hysterical rescue nonsense. Relief carried out as part of ordinary programme. No danger. Love.' It was a heroically typical piece of self-deprecating understatement.

Courtauld's parents had been understandably worried to hear that he had not been relieved after four months, and that Scott had failed to find the ice-cap station. As Gino was preparing to lead the second relief party to search for Courtauld, he sent a cable to London to report the situation, doing his best not to sound the alarm. But he felt bound to add a warning note: 'There is always the possibility that Courtauld is not alive, or unwell, in which case the station is probably covered.' There was alarm at the RGS, and Courtauld's father instructed the secretary of the expedition committee, Ralph Rayner, to charter an aeroplane to look for his son.* *The Times*, with its press rights to the

---

* Captain Rayner, a young Army officer, was engaged to Courtauld's sister Betty, whom he married six weeks after her brother's return to base. Courtauld blamed his new brother-in-law unfairly for the 'hysterical rescue nonsense'.

expedition, carried a report with the restrained headline, 'Anxiety for Safety of Mr Courtauld'.

Then the rest of the press got going. 'Millionaire's Son Alone on Ice', announced the *Daily Express*, which soon found Mollie, 'The Woman Who Waits', in Essex. The *Evening Standard* excelled itself, inventing a desperate message from Courtauld – 'Absolutely Without Food' – regardless of the fact that he had no wireless. A French newspaper described the *cauchemar* of a lone woman, Mademoiselle Augustine Courtauld. By now three aeroplanes were involved and the Danish government sent a ship to the edge of the Greenland pack ice. Gino, without radio contact, was unaware of the fuss as he, Rymill and Chapman proceeded with all speed towards the ice-cap station. Only one aeroplane, chartered by Rayner and piloted by a Swede, Captain Ahrenberg, flew over the ice cap. He spotted a party of four returning to base, and so was able to report that Courtauld was alive and safe.

Courtauld's annoyance and embarrassment at all the publicity and expense generated by his ordeal were tempered by the knowledge that he could stay on in Greenland undisturbed for the summer. Mercifully for him, the press did not have the ingenuity or the resources in those days to get to the east coast of Greenland. Had he been subjected to interviews – 'How did you feel when you heard your rescuers arrive?' – or, even worse, to counselling, he would have wished himself back on the ice cap, where five months of solitude had given him freedom. He had not suffered from his time alone, but rather had been strengthened by it. And he had no wish to exchange his private experience for public acclaim.

He had had enough of the ice cap and hazardous journeys, and was looking forward to returning to England with the ship which would call at Angmagssalik at the end of July. Further summer journeys were planned to round off the expedition – two from east to west across the ice cap and one by boat down the east coast and round the southern tip of Greenland. Gino himself was going on the boat journey, together with Percy Lemon, and he wanted a third person. Courtauld was good at survey work and good with boats, Gino asked him to join them, and Courtauld, despite his resolve when he came back from the ice cap, said yes. When he sent a message home to say he would not now be returning until November, his parents were furious and Mollie, to put it mildly, was very upset. 'I feel a frightful rotter about it,' he wrote to her.

'But I know what you would have me do in your heart of hearts. You wouldn't have me run out before the show is over… . Various things may go wrong, but they can only cause delay and not disaster.'

Various things did go wrong, not all of them unavoidable. Courtauld thought it was 'suicidal folly' to take one open whale-boat, with not enough room for both fuel and food, down an unmapped coast. If the boat was wrecked they would have to winter on the coast or try to cross the ice cap. He wouldn't have gone with anyone else, but Gino was very persuasive. Courtauld argued for a second boat, Gino agreed and they took with them three kayaks and two small sledges. The food which they carried with them consisted of little more than emergency rations (pemmican), porridge and sugar.

The three men did not set off until the middle of August. It was vital to push on as fast as possible before they were hit by autumn gales. But when they stopped at an Eskimo settlement at Umivik for a couple of days, and Gino took the opportunity to stock up their larder by shooting birds and seals, they stayed there for a week – an unnecessary, not to say irresponsible, delay which could have proved fatal. Courtauld became increasingly frustrated but Gino wouldn't move on. It was almost as if he and Lemon wanted to remain with the Eskimos and winter there. Courtauld thought they were in danger of 'going native' and possibly taking another two Eskimo mistresses, while he was anxious to get home and marry his English rose.

When finally they did take to the boats again, the weather broke and they were battered by strong winds, driving rain and seas made rougher by the lack of drift ice. The outboard engines broke down, they got lost in fog, they drifted among icebergs and were threatened from the shore by a calving glacier. After a few days, with no improvement in the weather, Gino and Lemon talked about wintering on the coast, while Courtauld became more miserable at the prospect and consoled himself by re-reading *Moby Dick* and making a pudding with porridge, black crowberries gathered at Umivik and his beloved suet. (He particularly did not relish the thought of having to use a kayak, in which he was less than expert. In the only known photograph of him in one of these canoes, he is sitting quite still, with his pipe in his mouth.) Gino decided to abandon one boat, but the one in which they huddled, overloaded now with fuel, sledges and kayaks, leaked all the time and its engine continued to break down.

'The next ten days were a nightmare…. It is getting sickening to the point of desperation,' Courtauld wrote in his diary, using stronger words than he ever employed in describing his five-month ordeal on the ice cap. 'It really begins to look like having to winter. If so, it isn't too good as the kayaks are getting rotten with all this wet, and if they become unusable we haven't a hope of being able to feed ourselves.'

The rain fell incessantly and now they had to contend with brash ice as well as everything else. They had to wait several days before they could get round it, going miles out to sea in an unseaworthy boat. They also had to negotiate a notorious glacier called Puisortok, of which the Eskimos said, 'Do not speak, do not eat, until Puisortok is passed', because huge pieces of ice were inclined to break off the glacier under-water and shoot to the surface like missiles. ('Puisortok' means 'the thing that comes up'.) Then the engine failed again, the wind rose and they sheltered on a small island. Lemon spent all the next day trying and failing to fix the engine. It seemed as if they were finally beaten but Courtauld, in a moment of inspiration, disconnected the silencer and the engine roared into life. 'Our spirits rose vertically, we really were going to get there.' From then on they kept going, while bailing continuously, until they passed through Prince Christian Sound to west Greenland and came to a settlement. It had been the hairiest of journeys, a distance of nearly 600 miles, and they were very lucky to make it.

Recollected later in tranquillity, Courtauld mused on this experience:

A journey is like the life of a man. The labours of its birth are heavy, it youth is full of ideals and hopes, its main course leads swiftly to harsh reality and its end, whether of failure or success, is bitter…. It is here that we realise the futility of our endeavour and the smallness of our achievement. For this is the time of parting from the fellow-sharers of our joys and disappointments, parting from the life of grand uncertainty, parting from a country and a people that we have grown to know…. It is only when we dig up those faded records, which once written are stored away unread, that we remember with a shock the truth of those days, when weary in body we gave expression to the anxiety of our minds…. One had forgotten…about the untimely breakdown the leaky boat, the just-avoided calving of the iceberg, the all but unweathered storm.

Courtauld came home with Gino via Copenhagen, where he had to endure an official Danish welcome. He had already written to Mollie, whom he longed to see waiting for him on the quay, to advise her against coming to Copenhagen, as 'there is to be some awful sort of reception ... these Danes are such fans at formal entertainment.' In his diary he wrote: 'There is a rumour I may have to say something. Heaven forbid! It is going to be a horrible show.' He had no wish to be thrust into the limelight but he was, as soon as he stepped ashore, by a man from the British embassy with a microphone who thanked Denmark for having rescued Mr Courtauld and invited him to say a few words. Courtauld obliged: 'I only want to say that what the last speaker has told you is entirely wrong. I wasn't rescued by anyone.' But he later spoke publicly of his affection for the Eskimos and his admiration for the way the Danish administrators looked after the country for the benefit of its people.

Six weeks after returning from Greenland, he and Mollie were married, having decided, in Courtauld's words, 'to get it done at Southwark Cathedral'. The night before, at his bachelor party, he went from the Café Royal to the funfair at Olympia where he climbed unsteadily into a motor boat as it sank to the bottom of the pond. Following his boating experiences of the previous autumn, it was an appropriate end to his carefree days as a single man.

He went back to Greenland once more in 1935, again taking the *Quest*, with a small party which included the geologist Lawrence Wager, with whom he had been loath to spend the winter on the ice cap four years earlier. His idea was to 'get up an expedition to have a stab at the mountains Gino had discovered' when he spotted them from the air in 1930. Courtauld was surprised to find himself leading an expedition and, in his typically self-effacing way, he gave the credit for its success to his companions. He took two mountaineers who had recently been on Mount Everest (Wager and Jack Longland), three Danes, and he put his own unconventional stamp on the composition of the party by including women. 'I thought it would be nice for Mollie to see Greenland, so I asked the married men to bring their wives. Everybody said it was bound to be an appalling failure' – which of course ensured that Courtauld would go ahead with his plan. 'The four girls survived all right and I think they enjoyed it; they certainly made themselves very useful.'

For Mollie it was an exhilarating experience, despite being trapped in pack ice for several days some miles from the Greenland coast and being told by the captain that they might have to abandon ship as the *Quest* was at the mercy of the huge icebergs around them. When they reached the coast the girls did their best to communicate with the Eskimos – the women would run their fingers through Mollie's hair – while Courtauld and his men made the first-ever ascent of the highest of the Watkins Mountains. The mountain wall, in the estimation of Wager, recently returned from the Himalayas, was the most impressive he had seen. It was a strenuous climb to 12,250 feet, the peak of the Arctic, where British and Danish flags were planted on a ski stick. 'It was a great satisfaction that it had been climbed by two of Gino's men,' Courtauld wrote. As the *Quest* set sail for home, Courtauld and his wife witnessed a scene of extraordinary beauty at sunset as the Watkins range climbed out of the sea and they could make out all the high tops. 'All the ice floes became a very pale rose while the water between them was the palest green ... the sky yellow and gold behind. The air was quite still with no sound.' In the twilight mirage changed the distant icebergs into unearthly shapes and the mountains appeared to stand on their heads. More than seventy years later, at the age of 101, Mollie recalled the sensation of saying goodbye to another, almost fantastical world as their ship headed across the Denmark Strait to Iceland and on to Scotland and 'civilisation'. They were returning to their two small children and a world threatened by Hitler and Mussolini.

Having been turned down for the Navy some years before, Courtauld was not very well disposed towards the Admiralty when he got a job in naval intelligence at the beginning of the war. He was not suited to a desk job; active service was what he wanted, but it was a year before he was given command of a motor torpedo boat, on air-sea rescue duty in the English Channel. Too much time was spent ashore for Courtauld's liking; he thought he was having too easy a war, but it was not lacking in activity. Commando training followed in the Shetlands, then a voyage to the United States to bring an infantry landing-craft across the Atlantic for the invasion of Sicily. He served as first lieutenant in an escort destroyer, and at the end of the war was sent to Copenhagen to oversee disarmament in Denmark. He was offered promotion to lieutenant-commander but turned it down because, he said, he couldn't be bothered to change uniforms. When the war was over he was relieved that he could now go back to sea again in his own sailing boat, *Duet*.

Sailing was his principal occupation and passion in the postwar years, whether off the East Anglian coast, across to France or round the coast of Scotland and the islands. Courtauld's intention to cross the Atlantic in *Duet* to Jamaica, leaving England in October, was not surprisingly frustrated by bad weather, and he had to turn back from Corunna (see pp. 115–16). Otherwise he lived the conventional life of a country squire while taking on public duties of county councillor, Deputy Lieutenant and, when his turn came, High Sheriff. His particular favourites among charities he supported were the Essex Association of Boys' Clubs and the Royal National Lifeboat Institution.

His continuing interest in polar exploration encouraged him to read widely in polar literature and to compile an anthology of the writings of explorers covering some two and a half thousand years. It is an instructive and delightful collection, with valuable biographical notes, put together over the years after his return from Greenland. It was published under the title *From the Ends of the Earth* in 1958, the year before he died.

A form of multiple sclerosis, diagnosed in 1953, gradually and relentlessly incapacitated him. But he did produce one more book in the 1950s – a short memoir, *Man the Ropes*, which he dictated to one of his nurses, mostly from his sickbed. His fellow Arctic explorer, Jimmy Scott, wrote a foreword, and the book is dedicated to his old friend with whom he travelled in the Sahara, Francis Rodd (who became Lord Rennell of Rodd). It is perhaps significant that the dedication is to the man 'whose leadership inspired my life and without whose care I should not be here', rather than to the memory of Gino, his leader in Greenland, 'whom we would have followed anywhere', as he had written to *The Times* in 1932. Was there an implied and not entirely forgotten criticism here of Gino's leadership on the open boat journey, when he put the three of them unnecessarily at risk by staying on at an Eskimo settlement at a critical time of the year?

There is no doubt, though, that Courtauld had been inspired by Gino. He had enjoyed and been stimulated by the life of grand uncertainty, as he put it in his Greenland diary, while sustained by his strong religious faith. But in his final years he faced only the certainty of a debilitating and incurable disease from which there would be no relief or rescue. After five months' isolation on the ice cap, Gino had shouted to him down the ventilator pipe and heard in reply what another of Courtauld's rescuers called the voice of a normal man. Now, in the latter stages of his crippling illness, that normality tragically deserted him. He was aged fifty-four when he died.

2

Sir Martin Lindsay, Bt, CBE, DSO
(1905–81)

'I say, Martin, do you mind going up with Jimmy and Quintin to relieve August? Are your moccasins in good shape, because it'll be hellish cold up there.'

The order, framed as a polite request, came from Gino, and Lieutenant Lindsay of the Royal Scots Fusiliers was proud to have been selected by his leader. It was the beginning of March 1931 and all the expedition members (except Courtauld) were, because of bad weather, confined to their coastal Greenland base. Lindsay, together with the other two (Scott and Riley), would battle against blizzards and winter gales for weeks on end, trying, and failing, to find the weather station in the middle of the ice cap where Courtauld had already spent three dark winter months alone. Lindsay respected Gino for this approach to leadership: 'He never adopted the pernicious habit of asking for volunteers – a proceeding which only overworks the willing horses. Instead he chose his man for every job of work and then asked him to do it in such a way as to inspire him to a relentless devotion to duty.' The devotion to duty was never in doubt, but Lindsay did later criticise his leader for failing to include a more qualified surveyor/navigator in the search party and for sending it out ill-equipped for the task.

It was perhaps because Lindsay was a trained army officer and not one of Gino's Cambridge cronies that he was the only person to draw attention to Gino's faults. For the moment, however, Lindsay had a serious job to do, in the most testing conditions. Gino had chosen him now because, in his early years of army service, he had already proved himself entirely suitable to be a member of a hazardous expedition.

Lindsay had a fairly conventional military background – father a Gurkha colonel, army scholarship to Wellington, followed by Sandhurst and a commission as second lieutenant in the Royal Scots Fusiliers. An accomplished horseman, he rode in steeplechases as an

46

amateur and, when he was seconded to the Nigeria Regiment for two years, he won that country's Grand National. In 1929, aged twenty-four and having finished his spell of duty in Nigeria, he announced his intention of undertaking a solo journey through the Belgian Congo. His colonel said it was not safe to embark on such a trip with fewer than twelve porters. Lindsay said he could not afford more than six, and the colonel refused to let him go. Lindsay then deployed his winning argument: 'Either I die, which is only my problem, or I get through, in which case it will reflect credit on the regiment.' Permission was granted and he survived, but years later he would say that this was the most arduous and perilous journey he ever made. In view of his experiences in the Arctic, it must have been some trek. Starting from Stanleyville (Kisangani), and walking for much of the time through thick rainforest, he eventually reached the shores of Lake Albert on the Uganda border. Having lost his way and nearly died, he abandoned plans to continue through Kenya to Ethiopia and instead linked up with The King's African Rifles in Uganda. The pygmy artefacts which he had collected in the Congo were presented to the British Museum.

Lindsay and Gino met at a weekend house party in Dorset. It was when Gino heard of his African journey, and after much badgering from Lindsay, that he invited him to join the British Arctic Air Route Expedition. The services were represented by one other army officer, Captain Percy Lemon, Royal Signals, as wireless operator, two flight-lieutenants – Narbrough ('Jimmy') D'Aeth (pilot) and Iliffe Cozens (pilot and photographer) – and Surgeon-Lieutenant Edward Bingham, Royal Navy, who acted as expedition doctor. Subsequently D'Aeth and Cozens became, respectively, air vice-marshal and air commodore; Bingham went to the Antarctic with John Rymill and led the Falklands Islands Dependencies Survey after the war; and Lemon attempted suicide shortly after the end of the expedition and died not long afterwards.

With his military training, Lindsay was slightly bemused by the coterie of young Cambridge graduates, easily outnumbering those from the services, who gathered in a room at the Royal Geographical Society in London to plan this expedition to the Arctic. Earnest discussions were held and detailed preparations made, but at the same time there was an air of almost juvenile high spirits. Gino might be leaning back languidly in a desk chair while jazz music was playing on a wind-up gramophone. Passers-by in Kensington Gore below might hear through the open window the newly fashionable Duke Ellington band playing 'Cotton Club Stomp'. The debutante and party season was beginning, and almost every evening Gino and Jimmy Scott would put on white tie and tails to dine and dance much of the night away. Around dawn they would often run back from the West End to the Watkins home in South Kensington. It was an unorthodox way of getting fit for dog sledging on the Greenland ice cap.

Lindsay shared the view of his companions that polar exploration should be more of an adventure than a quest for scientific knowledge. 'Rather it is something between an art and a sport.' In whimsical mood he compared the monotony of sledging to a painting by Ingres; 'but both owe their success to the skilful arrangement of the smallest details, and both for that reason intrigue us.'

> The technique of sledging is more intricate than that of any other form of travel.... The efficiency of the equipment is of supreme importance, since the penalty for an error leading to the break-down of an article on a journey may be death by cold or hunger. Misfitting dog harnesses or the loss of a primus pricker might make all the difference between success and disaster. Under these conditions there is no room for anything but neatness – neatness of thought and neatness of execution. An untidy person is not only a nuisance but a very real danger.

There was one particular occasion on the ice cap when he himself was anything but neat. He was trying to chop up a frozen block of dog pemmican with an axe. With the pemmican on the ground, it merely sank into the snow, so he put it on a petrol can containing the party's supply of paraffin for their journey. He split the pemmican block all right but also the can, losing most of the paraffin and the means of cooking food and keeping the tents warm. One suspects there must have been plenty of other instances of his inefficiency or hamfistedness. August Courtauld described him as 'an unfailing source of mirth; he does everything and says everything wrong with the completest good humour and cheerfulness'.

Certainly, neatness was one of the qualities which Lindsay admired in Quintin Riley. Having shared a cabin on the *Quest* taking them to Greenland, and a tent on the way to set up the weather station on the ice cap, they were quite happy to be left alone together to build snow-houses and tunnels and a wall round their encampment. Their dome-shaped tent was neatly arranged, principally by Riley, with reindeer skins spread on the floor and two sleeping bags (made of the same material) separated by a ration box. 'This funny little dwelling was a very happy home for us, and Riley and I look back on the days we spent there as being amongst the most enjoyable of the expedition.'

The two men shared few interests – chess was one – but they did share traits of character. While they differed in temperament, both were independent, self-reliant, outspoken. Riley may have been a more complex character than Lindsay, but they both knew right from wrong; they looked at life, and expressed their opinions, in black-and-white terms. Shades of grey seldom intruded; yet neither of them was arrogant or given to bragging.

> During our five weeks together at the ice-cap station Quintin and I never got tired of each other's company; and I believe had we stayed there another six months we should have got on just as well. There was nothing at all forced in this companionship; we always behaved quite naturally, and no efforts had to be made to 'give and take'. ... Although the days we spent together on the ice cap broke down all barriers so that we learnt just everything about each other, we have, strange to say, never returned to the same intimacy.

It is not really so strange because, once back in England and having retired from polar exploration, they moved in quite different milieus, with friends who would have had nothing in common. What Lindsay and Riley had in common was a taste for adventure and isolation, and a respect for each other's strength of character and ability to endure hardship. And their friendship did survive: they served together briefly at the beginning of the war, Riley was godfather to Lindsay's second son, and in their mid-sixties they returned to Greenland together (this time by air).

In their shared tent on the ice cap, after a day spent constructing a snow-house, clearing drift snow and taking weather readings, Lindsay would light a candle, fill the teapot with snow and relax on his sleeping bag. Riley would be at the primus cooker while Lindsay might read aloud from the *Oxford Book of English Verse*. He would muse on the

pleasures of a winter fireside at home after a day's hunting – warm
hearth-rugs, scalding tea, rain lashing the windows and a strong wind
sweeping across the park. 'These joys Quintin and I to some extent
experienced when we came inside after the day's work was over. ...
Lying there in our sleeping bags with the primus burning between us,
we could feel none of the bite that was in the air outside. Comfortable
and warm we read and talked, played chess and read again, until we
fell asleep, happy and contented.'

It would be very different in six months' time when the two of them
were searching the ice cap, in blizzard conditions and with an increasing sense of desperation, for their 'funny little dwelling' in which Courtauld was buried and, they thought, quite possibly dead. For the
moment, however, Lindsay and Riley could enjoy the sunset on most
evenings when, as Lindsay wrote in a fine, descriptive, almost lyrical
passage:

> The western sky floods slowly into the most extraordinary
> extremes of colour – brilliant contrasts of pink, pale blue and
> orange, purple and gold. ... The stillness is unbroken save by the
> flapping of the flag as the wind comes and goes, and sometimes
> the sighing of the snow as it speeds along the ground. Ten o'clock
> has its delights too, in the beauty of the northern lights, a muster
> of dim lances, close serried, standing erect in the sky.

Lindsay had always wanted to be a published writer, ever since he won
the school essay prize at the age of twelve. For the next ten years he
wrote 'for the wastepaper basket'; rejection slips followed him until an
article he had written while in Nigeria was published by *Blackwood's
Magazine*. His first book, *Those Greenland Days*, was published, also
by Blackwood's, a year after he returned from this expedition, and
described by *The Spectator* as 'written with spontaneous vigour ...
quite free from any touch of boastfulness or self-pity'. He had *Fowler's
English Usage* with him at the ice-cap station, and enjoyed reading
Vanity Fair, *Guy Mannering* and De Quincey's *Confessions of an
Opium Eater*.

The one thing which seems to have concerned Lindsay, or at least to
have been a frequent topic of conversation with Riley, was what they
should do if the relief party failed to arrive. They had full rations for
five weeks but found they could happily exist on less. There was an

understanding among all of them that if a relief was long overdue, the occupants of the station could start the trek back to base without any dishonour. Lindsay and Riley did not seriously think that the relief party would be lost in a crevasse, but at the same time they agreed there was no point in their staying on until the last ration-box was finished and they became what Lindsay described as 'a total loss. Neither of us intended to be martyrs to meteorology.' Following the flags and skiing or walking downhill all the way, they could have got back to base in ten days.

This they did, with John Rymill and Freddy Spencer Chapman, who had arrived to relieve them, in early October, leaving Ted Bingham and Jimmy D'Aeth to take over the station. For Lindsay those first moments of the return to their coastal base after a sledging journey were unforgettable: 'Everybody used to welcome you and do all the little things they could to make you comfortable. One man filled your pipe and another hurried up the tea, while the girls pulled off your boots and made you buttered toast.'

'The girls' – Arpika, Gertrude and Tina – were welcomed by Lindsay for the cooking and cleaning they did and for their lively company. 'Most of us were on very playful terms with them. … We treated them exactly like children; but we brought them up in the way that no children should go.' Like Riley he did not approve of them sharing their employers' beds. 'The female servants of an expedition should be as prescribed for bedmakers in an old university statute – *horrida et senex* [ugly and old].' You might bed a young female servant in a French hotel, but in a crowded hut in the Arctic such behaviour was intolerable. It was conduct unbecoming an officer and a gentleman, and Lindsay was especially critical of his fellow army officer, Captain Percy Lemon (who had Arpika as his mistress), and of his leader (who generally slept with Tina) for setting a bad example. For most of the winter Tina slept in Gino's bunk, which was immediately above Lindsay's. 'Every time this bloody Eskimo girl got up into his bunk she had to put her feet within an inch or two of my face. I objected strongly, and so did some of the others, and if the ship hadn't come when it did we'd have formed up and said look here, Gino, this has bloody well got to stop.'

Lindsay was perhaps the one member of the expedition who had reservations about Gino which he was prepared to express. It was significant that when, after Gino's death, Lindsay proposed himself as Gino's biographer, Courtauld wrote to Margaret Graham (Gino's fiancée) in strong terms that he and Jimmy Scott agreed that Lindsay was not the right person to do it. It was not that Lindsay wished to belittle Gino – he was seduced by his charm, he admired the fertility of his ideas and many of his qualities of leadership – but he did consider that the eulogising of him when he died, universally acclaimed as one of the heroic figures of the age, was misplaced, or at the least exaggerated. In a letter years later Lindsay wrote that Gino's 'blemish, unforgivable in a leader, was casualness to the point of fecklessness'.

What Lindsay did admire Gino for was his willingness to learn from the Eskimos, and from the Canadian explorer Vilhjalmur Stefansson, how to survive and get around in the Arctic. He knew that they must use dogs for sledging and live off the country by shooting seals from a kayak, and so he learnt these skills and insisted that the others follow him. Also learning from the experience of the pre-war Antarctic expeditions, he improved the make-up of the rations which they would take when away from base (substantially increasing the fat ratio), and he designed a dome-shaped double tent for the ice-cap station.

In Lindsay's opinion Gino was undoubtedly a better explorer than Captain Scott of the Antarctic, but he was his inferior as a leader. In the epilogue, written a year before he died, to his little book, *The Epic of Captain Scott*, Lindsay lists the various mistakes that Scott made. He failed to learn the principal lesson of his first expedition – 'the limitations imposed by man-haulage' – and he neglected to learn, or to get his men to learn, how to drive dogs. The man he sent to Siberia to buy ponies and dogs knew something about dogs but nothing at all about ponies; both his choices were unsuitable for the Antarctic. The best sledge dogs (used by Amundsen) were those found in Greenland, and the ponies should have been selected by his cavalry officer, Captain Oates. It was not really surprising that Scott paid the penalty for his errors of judgement.

However, Lindsay goes on to praise Scott as 'a great and noble man', a leader of energy and determination who was always concerned for the welfare of his men, a man of strength, humanity, simplicity, 'invincible courage and unblenching fortitude'. Some of these qualities Lindsay clearly found lacking in Gino, though most of Gino's companions would have disagreed, preferring his more informal style of leadership to Scott's authoritarian approach and refusal to elicit the opinions of his men. As a leader Scott must be held to account principally for his irresponsible, and possibly fatal, last-minute decision to take five men on the last lap to the Pole rather than four, and for failing to take the fittest of those available.

'A scientist [Wilson], two sailors [Bowers and Taff Evans] and a soldier [Oates] – what better companions could a man have?' So says John Mills playing Scott in the 1948 film, *Scott of the Antarctic*. What was left unsaid was that all the planning had been for a four-man unit. The rations were made up for four men for a week; the tents held four men and the cookers four mugs, plates and spoons. Scott soon discovered, as he recorded in a naïve admission, that 'Cooking for five takes a seriously longer time than cooking for four; perhaps half an hour on the whole day. It is an item I had not considered when reorganising.' Apsley Cherry-Garrard gave his opinion some years later that a four-man party would have survived.

In Lindsay's view, Scott decided at the last minute to take Bowers because he could not bear to disappoint him. (Three days earlier he had told Bowers to leave his skis for the return journey, so the poor man now had to walk on foot for three months until he died.) It may also have been due to Scott's sensitive nature that, not wishing to disappoint them, he took Oates and Evans to the Pole when neither was 100 per cent fit. Oates had one leg shorter than the other (from a wound in the Boer War), and Evans had a badly cut hand. If this reasoning is correct, Scott was guilty of culpable weakness of character resulting in the deaths of the two men. It is at least arguable that the indefatigable Tom Crean (who four years later would make the epic journey with Shackleton across the southern ocean and the mountains of South Georgia) should have been chosen by Scott in place of Oates and Evans. He returned instead with Teddy Evans and Bill Lashly, and made a heroic trek to save Evans's life.

Lindsay did not accuse Scott of irresponsibility as a leader, though the evidence against him was clear. But he did level this charge against Gino when he asked Lindsay to accompany Jimmy Scott and Riley to find and relieve Courtauld on the ice cap. Three months had elapsed since Courtauld had been left alone in the middle of Greenland to endure its winter weather. While there was no cause for alarm, there was naturally concern for his well-being. No hint of criticism of Gino is

to be found in the pages of Lindsay's account in *Those Greenland Days*;
but he did let his views be known years later (in a letter to Nicholas
Wollaston, Courtauld's biographer): 'Any responsible leader would
have decided to lead the relief party himself, taking with him a first-
class surveyor-navigator, of whom he had the choice of several. But he
chose Scott and myself who had only done a crash course on the
subject. The excuse for not taking a time-signal set, because we had to
travel light, was phoney. Those sets did not weigh much.'

In fact Gino's 'casualness to the point of fecklessness', in Lindsay's
words, was such that he initially sent off only two men (Scott and Riley)
to make the 130-mile journey. They were back the next day having
broken a sledge and encountered the worst conditions they had known
– raging blizzards and an uphill surface as hard as marble. It was then
that Gino added Lindsay to the relief party, and one is bound to ask
why he didn't go himself. He knew of the severity of the weather – gales
and extreme cold had continued for most of the winter – and must have
appreciated the importance of relieving Courtauld as soon as possible.
He should also have suspected that the ice-cap station would be hard to
find in these conditions – the tent might be partially covered by drifts,
the wind might have torn away the Union Jack – and that a time-signal
set was necessary to fix its exact position. Yet he decided to stay at the
base himself and not to send an expert navigator (Rymill or Alfred
Stephenson) with suitable equipment. True, a time-signal set would
take up most of one sledge, but that did not stop Gino taking it when he
led the second relief party, with Rymill and Chapman, six weeks later.
With Scott and Riley, Lindsay was able to calculate latitude with their
sextant and theodolite, but without the time-signal set they could not
compute the longitude. They could navigate to within about a thousand yards of the ice-cap station, but since it was by now covered with
snow, with Courtauld trapped inside, it was invisible.

Once they had got to within a few miles of the ice-cap station, a blizzard blew for six days and they were unable to travel at all. They had to
endure the frustration of knowing they were close to Courtauld but
could not search for him. When Lindsay came back into the tent one
afternoon having just taken a temperature reading of minus 24° F, he
was greeted by Riley telling him this journey was very good for the
character. Lindsay's contemporaneous diary has not survived, but in his
book he writes rather matter-of-factly of Courtauld's situation. 'It was

difficult to understand how Courtauld could have come to let the station get so drifted over – unless he had met with some misadventure. A man wintering alone on an ice cap is hardly a justifiable insurance risk.' In fact he could not dig himself out because he had left his spade outside; by the time his would-be rescuers had got close to the station, he was already buried.

Although Lindsay was full of praise for the way Courtauld came through his extraordinary ordeal – and simply staggered when his first words on his return were to apologise to Lindsay, Scott and Riley for the hardships they had experienced in looking for him – he might not have been very forgiving of Courtauld's absent-mindedness in leaving his spade outside the tent. No doubt thinking of Jimmy D'Aeth's breakdown when his hands became badly frostbitten while returning from the ice cap, Lindsay made this typically outspoken comment: 'There can be no excuse for a man in good health getting frostbitten. It is only slackness on his part if he has failed to dry his clothing; and sympathy is the last thing that he should receive. At the best he becomes a beastly nuisance; at the worst he endangers the whole party.'

Here was the Sandhurst-trained officer hardened by his experiences alone in the forests of the Belgian Congo before going to the Arctic. But he had every sympathy for Scott who, as leader of their party, felt a heavy responsibility for not having found Courtauld, though he certainly could not be blamed in any way. When it was clear that the ice-cap station was no longer visible above ground, he took the decision to return to base as fast as possible so that another party of three, this time with a navigator and a time-signal set, could set off to the ice cap where, Gino had convinced himself, Courtauld was still alive.

Lindsay was pleased to have been chosen for this journey, but as they hurried home empty-handed one may imagine his feelings towards his leader who, in his opinion, should have been leading the relief party himself and with the necessary back-up which they had been denied. On the last day they did thirty miles on snowshoes; their spirits were low, especially Scott's, who dreaded getting back to base and having to explain his failure. He was both physically and mentally exhausted, and had to stop and rest twice in the last mile. Having wandered for forty days in 'the wilderness', as Lindsay put it, they finally reached the base hut at midnight on 17 April.

Chapman came outside and shouted, 'Who's that?' We told him. He then said, 'Have you got August with you?'

'No!' The answer went back to him like a pistol shot. We were too tired to give more than one explanation, and could not bear it if Chapman started to ask questions. So the word was flung at his head.

There was silence. A few seconds seemed to contain all the weariness of a lifetime. Then mercifully he said: 'I'll go in and tell Gino you've arrived.'

Gino appraised the situation quickly, told Scott he had been right to turn back, and set off as soon as the weather allowed. Three weeks later he was back, with Courtauld safe and sound.

Lindsay made no more extended sledge journeys for the next three months. When the ice left the fjord he went boating, with one of the girls to do the rowing. He would sit lazily in the sternsheets, smoking his pipe to keep the mosquitoes away. He enjoyed the company of the Eskimo girls – 'most of us were on very playful terms with them' – but continued to treat them like children and certainly not as bedmates. Gertrude occasionally irritated Lindsay by playing the same record continuously on the gramophone. When he finally lost patience, smashed the record and threw it away, she retrieved it and stuck it together again.

During the winter Lindsay would go and visit the neighbours in one of the small settlements nearby. He was enormously impressed by Eskimo hospitality, though less so when invited to eat raw frozen seal meat. At the base occasional culinary treats included seal liver, roast seagull, and once curried dog. The tinned beef brought for the dogs was found to be quite acceptable, or at any rate too good for canine consumption. A few tinned luxuries were kept for birthdays and to celebrate the return from a sledging journey. On Christmas Day the menu was hare soup, salmon, chicken, tongue, asparagus and Christmas pudding. Women were invited, and a photograph of several expedition members with Eskimo girls on their laps or beside them shows only Lindsay sitting slightly apart and by himself.

When journeys were being planned to end the expedition, Lindsay got together with Scott and Stephenson to cross the ice cap diagonally to the coast of south-west Greenland, a distance of about 450 miles. By the end of June he was happy to leave the base: it was not only the irritation of having Tina climb over him every night to get to Gino's bed above him, but there were one or two others who were getting on his nerves. While he was amazed that in general they all got on so well – 'I cannot recollect a single serious row during the whole of our thirteen months together' – little niggles were magnified in the close confinement of the base hut. 'One man was rather malicious, two were outspoken to the point of rudeness and a fourth had an ungovernable temper.' Jimmy Scott, with whom Lindsay had been on the March journey to the ice-cap station, was none of these. He and Scott worked well together, and Lindsay wanted to learn more from him about the art of dog driving.

One thing Lindsay had discovered about their dogs was that they loved, and thrived on, Horlicks mixed with seal's blood. Three teams of nine were taken on this journey. It was good experience for Lindsay in preparation for his much longer trans-Greenland crossing in 1934. 'The more you drive dogs the more, I think, you enjoy it. At first it all seems very strange. ...The dogs appear to be conspiring together for your discomfiture, and always get the better of your harassed self. After a little you feel more confident; you know your team well and take a pride in how you drive it. And now, after nearly a year with our dogs, we knew everything that was to be known about each one and how to make him do his utmost.'

He also came to know the characters of his dogs. Two of them he likened to wise old men, 'asthma-ridden lawyers' clerks', another to a barber's assistant who played left-half for the local football team, another to 'one of those persistent and persuasive gentlemen whom you meet in a place like Port Said'. This made it all the harder when, at the end of the journey, they were obliged to shoot all the dogs (except one which Scott took home with him). In south-west Greenland sledging with dogs was unknown, no one had any use for them and they would have been a danger to the cows and sheep. (One of Scott of the Antarctic's problems was that he could not bring himself to shoot dogs, or to feed dog to dog, though he was quite prepared to shoot his ponies.)

For most of the four-week trans-Greenland trek they travelled by night and slept during the day, when it was sometimes so hot in the tent that they lay naked on top of their sleeping-bags. The only thing Lindsay longed for was the hip-bath which he had brought to Greenland

and lost when it was blown away in a winter gale. Having reached their highest point on the ice cap, more than 9,000 feet, they celebrated with a jar of greengage jam given them by Courtauld and attached sails to their sledges for the downhill stretch to the coast at Ivigtut – as Nansen had done when he made the first crossing of Greenland in 1888.

In the previous twelve months Lindsay had grown up and learnt a lot. After an inchoate and undistinguished beginning to his army career, he had attained maturity in the Arctic. In the blank whiteness of Greenland his life had found its focus. Before going north he had never handled large fierce dogs, had never put on skis or rowed a boat, knew nothing of the working of a primus stove, and had hardly heard of a glacier. Though attached to the expedition as a surveyor, he had only done two months at the Royal Geographical Society (RGS) and admitted to having learnt very little.

It was in the teeth of opposition from the RGS that Lindsay led his three-man expedition to Greenland in 1934. His plan was to cross the ice cap from west to east, then to survey and map 350 miles of uncharted mountain ranges down the east side of Greenland, finishing at the base hut used in 1930–31. It would be the longest self-supporting sledge journey in history, exceeding a thousand miles, and the RGS refused to support it on the grounds that the project did not provide 'a sufficient margin of safety'. 'We considered Mr Lindsay's plans and considered them again,' said a subsequent president of the RGS, before deciding they could not endorse them.

'Nonsense,' said Lindsay. 'I was summarily dismissed by a body supposedly in business to increase geographical knowledge. But they did their utmost to obstruct a notable piece of exploration.'

Lindsay suspected that inquiries had been made of members of the first expedition, who may not have given him their unqualified support. He spoke his mind, he could be abrasive and – worst of all – he was not the most faithful follower of Gino and all his works. Lindsay was petitioning the RGS within months of Gino's death, and his memory was sacrosanct. Having come up against the brick wall of the RGS, Lindsay then used his considerable initiative and enlisted the support of the colonel of his regiment, Marshal of the Royal Air Force Lord Trenchard. Having himself soldiered in Nigeria at the beginning of the century, Trenchard had been impressed by Lindsay's trek through the Belgian Congo, and he agreed to use his influence to arrange for the Foreign Office to apply to Denmark for permission for the expedition to proceed. He also persuaded the Prince of Wales, Colonel-in-Chief of the Royal Scots Fusiliers, to be patron of the expedition, to the intense annoyance of the RGS. With a notable lack of good grace, the RGS agreed only to lend Lindsay some instruments.

So Lindsay assembled his team: Andrew Croft and Lieutenant Daniel Godfrey. Croft, a parson's son who had been the first head boy at Stowe when the school was founded (and who would become Quintin Riley's brother-in-law), went on ahead to Greenland to buy and learn to drive the dogs. (A few months earlier, travelling in Germany as a student, he had been perhaps the only Englishman to witness the burning of the Reichstag in Berlin.) Godfrey was an Eton scholar, a Royal Engineer and a qualified surveyor. Roger Pettiward, a talented artist and cartoonist who had recently been with Peter Fleming on his Brazilian Adventure (the title of Fleming's subsequent book), was due to go to Greenland with Lindsay, but the recurrence of a tropical disease contracted while in South America led him to suggest that Croft, an old friend from Oxford, should go instead.

The three-man expedition sledged for more than a hundred days and achieved its aims. It was a complete success and gained an entry in the Guinness Book of Records. *The Times*, in a leading article, declared it was one 'which for daring and success will rank high in the long annals of polar exploration'. The position of the highest mountain in Greenland (which Gino had photographed from the air in 1930) was established, and a new range of mountains discovered. On their return the RGS, while not exactly admitting its mistake in withholding support, did invite Lindsay to give a lecture to the Society, and a new president congratulated him on his achievement. James Wordie, the distinguished explorer in Greenland and the Antarctic, was present and paid a thoughtful tribute to Lindsay: 'I am not at all sure that a wholesome douche of discouragement is not the best incentive to spur on a young explorer. A man has to be set upon his mettle, and there is no more delightful outcome of effort than to prove that those whom one has been taught to respect were wrong, when this is done by carrying out to the letter the almost impossible exploits which were planned beforehand. That Mr Lindsay has done.'

Lindsay was generous in praise of his companions, in particular the proficiency of Croft's dog-driving and the precision of Godfrey's mapping. But the journey was not without occasional friction. Years later Croft wrote of Lindsay: 'Martin was something of a slave-driver and Daniel astonishingly unfit. Neither of them ever became much good at driving dogs and to crown it all Martin had economised on weight by bringing only a single-skin tent, which meant that we could never avoid hoar-frost and spent virtually every night in damp discomfort.'

Having already spent a winter in Greenland and laid a depot of dog food on the edge of the ice cap, Croft was frustrated by Lindsay's seeming indifference to the need to get going on their journey. 'My patience was tried almost beyond endurance while Martin calmly sat and wrote articles for *The Times*, and the spring thaw rang no danger bells in his ears. ... I felt totally disgruntled and so – I am afraid – did my Greenland friends who did not take kindly to Martin's autocratic ways.'

When Lindsay decided that the time had come to start their climb on to the ice plateau, 'he began ruthlessly to discard anything which in his eyes was not essential. He scrapped most of the medical equipment and carpentry tools, retaining twelve screws but no nails. We were allowed only one spare shirt, one pair of pants and one book.' However, Croft disobeyed orders and smuggled in a packet of tea, a spare suit of windproofs and *Hamlet* and *Macbeth* along with *Barchester Towers*. (Lindsay claimed not to understand the language of Shakespeare. He enjoyed early Victorian novels, but was happiest with a pocket atlas.)

By comparison with the Gino Watkins approach, Lindsay's was a quite different style of leadership – issuing orders, imposing discipline rather than choosing an individual for a task and then leaving it up to him. Gino's method inspired devotion while Lindsay's, derived from his army training, gained him respect. Yet in writing about his expeditions, in his often humorous narrative style and with an endearing modesty, he betrays no authoritarian tendencies. Perhaps it was the responsibility of leadership which brought out the soldier in him.

Lindsay's criticism of what he saw as Gino's irresponsibility in not leading the first relief party to rescue Courtauld from the ice-cap station was redoubled when he learnt, at the end of the expedition, of Gino's behaviour during an open boat journey which he made with Courtauld and Percy Lemon down the south-east Greenland coast. Gino had insisted on delaying the progress of their trip by staying for a week at an

Eskimo settlement instead of pushing on while the weather held. This, according to Lindsay, put their lives unnecessarily at risk: the autumn weather inevitably deteriorated, the seas got rougher, the boats broke down and they were nearly marooned in Greenland for another winter, with the prospect of having to shoot seals to survive. And yet here was Lindsay, according to Croft sitting around writing articles while the snow thawed, behaving in a similarly casual manner and failing to anticipate the consequences.

These occasional differences in no way prejudiced the success of the trans-Greenland expedition. 'As a party,' Lindsay wrote, 'we were as hard as nails and in perfect compatibility.' They reached the east coast (where Lindsay had been based four years earlier) on almost exactly the day, in early September, which he had calculated for the end of the expedition. He had asked the skipper of an Aberdeen trawler, the *Jacinth*, if he would give them passage home; but the pack ice, which was unusually early that year, was fast closing in. Had they been a day later, the trawler would not have been able to get in close enough to take them off and they would have had to stay for most of another year in east Greenland. (Jacynth was the name Lindsay gave his daughter, born within a year of his return home to his wife Joyce, a distant cousin whom he had married in 1932.)

Croft found himself in Finland at the beginning of the war, assisting that country in its struggle against the Russian invasion. Lindsay was charged with forming a battalion of skiers to support the Finnish resistance – three of his previous Arctic companions (Riley, Scott and Chapman) briefly served under him – but it was soon disbanded when Finland capitulated. A month before the outbreak of war, Lindsay had been recruited by his friend the author and adventurer Peter Fleming to go to China on assignment from the War Office. Their mission was to report to Chiang Kai-shek and help foment guerrilla warfare against the Japanese; but it was cancelled before they were due to leave. Lindsay was proposed by Fleming because he had learnt a bit of Chinese when he went to Shanghai with his regiment after returning from the Arctic in 1931. He and Fleming met in Moscow (Fleming was about to embark on his journey on the Trans-Siberian Railway which he recorded in *One's Company*); and they dined together in London on the night before Lindsay left for Greenland for the second time. Fleming said he wished he were going too; had he done so there is little doubt that, with his sense of comedy and his talent for mockery, of self and others, many of the orders issued peremptorily by Lindsay would have been ridiculed or ignored. 'Martinet Martin' might have featured in Fleming's account of the expedition.

When Germany invaded Norway in April 1940, Fleming and Lindsay came together once again, the first British soldiers to land on Norwegian soil. The commander of the reconnaissance force, the one-eyed and one-armed General Carton de Wiart, was delighted: 'Whoever may have been responsible for sending them, I thank him now, for there and then I appropriated them, and a better pair never existed.' The Norwegian episode was a fiasco, but Lindsay wrote two personal accounts of his experience of German bombing, in *The Spectator* and *Time and Tide*.

The war went on, Lindsay went to India, then to Normandy in July 1944, where he commanded a battalion of the Gordon Highlanders. He continued through France and into Germany until the end, was awarded the DSO and finished the war as a lieutenant-colonel. He never used his military rank again and, having never been very religious, he ceased believing in God after he had entered a concentration camp in 1945. He never regarded his war service as something to boast about, saying that his Polar Medal was the only gong he had really earned.

For the next twenty years Lindsay was MP for Solihull (he had been adopted as candidate for Brigg in Lincolnshire before the war), having won the seat in the Conservative interest against Roy Jenkins, and against the general trend to Labour, in the 1945 election. He was not always a wholehearted supporter of the Macmillan government, and it was no surprise that he was never offered a ministerial post. He did not toe the party line, in the same way that he did not toe the Gino Watkins line. He may have suffered for it, he was often outspoken, but he remained true to his principles. Having tabled a House of Commons motion condemning Lord Beaverbrook for his 'sustained vendetta' against the Royal Family in his newspapers, Lindsay was himself attacked in the *Sunday Express*, which suggested he was 'after a rich widow'. He had been left a large bequest and a flat in New York by a wealthy American woman, and had been divorced three years later by his wife. The Press Council upheld his complaint against the newspaper; not long afterwards he married a rich divorcée, Loelia, Duchess of Westminster.

Above all, perhaps, Lindsay was a man of courage – in Africa, in the Arctic, in the war and in public life. The year before he died at the age of seventy-five, he was about to undergo an operation for cancer and was offered a sedative the night before, which he declined. 'I always slept well on the night before a battle during the war, and I propose to do the same now.'

3
Quintin Riley (1905–80)

Whether in appearance or behaviour, Quintin Riley was not one's idea of an Arctic explorer. He was short, slim, with an air of vulnerability. In his dress and habits he was fussy, meticulous, in his speech dogmatic and often mischievous. From his father he had inherited a strong religious belief, in the Anglo-Catholic tradition, and his faith gave him self-assurance and helped him overcome an innate pessimism. He was the natural padre of the Greenland party and would conduct Sunday services at the base.

The other members of the expedition thought it amusingly appropriate that Riley should have been given the names of Quintin Theodore Petroc Molesworth. The last two were Cornish: his mother, Andalusia, was the daughter of Viscount Molesworth, who was rector and patron of the church of St Petroc in Little Petherick, a village near Padstow in north Cornwall. At the end of the nineteenth century Riley's father, Athelstan, bought the patronage from his father-in-law and proceeded to turn the church into what Betjeman has called 'a shrine of Anglo-Catholicism'. He employed Sir Ninian Comper to embellish it with a painted rood screen, a new high altar and reredos, and stained glass. After his wife's death Athelstan Riley added a chapel and commemorated her with a bronze effigy, also some sixteenth-century vestments and chalices. His heart was entombed in the chapel when he died.

Athelstan never took orders but he was active in ecclesiastical affairs for most of his life. He collaborated with Vaughan Williams on the English Hymnal, took a close interest in the Greek, Russian and Armenian Orthodox Churches and visited the Assyrian Christians in Kurdistan. He also went to Mount Athos and wrote an account of the monasteries. Soon after the birth of Quintin (his youngest child), Athelstan bought the Manor of La Trinité in Jersey and with it the right to call himself 'Seigneur', which also imposed on him the duty, whenever there was a royal visit to the island, of presenting the monarch with a brace of mallard.

Young Riley revelled in his father's eccentricity as much as in his passion for Anglo-Catholicism, and he loved telling his Greenland companions about his family. He followed his father in so many ways: in his insistence on correct form in church services and his opposition to any reform in the liturgy; in his membership of the Church Assembly; in his fastidious manner; in his preference for Turkish cigarettes. Unsurprisingly, the choice of public school for Riley's education was Lancing, one of the schools founded by a Tractarian and Anglo-Catholic priest, Nathaniel Woodard. Evelyn Waugh was a contemporary at Lancing, but not a friend. Riley's fellow-pupil who soon became his closest friend was Gino Watkins. At school they shared an aversion to work and ball games and a sense of the ridiculous. At Cambridge they went to different colleges and read different subjects, but continued to spend time together. Riley was the slightly less irresponsible of the two – unlike Gino, he did at least get a degree – but the social life of post-war 1920s Cambridge took up much of their time. They both did a spell together as special constables in London during the General Strike, and were disappointed not to get involved in any riots.

Three of the most distinguished living Antarctic explorers were teaching in Cambridge at this time. Professor Frank Debenham had been on Scott's last expedition and was now first director of the Scott Polar Research Institute; James Wordie had been with Shackleton on his *Endurance* expedition; Raymond Priestley had been with Shackleton on his previous, *Nimrod*, expedition, then with Scott when the South Pole party perished. While Riley would have met these men, probably with Gino, or at least attended their lectures (he was reading geography), they did not immediately fire in him an ambition to be a polar explorer. (Gino was inspired by Priestley to go to the Arctic and by Wordie to lead an expedition to Spitzbergen in 1927, at the age of twenty.) Riley enjoyed coxing the Pembroke College VIII, and in the holidays sailing in Jersey and Cornwall. When he left Cambridge he rather wondered what to do. His father suggested the Colonial Service, but instead he went to work for Gino's father, Colonel Watkins, who had an interior decorating shop in Chelsea called Renaissance Traders. Riley spent almost two years there, selling wallpapers and lampshades, and earning £2 10s. a week.

It was not a job that gave him much satisfaction, and when Gino returned to England after nine months in Labrador and asked him to come to Greenland – 'I have planned a marvellous expedition' – Riley jumped at the idea. Jimmy Scott would be going – he was known to Riley as Gino's sister's boyfriend – and so would Courtauld, whom he had known when they were at prep school together in Eastbourne. It sounded like a jolly Cambridge party. But this would be a serious expedition, and Gino said he would have to learn something scientific. 'So I went off to Kew Observatory, at Gino's suggestion, to learn the rudiments of meteorology – taking observations, estimating the height of clouds and so on. The course lasted less than two months, but I learnt quite a lot in that time.'

Gino knew where Riley's strengths lay. Not only would he be conscientious and thorough with his weather readings, he would be the ideal person to put in charge of assembling all the stores and equipment which they would need to take with them. So Gino made him quartermaster, and in his neat and meticulous way Riley recorded and checked all the equipment – scientific instruments, aircraft parts, tents, food, clothing – as it was delivered to St Katherine's Dock in London, where the *Quest*, Shackleton's old ship, was waiting to take the party to the Arctic. Only the Energen rolls were left behind. When they were offered to the expedition, Riley told the company that made them of their total requirement for a year, and then forgot about it. The huge consignment of Energen rolls, filling several lorries, had to be politely declined when it turned up at the docks shortly before the ship sailed. As the *Quest*, dressed overall, prepared to cast off, Riley's father, his sister Morwenna, and Nana, his old nanny, waved him goodbye. Half an hour later, still suffering the effects of the farewell party the night before, he was sick.

Riley met his first Eskimos when the *Quest* put in to Angmagssalik, on the east Greenland coast and he visited one of their tents. It was made of sealskin, the smell of which he found very offensive; nor was he impressed by the accommodation, or by what was cooking in a tin wash tub on the stove. 'I was very afraid they would offer us something to eat, but they didn't.' However, it didn't take him long to appreciate the virtues and the taste of seal meat. In an article written during the war when he was training commandos in Arctic warfare, he compared it to mutton and recommended the tongue, liver and brains of a seal as being particularly good. And for a special delicacy, 'the liver of an unborn baby seal, lightly cooked and served on toast is an excellent breakfast dish'. He did admit that raw seal brains were an acquired taste.

Within two weeks of finding a suitable place to build the base hut, Riley and four others, led by Scott, set off on their pioneering journey which would take them 130 miles inland, climbing from the coast to 8,500 feet in the centre of Greenland. It was an exciting but a daunting prospect as they looked up at this vast white desert which reached down towards the sea and was seemingly held back by the dark, bare mountains of the coast. First they had to climb rocks to the foot of the glacier, then up what one of them described rather whimsically as 'an ancient giant's stairway' (and all of them called Buggery Bank), and through a maze of crevasses on to the ice cap proper. As he was the short man of the party and the lightest in weight, Riley had the hardest task when it came to pushing or hauling the sledges up the steep ice bank, and he was sometimes on his knees, though not in prayer. When his sledge was almost at the top, he suddenly began to descend, head first and on his stomach, passing Martin Lindsay 'with a look of pained surprise on his face'.

Only Scott had previous experience of driving dogs, and the crevasses were more treacherous in summer, when the snow was wet and slushy. But once they had marked the route through the crevasses with red flags, they were on the ice plateau and the going improved. Now the problem was seeing the way ahead on this white sheet. The moving clouds and the shadows of the snowdrifts were the only things to focus on. Riley was able at times to ride on the sledge while driving the dogs and enjoying what for Greenland was warm summer weather. Disciplining dogs with a whip, however, was against his nature and he took time to get used to it. 'Learning to use the whip, I have managed to whip most parts of myself – quite painful too.'

He was more concerned that he had left his prayer book behind at the base. This was most unlike Riley, who normally prepared and packed everything so carefully before a journey. Someone suggested that he wouldn't need to say his prayers on the ice cap.

'Of course I do.'

'But can't you say prayers without a prayer book?'

'Yes, only I like to remember the saints' days. It makes it so much more interesting.'

(Later, when the two men were on their own together setting up the weather station, Lindsay asked Riley why he should want a prayer book in the middle of Greenland. 'In case you die' was Riley's response.

His faith meant a great deal to him, but it was not in his character to belabour others with it. There was invariably a twinkle in his eye.)

It had taken a week to get on to the ice cap, and it would be another ten days before they reached the place, at the agreed height and distance from the coast, where the weather station would be established. Three of them would be returning to base, but for Riley and Lindsay it was a relief to be staying put. 'Well, here we are for several weeks. A lovely view, just nothing stretching in front of us. The party left lickety split about 4 pm. It was getting cold so Martin and I went back and had a cup of cocoa. We tidied up a bit outside and settled our things inside. After supper Martin and I played chess in which he thought of a very pretty mate. A chapter of *Vanity Fair* and so to bed.' So unworried and 'laid-back', Riley might have been describing the first evening of a weekend at a fishing lodge in Scotland. One would hardly think they were virtually in the middle of nowhere and would see nothing or no one for at least a month.

Gino had made an interesting choice of the two men who were to set up the station. Riley was fastidious, methodical, tidy-minded, a good person to organise a tent and the space required for cooking and sleeping. Lindsay was quite different – a soldier who was personally undisciplined, prone to losing things and getting things wrong. But he was very good at building the snow-houses which they added to the weather station – two for stores or living space, and an 'ice closet' with a sledge for a seat.

Until 1914 it was assumed that only Eskimos were capable of building snow-houses or igloos, which in extreme temperatures are much warmer than tents. It was Vilhjalmur Stefansson, an explorer of Canadian and Icelandic origins, who exploded this myth by building a serviceable snow-house nine feet in diameter and six feet high in three hours. He was something of a guru to the expedition and his books – *My Life with the Eskimo* and *The Friendly Arctic* – became bibles. Scott, who used to pen verses in Greenland for his and the others' amusement, wrote one piece of doggerel in tribute to Stefansson:

> There lives a hothouse breed of men
> Who wash behind the ear;
> Their meat is potted ham and hen,
> Their drink is bottled beer.

Such is the man I might have been,
But the one clear call to me
Was to chase the wily vitamin
Across the Polar sea.

There's very little you must know,
So long as you travel light.
Just read *My Life with the Eskimo*,
And you will be all right.

'We built the snow-houses with a spade in one hand and Stefansson's book in the other,' Riley recalled. He would neatly cut out the blocks of frozen snow, from about eighteen inches below the snow surface and using a long knife, while Lindsay did the building. When the snow wasn't cold enough, the blocks had a tendency to break up, and Lindsay would demand that Riley dig deeper into the ice. Another problem, as Riley put it in a light-hearted rebuke, was that Lindsay insisted on a cupboard in one of the snow-houses. 'I don't think Stefansson or Eskimos build snow-houses with cupboards.'

The two had almost nothing in common, in temperament or interests. Lindsay's principal sporting pastime was hunting; the only sport Riley enjoyed, having finished with his spell as a cox at Cambridge, was yachting. Riley's other main, indeed passionate, interest was religion, in particular the Church of England, while Lindsay's religious education and observance had never got beyond army church parades. But the two got on remarkably well. 'I feel Martin will be most admirable. Nothing upsets him and he is one of the most good-natured people I have ever met. In fact an excellent person for this sort of game. ... I hung my crucifix over my sleeping-bag and we hoisted the Union Jack outside, and so we have both Christian and national emblems erected.'

When they were not making improvements to the ice-cap station, clearing snowdrifts or taking regular weather readings with the various instruments – temperature, pressure, wind speed, depth of snow – Riley and Lindsay would read, play chess, talk about life. There was a code of private jokes which were repeated almost daily. The postman was late, the telephone out of order, and there was never anything worth reading in the newspaper. When snow fell from the roof of their tent, one would remark that the cat must be up there again.

Riley was happy to sit cross-legged in front of the primus stove; but there was not much variety in the food he was able to cook – porridge for breakfast, peas and pemmican for dinner, with prunes on alternate nights. He tried making cakes with pea-flour which tasted only of warm margarine, and once announced that he would make scrambled eggs from egg powder, which proved impossible. Chess was usually played after dinner. 'Two games of chess tonight, both of which I won. M. lost his queen in both of them. He doesn't seem much use without her.' And so to bed, with a book (*Jane Eyre* or *Wuthering Heights*) and for Riley a hot-water bottle. Always concerned for his creature comforts, Riley would not travel without his 'hottie'. On the way up to the ice cap the water from the bottle was used for making porridge the next morning (instead of melting snow for the purpose), but it was thought so disgusting that the practice was soon abandoned.

When the snow kept them indoors Riley's Brixham trawler might occupy his mind, as he made designs for improving its cabin space. On Sundays they rested from their labours, and though Riley could not persuade Lindsay to take part in any readings or prayers, he was happy alone with his bible. 'Nice and warm in the sun. I read a chapter of St Paul's Epistle to the Romans and St John's Gospel, also two or three chapters of the *Imitation of Christ*.'

After a month they calculated that if the relief party did not arrive by mid-October, they would have to walk out, giving themselves ten days' food to get back to base on half rations, but neither of them seemed unduly worried at this possibility. 'No sign of travellers,' Riley noted on 1 October. But the following day their peace was disturbed by the arrival of six of their companions, including Gino who congratulated them on the building of the snow-houses, which especially pleased Riley. One of them teased him about his crimson face and long beard and hair. There followed two days of talking, planning, singing, eating and pipe-smoking before Riley and Lindsay said farewell to the two who were replacing them and to the home they had shared for five weeks. During their time on the ice cap Hitler's National Socialists became the second largest party in the Reichstag, and unemployment in Britain exceeded two million – two grim pieces of news of which they were happily unaware.

Back at the base – a three-day blizzard on the return journey gave a foretaste of the winter to come – Riley was delighted to have his first bath in more than two months. 'It is very nice to be in plus fours and be a gentleman again. My fingers are getting better; the ends were a bit frost-bitten.' He was also pleased to note that there were now three Eskimo girls helping to cook and clean the base hut. Three of the party – Gino, Chapman and Lemon – were already looking on them to satisfy more than their domestic needs. To Riley, however, they were servants who should be kept in their place, and certainly not in his bed. 'The servants want a bit of looking after, they let the fire out if you don't watch them and you have to show them and tell them everything, which is difficult when one cannot speak the language.' However, he took the trouble to learn the language, particularly in relation to cooking. His diary also records details of Eskimo games and dances, and long vocabulary lists.

Riley's attitude, and that of the others, towards the three men who took the Eskimo girls to their beds was disapproving, but it was behaviour that, reluctantly, had to be tolerated. For Riley a sexual relationship with the natives was not British, not the done thing; though with his leader and great friend indulging himself, there was very little Riley could do about it.

One of Scott's verses, written at the base hut and entitled 'Quintin's Song', records his distaste for the idea: 'And dreaming of an Eskimette / Has never made my bedclothes wet.' It does, however, also allude to a physical relationship with Gino which, though shocking, is probably no more than a fantasy expressed by Riley, or rather by Scott imagining Riley's feelings. The question arises whether Riley was a repressed homosexual. He had had very little social contact with women, he did not appear at ease in their company, and though not exactly a misogynist, he considered women to be irrelevant to his life. By his own account he did not have a physical relationship with a woman until he got married, at the age of thirty-six, to the sister of one of his explorer friends. Gino had been his closest friend since school, and he looked up to this handsome, slightly effeminate-looking man as his role model – jealous of his way with the girls and his reputation as a ballroom dancer.

Whatever his emotional feelings at the time, Riley did not record them; and he was happy with his burgeoning life as a polar explorer. In the last week of October, when Chapman and his party had set off for the ice cap, he was alone at the base for a few days – except for visiting Eskimos who might sleep on the floor. On the 27th he celebrated his twenty-fifth birthday and 'a quarter of a century of my life irretrievably gone. Am I satisfied with it? On the whole yes.' He gave as examples his religious belief, 'though I might practise it a good deal better', and his good fortune in having 'a wonderful father and a family of whom I am very fond, and they of me'. 'Here I am in Greenland, having a wonderful time and enjoying every minute of it. Really, what more could one want?'

For much of the time Riley was working in his capacity as meteorologist, on occasion having to crawl out of the hut to read his instruments in stronger than gale-force winds. It was not, of course, in any way Riley's fault that the winter weather forecasts which had been given him by the Meteorological Office in London were wildly wrong. Based on the records of a meteorological station at Angmagssalik, the Met Office forecast an average of one gale a month, which led Gino to make plans for the relief of the inland weather station every four to six weeks. This proved quite impossible: gales became commonplace during the winter, and Riley's instruments recorded eighteen which exceeded storm force 10 (above 60 mph). Gusts were recorded of more than 130 mph.

What neither the Met Office nor Riley knew was that the place chosen for the expedition's base, only thirty miles west of Angmagssalik, experienced storms of a severity that was not found elsewhere. These winds, known as katabatic, flow out and down from the dome of the ice cap, gathering speed rather like a mountain torrent, and producing local storms as they reach the edge of the ice and funnel down the glacier towards the coast. The real problem was that around the base camp the ice cap came down almost to the sea. The topography was ideal for these katabatic winds, formed in the cold air above 8,000 feet, to rush down the ice, whereas the mountains behind Angmagssalik gave some protection. Nor did the wind strength at Lake Fjord, 100 miles north where the 1932–33 expedition made its base for a year, ever exceed 40 mph. At the central ice-cap station the gales were less frequent than at the base and, though severe enough, never exceeded force 9 (around 50 mph). Further north, where an ice-cap station was established by a German expedition during the same winter, the highest recorded wind speed was 40 mph. Though only an amateur meteorologist, Riley, with his sense of the meticulous, continued to take observations during all weathers; obligingly, the anemometer narrowly missed him when it blew away in an October storm. On his return to England he was congratulated by the director of the Met Office on his work and all the information he brought back.

Riley was soon to experience the worst of the winter weather hurtling down the ice cap as he struggled to get up the glacier and on to it. Two flights had been made during February in one of the Gypsy Moths with the intention of dropping food to Courtauld at the ice-cap station where he had now been alone for nearly three months. On the first occasion, although the weather was clear at the base, there was thick cloud over the ice cap, and the second time the Moth could not make enough headway against the force of the wind. Both aeroplanes were then badly damaged on the ground, so Gino decided that Riley and Scott should sledge up to find him. If all was well, the practical, phlegmatic Riley, who knew how to look after himself, would stay on alone for another spell.

Having already stayed at the weather station, he was sure that drifting snow would have covered the tent, but thought they might at least see the Union Jack marking the spot. Riley was touched that the Eskimo girls were in tears when they said goodbye, sure that they would never see him and Scott again. In fact they were both back the next day: huge wind drifts of hard snow kept upsetting the sledges, which were so heavy they had to be unpacked before they could be pushed upright again. Then the runner of Scott's sledge broke in half. 'Gino was very upset at our return,' Riley noted. However, he should have realised that Riley would not have the strength, with only one other person, to right an overloaded sledge. If a sledge broke again, a third man would be needed, so that two would go on while the other came back. Lindsay was the man chosen, but they made another false start because the wind and visibility were so bad they could not reach the depot at the top of the glacier where all their food for the journey was stored. Unsurprisingly, Riley was the one person to have anticipated this, and had taken the precaution of packing 'a few biscuits for lunch' – in fact about thirty biscuits and some chocolate, which had to last them for three days before they were driven back to base.

They finally got away on 9 March and returned forty days later having failed to find the ice-cap station. The wind and cold were extreme for most of the time – temperatures were recorded down to eighty degrees of frost – and one blizzard prevented their travelling for six days. The meteorological records of the journey kept so assiduously by Riley led Gordon Hayes, in his book *The Conquest of the North Pole*, to judge that the conditions 'approached the limits of human endurance'. It was certainly colder than the journey to the ice-cap station led by Chapman the previous November.

In the first week of April, having already been in the area of the ice-cap station for several days, but for most of the time confined to their tents in appalling weather, Riley commented: 'Things begin to look rather serious.' On Easter Sunday, 5 April, visibility improved but nothing was seen. Riley read the Communion service after breakfast, and said a special prayer for Courtauld. 'I wish I was able to make Communion. I do miss it. ... We can look for the station for three more days only and then we shall have to return to the base. I pray God we find August first for it will go hard with him if we don't.'

Since there was now no question of leaving Riley at the ice-cap station, he gave Scott and Lindsay an Easter present of tobacco from his reserves. They all had an Easter tea with marmalade, and then, because dog food was getting short, it was reluctantly decided that one animal would have to be killed to feed to the others.

The three men searched in vain for another four days. Without a wireless time-signal set to measure longitude against latitude, they could not pinpoint the position of the station, but Riley knew they must have passed within a mile of it, and that it would have been visible from that distance. 'There is no more we can do without a time-signal set. ... I fear something has happened to August and he is dead. ... Poor August's people and Mollie. Unless he has walked out they will have weeks of suspense. If we can get back quickly now there may be another chance.'

The chance to which Riley was referring was that another party of three men, this time with a time-signal set, would find the station and perhaps Courtauld still alive inside it. But most of the dogs would be needed for the second relief journey, and they were now so hungry they were eating both the men's and each other's excreta. Scott, Lindsay and Riley were on two-thirds rations and it was imperative that they get back to the base fast. They reached it in seven days, and it was midnight on 17 April when they gave Gino the bad news.

After the rescue of Courtauld, no more journeys to the ice cap were undertaken and Riley had little to do, apart from his weather observations, until he went home in August. However, he did make trips in one of the whale boats, sometimes to pick up supplies from Angmagssalik, and always recognisable by the yachting cap or trilby which he used to wear. His attempts to learn the art of kayaking were not entirely successful. On one occasion, while coming back to shore, he overturned, having put his paddle too far into the water. He could neither right the kayak nor get out of it. Fortunately Chapman was on hand to pull him out.

As the expedition's principal humorist and conversationalist he could be relied on to keep his companions entertained. One of them said of Riley that 'he can talk more volubly than anyone I have yet met, and tells a story in a most fascinating way'. He also loved to start an argument about something trivial, which often engendered a lot of heat and might last, off and on, for days. The most memorable, if pointless, concerned the description of a cooked breakfast. Eggs and bacon, or bacon and eggs? The former was eventually adjudged the more acceptable, by a narrow majority.

Later that year Riley, together with Scott, Pam Watkins and Gino's nanny, went to Copenhagen to greet Gino on his return. (Colonel Watkins told Scott and Pam they were not to go unless Riley accompanied them as chaperone.) Gino and Courtauld had completed their hazardous open boat journey round the southern tip of Greenland, then linked up with John Rymill and Wilfred Hampton who had crossed the ice cap to the west coast. This was the end of the expedition, marked by much celebrating and carousing. Riley recalled a party in the Tivoli gardens, where he ended up dancing ring-a-roses with Prince Knud.

Riley was back in Greenland the following summer, with Gino, Rymill and Chapman, to spend another year taking meteorological readings and doing coastal surveys, on behalf of Pan-American Airways. His father accompanied him to Copenhagen and went with the party as far as Elsinore on the Danish ship *Gertrud Rask* taking them north. Once it had dropped them off at Lake Fjord, they were able to get around in Riley's motor boat, the *Stella Polaris*, which he had brought to Greenland (it would also go with him in 1934 to the Antarctic). Lake Fjord, so named when it was discovered during the first expedition, was not only ideally sheltered for their base but might, Riley mused, suit their sponsors very well, as a place for landing sea planes and building fishing lodges and a hotel round the shores of the lake.

Due to the lack of sponsorship for this expedition (less than £1,000), the food which was brought from England was kept to an emergency minimum. Riley was able to supplement their diet in the first few days when he went on board an Aberdeen trawler and was given fresh cod, salt cod and a large halibut; but Gino was intent on spending much of his time hunting seals from his kayak. After only a week, however, his empty kayak was found floating half a mile from the shore. Riley's leader, mentor and closest friend was dead and his body never found.

That morning Riley was at the base camp, making a floor for one of the tents, while Gino went off alone after seals and Rymill and Chapman took the *Stella* to do some mapping in the fjord. Several Eskimos turned up and were given some seal-meat for lunch. Riley was 'tidying up' when the boat returned at three o'clock with Gino's kayak on board. He knew that Gino soon got cramp in cold water, even in England, and could not have survived for long in freezing water, especially as his trousers were found on an ice floe. In his diary Riley betrayed none of his feelings in his account of how he thought his friend must have met his death. His concluding note was written that evening, after he had gone out, in his methodical way, to count the number of fish in the net below the camp: 'After a meal we went to bed. I cannot realise that Gino must be dead. Thirty-five salmon in trammel.'

Only a few days later, returning from Angmagssalik where they had gone to report Gino's death and communicate with their sponsors, Riley had what he described as 'the nearest approach to death I have ever made', on board the *Stella*. The three of them were being thrown around in a huge sea; both the engine and the pump failed. Riley was steering his boat, in Chapman's words, 'with white set face, whirling the wheel round trying to keep bows on to the waves – and what waves – coming off the bergs at all angles. Soon the seas got worse … I saw Quintin turn the boat somehow between two waves, and with the northerly wind we started drifting helplessly towards a rocking berg. …With Quintin's masterly handling of the sail in alternating winds, we gradually drew away from first one berg then the other.'

Once back at their Lake Fjord base, a cross was made in memory of Gino and placed on a headland overlooking the fjord. At the end of the expedition, which continued for another twelve months, Riley allowed himself a more emotional farewell for his old friend as he left Lake Fjord, and Greenland, for the last time: 'I felt very sad at leaving Gino behind when we passed his cross. My thoughts and prayers were full of him. Now back to the civilised world without him – what next? It seems that all the kick in life will be gone. Gino gave me my calling and so I must go on.' When he got home Riley found a letter from Gino's father, who died two years later at the age of fifty-five, referring to him as 'Gino's greatest friend'.

It is no exaggeration to say that Gino was responsible for the course of the rest of Riley's life. He spent three years in the Antarctic (there were five of Watkins's boys on this expedition), followed by irregular warfare in several theatres of the Second World War, making good use of the Watkins way of leadership and of encouraging individual initiative. In his later years his activities and interests, aside from the Church of England, were almost entirely to do with polar matters.

Riley liked to say that he joined the British Graham Land Expedition, led by John Rymill, because he enjoyed housekeeping. In addition to his job as meteorologist, looking after and distributing the stores were his department; so too were controversy and prejudice. On the way to Antarctica, the ship carrying Riley and the rest of the expedition was commanded by a naval officer, 'Red' Ryder, whose views on discipline were anathema to those trained in the Gino Watkins school. Their attitude to the voyage was that, while Ryder was of course captain of the ship, there was no need for naval regulations or the issuing of orders. Ryder, on the other hand, 'felt that the Admiralty would look to me to maintain the high level traditional to the naval service'.

Riley had a healthy disrespect for naval discipline, though he was careful (or perhaps Rymill advised him to be careful) to restrain his argumentative tendencies. He was contemptuous of the inefficiency and time-wasting on board which, as he saw it, was 'entirely due to things being run on Service lines. In the Services when dealing with brainless people (includes all ranks) no doubt you have to do things in a peculiar way.... God preserve us from Service people. ...does it surprise one that mutinies occur in the Navy? I remember Gino saying he would never have Service people in command of anything.'

Once the expedition established itself on the long peninsula known as Graham Land, which hitherto was thought to be an archipelago of islands, Riley got on much better with Ryder. He also struck up a friendship, albeit at times a disputatious one, with Launcelot Fleming, a geologist and the expedition chaplain (he had been ordained the previous year). Religious observance was quite a feature of this expedition: two services every Sunday, with Riley playing the hymns very slowly on his accordion, and a sermon from Fleming. 'Launcelot preached on miracles. He really is extraordinarily good. It caused a discussion from 6.45 to 11.30 on the subject.' On Christmas Eve Fleming heard Riley's confession, in the meteorological hut on top of the hill.

They disagreed, however, on the forms of service, Fleming being in favour of an informal, ecumenical service, while Riley insisted on sticking to the Book of Common Prayer and taking Communion , which he sometimes called Mass, in the early morning. When the two men shared a tent, and a blizzard made sledging impossible, they would engage in debate – perhaps uniquely among polar explorers – on the liturgy and other ecclesiastical matters. 'Although a man of no principles (I allude to his lunching, and shaking hands, with the Bolshevist naval attaché in London), Launcelot has many ideas which lend themselves to long discussions, so pleasant for this kind of weather and beneficial to the intellect.'

Fleming was entertained, stimulated and sometimes exasperated by Riley's prejudices and his dogmatic expression of them. He remarked that one eccentric on an expedition was quite enough: 'to have had a second man of similar characteristics would have been to invite disaster.' He did not share all Riley's religious views, which 'may appear in some respects narrow and partisan – part of this was I think a kind of pose, part of it inherited from his father whose memory he deeply honoured – but there was a wonderfully firm root of spiritual devotion and trust, a strongly held Christian loyalty'. And his faith must have given him comfort during his various ordeals, on the Greenland ice cap and on the sea ice of the Antarctic.

Under Riley's supervision, the keeping and distribution of the stores, in Fleming's words, 'contributed to the success of the expedition and the wellbeing of its members'. He particularly enjoyed arranging the occasional handout, at Christmas or to celebrate a birthday, of a reserved bottle of port or sherry. (Alcohol was only drunk on special occasions but music was available on a wind-up gramophone operated by Riley. Evenings were normally spent reading or in some debate or argument initiated by him.)

Some of Riley's eccentricities were recalled by fellow members of the expedition. If it was snowing when he had to climb up to the meteorological hut to take readings, he would take an umbrella with him, returning downhill on skis under cover of his umbrella. One day, when a loud noise was heard from his tent and he was asked what was going on, Riley replied that he was having an argument with a Roman Catholic nun, and that he was winning. He kept with him a copy of *Whitaker's Almanack* in order to settle any factual points which might arise in the arguments with his companions which he so enjoyed provoking. And he was particularly pleased when the news of King Edward's affair with Mrs Simpson was announced on the wireless and he was the only one to say that the king would abdicate. He won several bets, which were paid in chocolate.

When war came and Riley joined the Royal Naval Volunteer Reserve, he had to bow to naval discipline – but only up to a point. The attitude to conventional notions of discipline instilled in him and his Arctic companions by Gino, and their experiences in Greenland, made them ideal candidates for irregular operations where their training, their ability to take decisions under stress and to survive by their wits might be critical. Four of Watkins's boys – Lindsay, Chapman, Scott and Riley – came together in January 1940 to form a battalion of the 5th Scots Guards to undertake covert attacks against the Russians in their 'winter war' with Finland. But it never got off the ground, and Riley went on to combined operations in Norway, then an Arctic commando where he teamed up again with Commander 'Red' Ryder. Ryder was involved, with Lieutenant-Commander Ian Fleming, in the formation of intelligence assault units, one of which was commanded by Riley, who succeeded in capturing large quantities of enemy intelligence during the landings in Sicily and Italy. He spent 1944 in Burma and India, then joined the British forces advancing through Germany. For someone who would not have been at home with the discipline of a hierarchical military unit, his talents had been well employed in small-scale operations. He had had a good war, but he received no honours or decorations.

Much more important to him, during the war he married Dorothy Croft and they had a daughter. Dorothy was the daughter of a parson and sister of Riley's old friend Andrew Croft (they had been at Lancing together), who was himself a distinguished Arctic explorer, making a 1,000-mile trek across Greenland with Lindsay in 1934.

Riley never had another day job but, following the calling that Gino gave him, he continued to be concerned with polar affairs. He was chairman of the Friends of the Scott Polar Research Institute, a member of the Arctic and Antarctic clubs, a founding member of the Reindeer Council, and author of a children's book, *The Discovery of the Poles*. The discovery of the South Pole, and the death of Captain Scott and his companions, was the subject of a film, *Scott of the Antarctic*, for which Riley was hired in 1947 as technical adviser. As a stickler for detail, he enjoyed insisting that the sledges, clothing and equipment should all be reproduced with complete accuracy, and despite occasional disagreements on how things should be done, he soon gained the affection of all involved in the making of the film. John Mills, who played Scott, said Riley became an old friend in a remarkably short space of time. His help and encouragement on location in Switzerland and Norway were especially appreciated.

It is not known whether Riley gave anyone on the film set the benefit of his opinion of Scott. He was not a fan of Scott's style of leadership, nor of his refusal to use dogs for sledging and his reliance instead on ponies. As a Victorian naval officer, Scott imposed naval discipline on his expeditions. Ward-room and lower deck were separated, he was in command and he gave orders. He never discussed his plans, even with his closest companion, Bill Wilson. This was not the way to run an expedition, in Riley's view, brought up in the much more relaxed and inclusive Watkins school. Gino had also learnt by Scott's mistakes, teaching himself to drive dogs because there was no other sensible way to travel in the polar regions. Scott couldn't drive dogs, didn't want to learn, and the dogs that he imported to Antarctica were the wrong sort – Siberian rather than Greenland huskies. Riley of course respected Scott's heroic trek to the Pole and back and the manner of his death (which were suitably portrayed in the film), but he did not admire his methods.

Riley represented perhaps the most enduring link with the Watkins boys in their later lives. He organised a dinner to mark the twenty-fifth anniversary of the expedition, remained a good friend of Chapman, kept in touch with Rymill's widow after Rymill's death, and went back on a trip to Greenland with Lindsay in 1973. As a man so devoted to the Church, it was perhaps unsurprising that he was selected as a godfather both to one of Lindsay's sons and to Jimmy Scott's second son.

And he was never averse to passing on a bit of mischievous gossip, such as how the expedition's pilot, Jimmy D'Aeth, having become an air vice-marshal, decided at the age of fifty-eight to go into the Church. He made the announcement, according to Riley, at an RAF dinner – 'Having served King and country, I am now going to serve God' – and departed leaving a large number of debts in the mess.

It was through Captain Scott's son, the naturalist Peter, that Riley became interested in the Loch Ness Monster, or what they called an 'unidentified animate object, in the depths of the loch'. For several years he would make summer trips to the shores of Loch Ness, to spend all day watching and making written notes of every passing boat, bird and floating log, in the same meticulous way that he used to record his weather readings in the Arctic and Antarctic. He would also talk a lot and ask a lot of questions, especially of young people whose attitudes, ambitions and morals interested him. As a county councillor and a school governor in Essex, he made sometimes controversial contributions to meetings, but his enthusiasm was welcomed.

Always conscious of his father's example, Riley's passion for all things ecclesiastical never faded. Having been a member of the Church Assembly, he was elected to the General Synod and re-elected in 1980, the year he died – killed in a car crash on Christmas Day. Among the tributes David James, MP, also a Loch Ness enthusiast and an Antarctic explorer who helped with the Scott film, wrote to Riley's widow Dorothy:

> At moments he must have been exasperating – and I had my odd moments of controversy with him ... but however irate and worked up he became, I found him incapable of unfairness or lack of personal compassion. And always there was that glint of humour in his eye that turned away any possibility of wrath. But certainly only you could have transformed an 'eccentric' into a 'character' in the richest meaning of the word. He loved, of course, to stir things up, which is what made him such marvellous company.

Riley's old Antarctic companion, Launcelot Fleming, who became a bishop and afterwards Dean of Windsor, wrote an appreciation in *The Times*, in which he commented on Riley's 'inexhaustible capacity for argument which revealed many assumed prejudices. ... He will be remembered with affection as a tremendous character – opinionated on most subjects, provocative on some – and as a man of faith, courage and dedicated loyalty.' Fleming also wrote to Dorothy: 'No expedition with Quintin as a member could be dull. ... He was always good company, and extremely able in many respects: as a sailor, dog driver, traveller... . He was very tough but never posed as such.'

The posing manifested itself in his prejudices, also in his supposed amateurishness and his seemingly light-hearted approach to adversity. These qualities, together with an inner ring of steel, had impressed themselves on Gino when they were boys at Lancing together. In character and attitude he remained a lifelong follower of his great friend.

4

John Rymill (1905–68)

We were still 130 miles from home, but this first sight of well-known landmarks and the sea – always a thing of life even when frozen – gave us a pleasant sensation of familiarity which was a relief after the austere country through which we had been travelling for the last forty-five days: a country which had known eternal peace until we, two puny little black dots in its vastness, had the impudence to lift the curtain for a few brief days and look upon its beauty. Now that we were leaving it behind I had a feeling of intense pleasure in knowing that we had travelled its glaciers and scaled its mountains and come through safely. But this feeling was tinged with one of loss as though a friend had died, for the curtain had again dropped and in dropping had hidden a scene difficult to put into words. Day after day we had travelled through silence which was absolute, not a depressing silence as of the dead, but a silence that had never known life. Even more impressive had been the sheer immensity of the country, and the atmosphere of mystery which seemed to dwarf us.

John Rymill is in fact writing here about the Antarctic, and the expedition he led to Graham Land in the mid-1930s, but his words are equally applicable to the Greenland ice cap over which he had travelled with Gino's expedition in 1930–31. For a burly Australian sheep farmer who weighed sixteen stone and looked like a rugby player, reticent in speech, dyslexic and seldom given to express his thoughts in writing, this was a remarkable passage in his otherwise dry and succinct official account of the British Graham Land Expedition (*Southern Lights*). It testifies to Rymill's deep affinity with the polar regions.

He was brought up at the family homestead of Penola (in South Australia, between Adelaide and Melbourne), but without a father, who had died in a car accident when he was barely a year old. Having completed his education in Melbourne, Rymill came to England with his mother in 1923 and embarked on a number of studies and activities, beginning with a course of lectures in ethnology.

'At the same time I did survey work and navigation at the Royal Geographical Society, went through the De Havilland School of Flying, and went to college in London to do accountancy... training myself for all the things, including cooking, that I considered necessary for the running of a polar expedition.' At the age of eighteen the single-minded resolve was already evident – not only to travel in the polar regions but to become a leader of men. It was also strengthened by the subconscious need to prove himself to his only parent, who thought more highly of his cleverer, non-dyslexic elder brother.

From his Australian childhood Rymill had already acquired certain practical bush skills: hunting, camping, tying knots, working dogs. Some experience of snow and ice would clearly be a good idea, so he took himself off to Switzerland, Austria and Norway to ski and climb, every winter and summer for four or five years. And in 1928 he went with his brother on a hunting trip to the Canadian Rockies, climbing and testing his skill with a rifle.

It was after a second trip to Canada, an ethnological expedition to study the relationship between American Indians and Eskimos, that he decided to consult his friend and mentor Edward Reeves, map curator and instructor in survey at the RGS who had just been awarded the Victoria Medal for fifty years of service in the field of exploration. He knew of Rymill's ambitions and told him: 'You've come just at the right moment. Young Gino Watkins is planning a major expedition to Greenland and I'm sure there would be a place for you. Come along and I'll introduce you.'

Gino and a few Cambridge friends were making their plans in a room which the RGS had lent him. A trestle table served as a desk and was strewn with papers – letters, schedules, estimates, maps, calculations. There was a gramophone and a pile of dance records, a box of tea-cakes and an apparently light-hearted atmosphere. Rymill was somewhat bemused when a fair-haired, thin-faced foppish young man rose to greet him. Gino said he gathered from Reeves that Rymill was a keen skier. 'Would you like to design a ski binding for me that we can use on a soft boot, and bring it back tomorrow?'

So Rymill went back to his mother's flat off St James's Park, did as he was asked and produced his proposed design the following day.

The room at the RGS was again full of conversation and laughter and an impression of general disorder. Gino liked the design for the binding: 'We'll adopt that – now go and get it made.' No formal invitation was extended, but Rymill reckoned he was now a member of the expedition.

While several of Rymill's future Arctic companions, recently graduated from Cambridge, partied in London as they prepared for Greenland, he went to Cambridge to learn more about polar travel from a fellow Australian, Professor Frank Debenham, a scientist on Captain Scott's last expedition and now director of the Scott Polar Research Institute. Debenham's recently published book, *The Polar Regions*, became required reading and re-reading for Rymill, and by the time the expedition was launched there was no one better prepared.

Though Rymill – gentle, quiet, a bit of a loner – was quite different in character from Gino and many of his companions, the fact that he was the only one neither from Cambridge nor in the services gave him a unifying presence among his fellows. And he was soon both popular and much respected for being someone you could depend on. He was, according to Quintin Riley, his companion on two expeditions to Greenland and later in the Antarctic, 'a giant of a man, 6 ft 4 in. in height and enormously broad-shouldered. He was calm and methodical, as befitted his huge build, and utterly reliable.' When the *Quest*, the ship that brought them to Greenland, was being unloaded, Martin Lindsay noted that 'although exceedingly unpleasant, it is not impossible to take a load of 120 lb. John Rymill never thought anything of a weight like that; he was the biggest and probably the best of several good men at this kind of work, and he sometimes used to carry as much as 160 lb.'

Rymill's self-confidence and determination were qualities he shared with Gino, whom he also admired for 'that wonderful gift that very few people have of making every person on his expeditions feel really important and responsible for something. He never threw his weight about and, in the years I was connected with him I never once heard him lose his temper or raise his voice. A particularly selfless person, one would have followed him anywhere … I was very fortunate in being under a man like that.' He watched and learnt from Gino's informal approach to leadership, acknowledging his exceptional talents and skills. When the time came for Rymill to lead, he inherited

Gino's qualities while being himself more practical, more reliable, less volatile. Unlike Gino, Rymill was determined to leave nothing to chance.

Freddy Spencer Chapman thought Rymill somewhat lacking in imagination when he took over as leader of the second Greenland expedition after Gino was drowned. But the mercurial, occasionally unbalanced Chapman and the solid, placid Rymill were never natural soul-mates. They did, however, have a similar attitude to physical heartiness. Rymill had, in August Courtauld's words, 'a frightful habit of taking all his clothes off and sluicing himself with cold water, or running about on the ice stark naked, cracking a whip'.

No doubt Riley would have taken a similarly dim view of such behaviour. The difference in Rymill's and Riley's attitudes and interests, one might think, was as large as the physical gap between them. Yet they became firm friends. While not sharing Riley's religious and other dogmatic beliefs, Rymill admired his precision, his meticulous preparation, his attention to detail (and his own comfort), his repartee and the pleasure he took in argument and debate. For Riley Rymill was his rock, especially after Gino died, and he willingly followed him to the Antarctic in 1934. It is testament to Rymill's character that four men from Greenland – Riley, Ted Bingham, Wilfred Hampton, Alfred Stephenson – were prepared to spend three years on the Graham Land expedition under his leadership.

The pity is that, perhaps because of his dyslexia, Rymill kept no diary of his time in the Arctic and Antarctic. Little is known of his feelings towards his companions or of his thoughts on his various experiences and hardships. What is clear, however, is that from an early stage Gino had Rymill marked down as his deputy, as the safest pair of hands and the one to whom he would look first for the most important jobs. As surveyor and navigator, Rymill was given the responsibility, on the first journey to the ice cap, of positioning flags every half mile to mark the route to the ice-cap station 130 miles inland. And when the chosen place had been reached, it was Rymill who fixed its position with theodolite and time-signal set and who would be the man to find it again eight months later when Courtauld was buried in his tent beneath the snow.

On the first trek up the glacier Rymill developed a poisoned wrist, resulting from a cut while unloading packing cases from the ship, but

Bingham, the expedition doctor, was on hand to lance it. When they reached the top Jimmy Scott, who was leading the party, and Rymill were roped together to find a way through the crevasses. Once safely past them, they made a depot known thereafter as Big Flag and Rymill led the others on skis, gradually climbing over the featureless ice plateau on a surface which Scott described as 'like a rippled ocean swell'. With Scott, Bingham and Riley and Lindsay (who would be left to man the weather station) behind him, Rymill was the first to put his prints on this virgin territory.

> From now on [wrote Scott] the scene changed to what most of us will carry with us always as the most intense and lasting memory of Greenland. The dark tops of the coastal mountains gradually disappeared below the encircling horizon of snow. No rock or patch of earth nor any living thing broke the monotony of this featureless plain of dead white. The moving tracery of the high cirrus clouds above and the shadow of the snowdrifts below were all that anyone walking ahead of the sledges could focus his eyes upon.

The return journey to base by Rymill, Scott and Bingham, with nine dogs to each sledge, was completed in four days, a time not bettered during the expedition. Rymill narrowly avoided being lost down a crevasse by grabbing the handlebars of his sledge and hauling himself out. Gino's first plan was that Rymill and Percy Lemon, with wireless transmitting set, should relieve Riley and Lindsay. But with the approach of winter he decided that fuel and stores were more important than radio communication, and he realised that Rymill, with his strength and various skills, would be much more valuable when not sitting in a tent taking weather observations in the middle of Greenland.

He was already becoming a very competent dog driver, and so Gino asked him to take Chapman, with a load of provisions, back to the ice-cap station, while Bingham would travel up with Jimmy D'Aeth, accompanied by Gino and Scott, to relieve the two men there. Rymill and Chapman left after the others and impressed Gino by catching them up. This was Chapman's first experience of sledging with dogs, which he quickly learnt and loved, but the incipient friction between the two men led each to accuse the other of taking up more than his share of tent space. Careful measurement showed both of them to be in error. Once they had all reached the ice-cap station to find Riley and Lindsay in good spirits, Gino and Scott decided to head off on a journey south before returning to base. In Scott's account, 'Gino told Rymill to send up Chapman from the base as soon as possible, with a large sledging party, wireless equipment and as much food as they could haul.' Clearly Gino was putting Rymill in charge in his absence; he had passed his leadership tests.

The weather on the way back was very different from what it had been a month before. The journey which had taken Scott and Rymill four days at the beginning of September now, in October, took Rymill, with Chapman, Riley and Lindsay, more than twice as long. The winter gales and blizzards were beginning, and they were confined to their tents for three days. 'You can see only 35 yards. Wind shakes tent about so much one can't hear or keep candle going,' Chapman wrote in his diary. He had only twelve days back at base to turn round and make preparations before setting off again, and taking five weeks to reach the ice-cap station. Rymill helped Chapman's party up Buggery Bank and through the crevasses before returning to base. He guided Lawrence Wager, a future Everest mountaineer, probing with great care to establish the size of every crevasse he went over and earning praise from Wager: 'He is amazingly sound.'

Back at base Rymill was the handiest of handymen, repairing sledges, splicing traces, doing anything which required physical strength. 'He could also do all sorts of strange things with a piece of rope, and was an expert carpenter,' someone commented. He made a few short journeys, hunting seals with the Eskimos, but had to spend much of the winter working, with Hampton, to repair the expedition's two damaged Moth aeroplanes. The plan was for Gino and Rymill, together with the two principal pilots, D'Aeth and Cozens, to fly the proposed Arctic air route from Angmagssalik to Winnipeg in Canada, via Baffin Island, but this had to be abandoned. Had Gino taken Rymill off his repair work on the aeroplanes and sent him with the first relief party in March to the ice-cap station, it is likely that, with his navigating skills and a time-signal set, Courtauld would have been found at least a month before he was in fact rescued.

As it was, when Scott returned disconsolate and without Courtauld in mid-April, Gino knew he needed his two best men, Rymill and

Chapman, for this crucial ice-cap journey to find the weather station and its sole occupant, alive or dead. As Gino said to Rymill: 'It was you who made the original position fix for the station last summer; now it's up to you to find it again' – a task made more challenging by the fact that the flags which had pointed the way over the ice cap at half-mile intervals were no longer visible. But spring was bringing better weather, and it took only twelve days for Rymill to guide his leader to a position which he believed to be no more than a couple of miles from the weather station. When the three men searched the ground in different directions to look for signs of the station, or of Courtauld, Gino and Chapman returned to their tent two hours before Rymill. 'With characteristic thoroughness he quartered the ground for twenty miles, but he too had found nothing,' Chapman wrote. Years later Rymill recalled, in a rare revelation of his inner thoughts, that during those hours he became convinced that Courtauld was still alive.

The next morning was sunny and clear, conditions similar to those of the previous August when Rymill had fixed the position chosen for the ice-cap station. Having set up the theodolite and time-signal set, with an aerial stretched between two upright skis, he took careful observations for longitude and latitude and, in his calm, unhurried way, calculated that they were less than a mile north-west of the station. It was only a short time before they spotted a dark speck in the distance which turned out to be the tattered remnant of a Union Jack. There was no sign of recent digging, or of any life at all. But a small bamboo ventilator was visible on top of one of the buried tents. Rymill and Chapman held their breath as Gino took off his skis, knelt by the ventilator pipe and called down to Courtauld. He was alive and he answered.

Gino was already planning future expeditions, and his chosen team would include the two who had accompanied him to the ice cap to rescue Courtauld. They would go round the Arctic by sledge, boat and kayak, traversing the northern latitudes of Canada and Siberia, or embark on an expedition to the Antarctic to complete the crossing of the continent which Shackleton had attempted. An ascent of Mount Everest was also on Gino's future programme. Where Gino led, Rymill and Chapman would surely follow.

To end this Greenland expedition, Gino proposed three longish journeys, choosing Rymill and Chapman to sledge across Greenland to the west coast, carrying kayaks which would be used to cross lakes and rivers into the fjord that would lead them to the coastal town of Holsteinsborg, just north of the Arctic Circle. These two might not have been ideal companions for a month alone together, with no one else for company; but fate intervened in the shape of a swollen and growing gland on Chapman's neck. Surgeon-Lieutenant Bingham advised against such a journey and told Chapman to go back to England to have it treated. So the choice fell on Hampton to accompany Rymill. They had worked harmoniously together for weeks on end while repairing the damaged aeroplanes, and their friendship was cemented by the trans-Greenland journey. Hampton then went with Rymill to the Antarctic, and he was Rymill's best man at the latter's wedding in 1938. Scott described them as 'our two heavyweights, strong, placid and reliable'. Hampton, a flying officer in the Air Force Reserve, served as the expedition's engineer, but he was much more than a mechanic.

They should have got away at the beginning of July, but because there was now a shortage of dog pemmican and serviceable sledges, they had to wait six weeks until the *Gertrud Rask* was able to reach Angmagssalik with more equipment and provisions. There was little for Rymill and Hampton to do except improve their kayaking skills and fish for sea trout and cod.

Soon after they had started their journey, six dogs fell down a crevasse and had to be rescued by Rymill climbing down on a rope and disentangling their harnesses so that Hampton could haul them up to the surface. After another accident with a sledge slipping into a crevasse, and having taken days to find the Big Flag depot where their rations awaited them, things got better as they travelled across the ice cap. But the worst was to come as they began their descent from the plateau to the west coast.

For six weeks they struggled over steep ridges, across lakes and rivers not always frozen, through driving rain and wind as well as snow. When needle-ice lacerated the dogs' feet Rymill and Hampton made eighty boots for the twenty animals. Hampton's own boots fell to pieces and he had to make new soles out of empty food tins, renewing them almost daily. Then they had to abandon the sledges, shoot the dogs and carry 100 lb loads – tents, bedding, fuel, food, rifles – in relays, as well as the kayaks. The going was always steeply undulating and slippery, and they were constantly soaked to the skin. Eventually they were able to paddle their kayaks down a fast-flowing river and shoot a few rapids. But, at a bend in the river, a violent cross-current caused them both to turn turtle. In their upturned kayaks they were swept under a projecting sheet of ice, lost their paddles and nearly their lives. When Rymill, still upside down, emerged into a patch of open water, he was able to surface in time to grab the ice on the other side of the river and heave himself out.

Lindsay described this as 'the most precarious of all our journeys, and only tremendous guts saved them from disaster'. Lesser men would probably have died of hypothermia and exhaustion. By now their rations were running dangerously low, so they felt the cold more acutely. One of the worst things about their near-starvation was fatigue. No sooner had they fallen asleep than they began to dream of sumptuous meals, and immediately woke up again. Although they saw tracks of caribou and hare, they never got close enough to shoot one. An Arctic fox provided some sort of meal when they were getting desperate, but it tasted so repulsive that it caused both of them to vomit. Eventually they kept the meat down and it gave some sustenance

It was at least encouraging to see some bird life – snow buntings, an occasional gull and a white-tailed eagle – and as they approached the fjord a stand of dwarf birch trees provided welcome fuel for a fire. The next morning, 15 October, a fishing-boat was sighted in the fjord. When they reached the shore, they were cheered by a party of Greenlanders on board who had been sent to look for them. The Danish governor of Holsteinsborg had been alerted to the fact that they were a month overdue, and the search party told Rymill and Hampton that they had long ago given them up for dead but hoped to find their remains. When the hospitable governor entertained them in his house, Rymill was intrigued to find his host reading a freshly ironed daily newspaper every morning at breakfast. The date on the paper appeared to correspond to the day's date, but it was in fact exactly a year old, since the supply ship only reached Holsteinsborg every twelve months.

Gino, meanwhile, with Courtauld and Lemon, had completed the hazardous open boat journey round the southern tip of Greenland to Julianehaab, and when there was no news of Rymill and Hampton's safe arrival, he and Courtauld went up the coast in the hope of meeting them. The town of Holsteinsborg was *en fête* when they arrived to a reunion with the two 'lost' explorers. Schooled in the tradition of self-reliance and understatement, Rymill and Hampton expressed mild irritation at all the fuss made merely because they had got to their destination a bit late, then sent reassuring messages to their families and took ship, with Gino and Courtauld, for Copenhagen and home.

Home for Rymill for the time being was London and his mother's flat in Queen Anne's Mansions, where her friends gathered for tea to meet the young explorer back from Greenland's icy mountains. He also spent time in Cambridge, discussing his next moves with Frank Debenham and James Wordie, and in Hampshire where he was invited to shoot pheasants. He was anxious to get going again – north or south, he didn't mind; he would go where Gino went. The idea of circumnavigating the northern latitudes of the Arctic was shelved – it was unlikely that the Soviet government would give permission for Gino to cross Siberia – but there was enthusiasm among the old explorers in Cambridge and at the RGS for his Antarctic venture, following Shackleton's aborted expedition in 1916.

The trouble, as Gino and his friends did not fully appreciate, was that these were the Depression years and the funds that he needed would not be forthcoming. While Rymill and Hampton had been crossing Greenland, in Britain a National government was formed and the pound was devalued by 30 per cent. The most that could be raised was £800, £500 of it from Pan-American Airways, to go back to east Greenland for another year of meteorological and survey work to provide more data on the potential for a commercial air route. For Gino, Rymill, and the other two who would be going north again, Chapman and Riley, the initial disappointment was mitigated by the prospect of going back together to the country they had found so challenging and rewarding. It was much better than taking a day job in England, and after a year the financial crisis might have eased and they would get the money to go south as planned. Little did Rymill realise how this was going to turn out.

Only ten days after setting up their base on the shores of Lake Fjord – 'where great glaciers came down through the mountains to form vast floating tongues of ice, several hundred feet high' – Rymill got the chance he had been waiting for since he had arrived in England nearly ten years ago. He would not of course have thought of it like that, but he had trained himself to run a polar expedition; and with Gino's death he became leader, albeit only of a three-man expedition. When they returned home a year later, Rymill's mother was to comment, 'He went out a boy and came back a man.'

When Rymill first saw the empty kayak floating low in the water, he had assumed that Gino must have been attacked, by a bladder-nosed seal or a polar bear, and thrown into the water. Whatever the precise circumstances, Rymill and the others still half-expected Gino to turn up a couple of days later, apologising for the trouble he had caused. Years later, he wrote: 'It was the first time that death had come close to any of us. ... I still remember wondering – childishly – how all this beauty could still go on with Gino dead, somewhere out there in the fjord.'

And so Elisha succeeded Elijah. With Rymill now in command, Gino's death had the effect of drawing the other three closer together. 'I think it was this harmony which made it possible for us to carry out the expedition's full programme.' But the programme did not actually amount to very much. Riley continued to take the meteorological readings, while Rymill and Chapman were to do the survey work, mapping the coast and the mountainous interior. But no mapping journeys were undertaken until the end of March, seven months after Gino's death. Much of the time was spent hunting for food, sometimes with Eskimo assistance, and sailing or sledging to Angmagssalik. In the spring of 1933 there was plenty of exploratory activity on the east coast of Greenland. The two best-known Danish explorers, Lauge Koch and Knud Rasmussen, were leading major expeditions, and Charles Lindbergh was making experimental flights over Greenland for Pan-American Airways, who had contributed to the British expedition, now somewhat overshadowed by the others.

Rymill, Chapman and Riley all had distinctly hair-raising experiences, on their boat and while kayaking in heavy seas. On one occasion Rymill was alone in the boat when 'he met the full violence of the gale and water started pouring in over the bows. For a time he faced it, unable to turn, working the bilge pump with one hand and holding the tiller with the other. Several times he tried to turn, but each time he had to veer back owing to the mountainous seas. He really thought there was no hope for the *Stella*.'

Not long after Gino's disappearance, Chapman and Riley were absent in the boat for ten days; Rymill remained alone at the base and, in Chapman's account, 'felt quite calmly certain that we were drowned.

The prospect of facing the winter with only two dogs for company did not disturb him in the least, as John Rymill is one of those self-contained people who prefer their own company to that of anybody else. When he came to putting up the sleeping-benches in the hut he at first decided only to build his own, but eventually he thought he ought to erect ours too, in case we turned up after all.'

All the time Rymill was learning what he could from the Eskimos and gaining experience – of sledging on pack ice, hunting seals and polar bears, driving dogs, living with the cold, and of leadership. With the expedition's limited objectives, and limited funds, Rymill looked on this year in Greenland as a preparation, a training ground, for his much larger goal – to lead a party to explore the Antarctic continent and fulfil Gino's dream.

The harmony between the three men to which Rymill referred was not always felt by Chapman. In his diary he criticised Rymill for being unenterprising; Chapman was inclined to be jealous of him and harbour grudges. Sometimes the three of them would argue heatedly about trivial things, such as the use of words – 'pants' or 'trousers', 'pots' or 'pans'. Chapman knew he was too sensitive and Rymill later admitted he could be bloody-minded towards him. But the two generally got on well during their sledging journeys together, and Chapman would often read aloud to Rymill in their tent – choosing Stevenson's *The Pavilion on the Links* or something by Conan Doyle or Dumas.

When they were struck by a storm in the *Stella*, 'John, who really wakes up and comes into his own on such occasions, tore up the floorboards and started bailing furiously'. Tacitly acknowledging his own tendency to be unsound, Chapman called Rymill 'a good sound man', the man for a crisis; pragmatic, even phlegmatic at times. He admired his reaction when one morning they were woken to the dread sound of the ice breaking up beneath their tent. 'It can't be,' Rymill commented; 'we haven't had breakfast yet.'

At the end of the summer, thanks to the generosity of Rasmussen (who died from pneumonia three months later), the three men were given passage to Iceland in one of his ships and were back in England by the end of September. Now Rymill embarked on the task of raising funds and preparing for the next three years, which would place him alongside the great names in the annals of Antarctic exploration.

Less than two years earlier, Gino had failed to get the financial support he needed for an Antarctic expedition. It was the Depression, he was told, and there was no money for grand polar jaunts. In 1933 the Depression was showing no signs of lifting – Ramsay MacDonald was saying that the continuing experience of unemployment and bankruptcies was 'a challenge to the wisdom of man' – yet Rymill felt he was equal to the challenge. Encouraged by his old mentor and friend the ethnologist Louis Clarke, and by the Antarctic trio at Cambridge – Debenham, Priestley and Wordie – he took his plans for an exploration of the Graham Land peninsula to the Royal Geographical Society. A grant of £1,000 was forthcoming, with official RGS backing, which led to a further grant of £10,000 from the Colonial Office (Graham Land was claimed as British territory). Another £10,000 was raised from companies and private individuals. (Twenty years earlier, Shackleton had been granted similar sums from the RGS and the government for his *Endurance* expedition, and had raised an additional £40,000 from other donors.)

So how did Rymill succeed where Gino had failed? The support of his fellow Australian Frank Debenham was a key factor. Debenham had co-founded the Scott Polar Research Institute, he recommended Graham Land as Rymill's objective and he had the ear of the RGS. He was also a good deal more impressed by Rymill than he had been by Gino. Though initially seduced by Gino's charm, and by the social circle in which Gino moved in London, Debenham was not amused when the restaurant bill always seemed to end up in his lap. He thought Gino was good at wheedling people, but that he was a bit of a charlatan, and potentially unstable. Rymill was judged to have more substance, more stability; and he had proved himself on two Greenland expeditions, the latter in difficult circumstances. He was, in short, a better bet than Gino, and so he got the funding to take fourteen men with him to the Antarctic for three years. Six were on full pay from the services, the rest unpaid.

Of course the Gino legacy remained. Rymill chose four men from the first Greenland expedition: Riley (who had also been on the second one), Hampton, Stephenson and Bingham. Chapman was also invited, but after some thought and indecision he took a job instead as a schoolmaster in Yorkshire. In view of their occasional differences the previous year in Greenland, one may wonder whether Rymill would have wanted the volatile Chapman with him for three years.

But his infectious energy and resilience would probably have compensated for his weaknesses of character – what Chapman himself called, quoting Tolstoy, 'the unreasoning sadness of youth'. Before starting his schoolmastering, however, he went to west Greenland to buy dogs for Rymill's expedition. Jimmy Scott agreed to be the contact in London to deal with, inter alia, requests for additional funding while the expedition was in the Antarctic.

Rymill bought an old three-masted topsail schooner which he renamed *Penola* after his family home. (A grandiose name, such as *Endeavour* or *Discovery*, would not have suited the modest Australian.) On the voyage south, ninety-eight days to the Falkland Islands, there were inevitable tensions between the ship's captain ('Red' Ryder, seconded from the Royal Navy) and his idea of a disciplined ship and the more relaxed attitude to authority of the Watkins boys. Though a disciplined and responsible leader himself, Rymill had been schooled in the Watkins method; and on this issue he was not going to take sides. Ryder recorded his impressions: 'What I found was an expedition crew composed mostly of university graduates or those brought up in the tradition of Gino Watkins. Most charming and delightful they were but to them the very idea of any discipline was anathema. I could tell that they felt superior to that sort of treatment. In this they had John Rymill's tacit agreement.' Disagreements between the two men (over the extent and the cost of refitting the *Penola*) would surface later in the expedition, but each man recognised the outstanding qualities of the other – which, in Ryder's case, culminated in the award of the Victoria Cross for leading the raid on St Nazaire in 1942.

Perhaps the most significant achievement of Rymill's expedition was to refute the claim of Sir Hubert Wilkins, made in 1928 as a result of his aerial survey, that Graham Land was an archipelago separated from the main Antarctic continent. Rymill confirmed that it was in fact a peninsula, also that channels reported by Wilkins did not exist. He discovered one new channel which it was intended to call after the new king, Edward VIII. But when news of his abdication came through on the stuttering wireless set, the name was dropped and changed, by royal assent when the expedition returned home, to King George VI Sound.

L. P. Kirwan, in his study of polar exploration, *The White Road*, credited Rymill with having 'carried out by land and air one of the most comprehensive exploring and scientific programmes (in geology, meteorology, glaciology and biology) of any mainland expedition between the wars'. The lessons of the Heroic Age, with its heroic failures, had been learnt – dogs used on sledging journeys, diet much improved, accidents more carefully anticipated – and now, with the advent of the Air Age, the aeroplane could be used to impressive effect in reconnaissance, in photography and in the dropping of supplies. It would be another two decades before the coming of the Scientific Age in the Antarctic and the establishment by Rymill's own country, Australia, of a permanent base on the continent.

More than 1,000 miles of previously unexplored coast were surveyed; journeys were made covering hundreds of miles, much of them over the sea ice (where the going was easier than overland, provided the ice did not break up). Towards the end of one long journey, with two days' travel left and enough food for only one meal, Rymill decided they should eat what they had and then press on until they reached base. As the cooking pot began to boil, a most unpleasant smell was given off, and a pair of socks was discovered in the water. They belonged to Hampton who, having got his feet wet on the ice the previous day, had taken off the socks he had been wearing for a month and put them in the empty pot to dry out. When the pot came to be filled with snow that night for the last supper, the socks were overlooked in the darkness.

There were more serious near-mishaps – when the ice broke up, when dogs fell down crevasses – but Rymill liked to say that accidents never happened; it was always somebody's damn fool mistake. On one occasion Rymill, Riley and Colin Bertram were sledging several miles off the coast when the sea ice began to break up. Years later Bertram wrote of Rymill that it was 'his superb leadership and technical excellence on the broken ice that saved us all. Had he failed all would have been lost.' Thanks to his expertise and the meticulous care with which he prepared and carried out every aspect of the expedition's living, travelling and work, it was greatly to his credit that he returned to England after three years with all hands alive, fit and sane. (Mindful of Percy Lemon's attempted suicide soon after he got back from Greenland, Rymill kept an eye on all members of his expedition, and kept them occupied, until he was satisfied they had readjusted to civilisation.) The citation for one of the several awards given to Rymill referred to his 'harmonious team of very modest gentlemen' – none of them more modest than the highly respected and responsible team leader. After Rymill's signal Antarctic success, one can perhaps understand why the RGS should have had more confidence in his rather than Gino's leadership of a three-year expedition.

Rymill had proved himself more practical and reliable than Gino, while both of them inspired the same confidence in the men they led. Gino was the optimist, never anticipating failure or contemplating disaster, while Rymill exuded a quiet competence and maturity of judgement. Neither of them was authoritarian, and each was able to perform the practical tasks of a polar expedition as well as or better than any of its members. Yet there was something about Rymill's reticence, his calmness, his methodical approach, his determination to achieve his goal, and what one friend called his 'disciplined vitality', that made him the more inspiring and successful leader.

Rymill had met Eleanor Francis in Cambridge before he left for the Antarctic. She had been reading geography at Girton and was working for Debenham. By the time Rymill returned from the Antarctic she had completed a fellowship at Berkeley, California and was back at Cambridge; a little more than six months later they were engaged. At the same time, however, Rymill was planning to go back to the Antarctic and make the crossing of the continent which had frustrated Shackleton twenty years earlier. Assuming that neither Hampton nor Stephenson would be able to come, he proposed that Andrew Croft, who was an outstanding driver and handler of dogs, should be his second-in-command.

Croft had crossed Greenland with Lindsay in 1934, had been back to the Arctic a year later, and had done some reindeer herding in Lapland. He was working for Louis Clarke in Cambridge in 1937 when Rymill, back from Graham Land, also stayed for a while at Clarke's house in Grange Road. The two had detailed discussions about the Antarctic project, anticipating that they would need to raise £30,000, and Rymill wrote to Croft on the last day of 1937, three days after his engagement to Eleanor was announced, to outline his plans and offer him £500 a year for a period of not more than three years. He intended to go back to Australia for six months, then spend a year preparing for the new expedition, which would head south in the summer of 1939.

Remembering that it was Gino's ambition to be the first to cross the

Antarctic continent, was this, subconsciously perhaps, to be the ulti-
mate fulfilment of Gino's dream? Rymill had been widely praised for
the success of his Graham Land expedition and no doubt felt confident
that sufficient funds would be made available. Eleanor would understand that an explorer had to go away and explore, and he might be
away for little more than a year. He did not know, of course, that the
approach of war in 1938–39 would make such an expedition almost
impossible to organise. But everything changed sooner than that.
Rymill was back at the Penola family estate at the end of May 1938,
and six weeks later sent a cable to Croft: 'Owing family business
another expedition impossible.' He returned to London to marry
Eleanor in September, but he had decided that his future lay in manag-
ing his 8,000-acre sheep station and homestead in South Australia. He
would never see snow and ice again.

His age, thirty-three, also had something to do with his decision.
Polar exploration, he concluded, was a young and unmarried man's
game. Shackleton was forty when he began his attempt to cross the
Antarctic, and Scott forty-three when he went for the Pole in 1911–12.
Rymill would tell his sons that most great achievements were accomplished by young men, citing Alexander the Great who died shortly
before his thirty-third birthday. There was also the question of Rymill's
physical fitness. He had suffered from sciatica while in the Antarctic,
and when he applied to join the Royal Australian Navy on the outbreak
of war, he was initially turned down for active service because of an old
knee injury. For two years Lieutenant Rymill had to endure the frustrating inactivity of office duties in Melbourne, plotting the movements
of Australian warships on a wall chart.

After the war he developed the farm, and in the 1950s sold the sheep
and restocked with Angus cattle. He became particularly interested in
pasture improvement and promoting equestrian sports. Occasional
trips were made to England to visit his old explorer friends, in particular the four who had been with him in the Arctic and Antarctic. His
fellow Australian explorer, Douglas Mawson (who had been a member
of Shackleton's *Nimrod* expedition, 1907–09), periodically tried to get
Rymill involved in the setting up of a base in Australian Antarctica, but
to no avail.

He and Eleanor had two sons; the elder, Peter, took over the manage-
ment of the farm in his mid-twenties, having just won the Australian

Showjumping Championship, and in 1968 started an experimental vineyard, which would later become the Rymill Coonawarra Winery. In the early part of that year Eleanor was diagnosed with a severe auto-immune illness requiring treatment in hospital in Adelaide. An ambulance was organised for the 250-mile trip and Rymill would follow in his car. Not many miles from Adelaide, the car left the road and hit a tree. The stress of his wife's illness and the fact that he had spent most of the previous night putting out bush fires had exhausted him, and he presumably fell asleep at the wheel. He was taken with Eleanor to hospital, where she was treated successfully, but he remained unconscious as a result of his injuries and never spoke again. Eleanor thought that he may have recognised her once during the six months before he died.

It was a tragic end, the more so for a man who used to say there was no such thing as an accident – 'it's always somebody's damn fool mistake'. With Gino's inspiration and example behind him, Rymill's legacy is significant and often overlooked. The science gathered in Graham Land gave early warning of the depletion of the ozone layer and of the threat of global warming. The American Geographical Society, awarding its gold medal to Rymill in 1939, said that his survey work 'constitutes probably the largest contribution to accurate detailed surveys of the Antarctic continent made by any expedition'. Following the much more famous names and expeditions of the Heroic Age before him, this was high praise indeed.

5
J. M. Scott (1906–86)

Jimmy Scott had been away from the coastal base for six weeks. He had left in the first week of March to sledge up to the ice-cap station and relieve August Courtauld, who had been alone there since the beginning of December. But now he was returning without him. He had failed – he had let his leader and friend Gino down, he had let Courtauld down – and he would never really get over it. The fact that what he saw as his failure was rather a failure of leadership on Gino's part never occurred to him. Such was Scott's hero-worship of Gino that he would never find fault with a man of whom he wrote: 'One liked him for himself and obeyed him instinctively because he was so much the better man.'

In personality Scott was very different from Gino. He had a Cambridge rugby blue; he was tough, hearty and drew his friends from the sporting field; he was socially awkward, especially in female company; he was conservative, conventional. Gino was quite the opposite: he hated organised games, he was irreverent and sceptical of tradition, he was somewhat foppish in his dress and appearance, and he gave the impression of being what the popular press calls 'fun-loving', with a passion for parties, jazz music and dancing. Yet Scott was drawn to Gino as soon as they met. It was the veteran Antarctic explorer Raymond Priestley who, knowing of Scott's wish to travel, told him one day in Cambridge that Gino was planning a trip to Labrador and that he should go and see him. He went to Trinity College and found Gino's rooms in New Court.

> I knocked and was told to come in; then apologised and prepared to withdraw. This rather frail, elegant young man lounging in an armchair could not possibly be a leader of exploring parties, nor could his companion who was dressed more simply in an open dressing-gown and a bath towel. I felt certain that I was in the wrong room. But the man in the armchair sprang up and called

me back with 'I'm Watkins – are you Scott?' The man in the dressing-gown disappeared and we began to talk.

Gino produced a map of Labrador and showed Scott the journeys he proposed to make, principally in unmapped territory. He talked about the country as if he could see it while he spoke. It consisted of forests, rivers and a barren coastline; he would travel by canoe in summer and dog-sledge in winter.

> I had come to Watkins's room in a spirit of vague curiosity: I walked home half an hour later with nothing in my mind except Labrador and him. The smooth course of my life had been changed by the youth I had been talking to. He came to tea with me the next week and said that he could definitely take me with him: so would I mind learning all I could about photography, geology and botany?

Scott was the son of an Edinburgh lawyer who became a judge and was sent to administer the law in Egypt. Young Jimmy went to live with cousins on the island of Mull and was educated at Fettes before going on to Cambridge, at Clare College, where he read natural sciences. He was popular at school, mainly because of his prowess at games. He was captain of rugby and cricket; and at Cambridge he got his rugby blue and played in the Varsity match in 1927. Now, only six months later, he was boarding the SS *Newfoundland* at Liverpool with a man who appeared to despise the sports at which Scott excelled and to mock his respectful attitude to authority. Was the attraction of opposites going to work for nine months in the wilds of Labrador? The only thing Gino and Scott appeared to have in common was their love of popular music. Scott may have been bemused at times by Gino's approach to life, but he was entirely happy to follow his new leader: 'I had met a man who might be hard to understand but was impossible to doubt.'

With a trapper, they mapped some of the unexplored country of Labrador – rivers, lakes, waterfalls – travelling by canoe and, in winter, on snowshoes and with sledge dogs. For Scott the expedition provided 'experience, self-discovery and a wider knowledge of life', under what he called Gino's 'ruthlessly competent though unobtrusive' leadership. Gino did all the survey work, but together they began to learn about dog-sledging in Arctic conditions, probably the first Englishmen to do so. At times they were dangerously short of food, subsisting on flour-and-water soup and biscuits, some of which they felt obliged to give to the dogs. Fortunately they were able to supplement their meagre diet with a fairly regular supply of porcupines, thanks to the skills of their trapper companion. Scott records that he got to know Gino only reasonably well in Labrador. They lived in close physical proximity, they exchanged stories and vulgar jokes, they knew each other's likes and dislikes. But at no time during the nine months of the expedition did they call each other by their first names.

When they got back to England, Gino decided that Scott should be introduced to social life. They went to parties in London, to night-clubs, to the Guards Boat Club at Maidenhead, often accompanied by Gino's sister Pam. (One hopes that by then the two men were on Christian-name terms.) Scott was included in a family skiing holiday in Davos, joined by Gino's father who was now living in Switzerland. Gino encouraged the growing friendship between Scott and Pam – they had first met before the expedition to Labrador and were in love before he set off for Greenland – but for some reason Colonel Watkins strongly disapproved. He wrote to Scott to say that 'if you marry my daughter it will be nothing short of a disaster'. When they did marry in 1933, they chose, as one of the hymns at their wedding service, John Bunyan's 'He who would valiant be 'gainst all disaster'. Having failed to see the joke, the colonel cut Pam out of his will – a spiteful as well as a meaningless gesture, as he had virtually nothing to leave to his children.

Scott avoided the final preparations for Greenland, in particular the checking and packing of all the expedition's stores, by going off to west Greenland to buy the sledge dogs, some weeks before the *Quest* sailed north. As the one man, apart from Gino, with experience of these dogs, Scott was the natural choice for the job. Gino put it to Scott in such a way that he couldn't refuse: 'I wonder if we could find a man who knows as much about dogs as you do.' Before he left, however, Gino insisted that they should both spend a week eating only the composite rations which he had devised for the Greenland ice cap. A third of the diet consisted of fat, which was difficult to digest and made them feel sick, especially when they were going to late-night parties. But they remembered how, when almost starving in Labrador, fat had been the thing they longed for most. Gino's conviction proved to be correct –

that the ration, consisting of 6,000 calories, was as welcome under Arctic conditions as it had been nauseating in springtime London.

Scott had bought fifty dogs, and was on his way with them to the Faroe Islands when Pam Watkins gave a cocktail party on board the *Quest* the evening before it sailed down the Thames. He was reunited with the rest of the expedition at a foul-smelling whaling station in the Faroes. A ton of raw whale meat and blubber was loaded on to the ship, together with the howling pack of huskies, one of which took a piece out of Scott's hand. Gino offered him his bunk, insisting he could sleep just as well on the floor.

It was of course inevitable that Gino should ask Scott, the one man with previous experience of dog-driving, to lead the first party on to the ice cap to establish the central weather station. Here was what he had dreamed of when he heard the call of the north in Gino's rooms at Trinity College. This was his opportunity of leadership into the Arctic unknown, entrusted to him by the man who had so inspired him from the day they met. But first he had to get himself, his four companions, their sledges and dogs up the steep glacier which would soon become known as Buggery Bank. The sledges skidded and slewed on the uneven ice surface, the dogs had to be fitted with boots which they chewed off when the sledges overturned, and Rymill, in urging the dogs on with a stock whip, succeeded in winding it round Scott's neck.

Having negotiated the maze of crevasses, which took them three days, Scott and his party emerged on to the ice plateau and started to make better time as they climbed the steady gradient towards a height of almost 9,000 feet. The coastal mountains soon dropped below the horizon, and there was nothing to be seen but snow and sky. As dog master and instructor to the others, Scott led his team in single file with all the nervous excitement and anticipation of a nineteenth-century pioneer explorer in Africa or the Arabian desert. To him this feature-less snowscape was like an ocean with a rippled swell – 'the ripples being wind drifts and the swell long undulations or dunes as much as half a mile from crest to crest. … But not even the ocean can make you feel so fragile and insignificant.'

However, the ice cap in summer was relatively benign; it had yet to deploy its weapons of cold and wind. The weather station was set up, Rymill fixed its position with theodolite and time-signal set, and Riley and Lindsay were left there to do the meteorological observations for the next five weeks. Scott, Rymill and Ted Bingham sped downhill, back towards base, with nothing to hold them up until the nine dogs of the leading sledge went through a snow bridge over a crevasse and, with their traces tangled, hung in the bottomless darkness. Rymill suggested making a windlass with rope and two upright skis to haul the dogs up, but to no avail. Scott decided he would go down on a rope and was able to harness them, one by one, so they could be brought to the surface. The following day another snow bridge gave way under Rymill's fifteen stone and he saved himself by grabbing his sledge. The first ice-cap journey was, according to Scott, 'a great success, with just enough hardship and danger'. There would be more than enough hardship and danger to come.

Less than two weeks after their return to base, Scott set off again, this time with Gino, to undertake a long journey south. But first they would go up to the ice-cap station to supervise the handover to the next two men to do their stint there. From the station the two Labrador veterans sledged off on a trek which lasted more than five weeks and came close to putting an end to their Arctic adventures.

The idea was to survey the ice cap south for 200 miles to a point where it bisected the line of Nansen's first crossing of Greenland, from Umivik to Godthaab, in 1888. Gino and Scott had discussed doing such a journey together when, earlier that year, they had been running across the fields of Cambridgeshire to get fit, and in London running round Hyde Park in an attempt to digest the fatty ice-cap rations with which Gino was experimenting. One may wonder what was the point of this journey to nowhere – to check the terrain and the weather for a more southerly crossing of Greenland by air? Or were they just trying to set an example, or show off, by travelling a great distance across a barren snowscape in the deteriorating autumn weather? Scott admitted afterwards that 'the scientific results of the journey were small' – rather pathetically, as if it was of any significance, he noted that they established that 'the altitude of our southern turning-point was 200 feet less than that of the ice-cap station'. But of course he did not think of questioning his leader's intentions or doubting his purpose.

Fortunately the dogs seemed to know they were being taken on a completely pointless, not to say irresponsible and doomed enterprise, and they saved the two men from their fate. Fifty years later, in his book *The Private Life of Polar Exploration*, Scott wrote of this journey: 'We

realised that if the dogs had gone at normal speed while we were travelling south, we would not have got back. So we owed our lives to their
strange behaviour.'

Largely because of the dogs' reluctance to pull with their usual
enthusiasm, Gino decided to turn back after less than half the distance
they had intended to travel south. They had used up more than half
their rations and had been giving some of their food to the dogs to
revive them. Scott was mystified and upset that the dogs he had chosen
and come to know would not do his bidding. He wondered if this was
because they had been overworked for the previous two months, or
they were changing their coats for the winter, or weakened by the lack
of fresh meat. The fact was that when they turned for home, the dogs
stopped being listless and appearing lethargic; their tails went up and
they pulled hard for the coast.

The problem now was the weather. It was late October, the first of
the winter gales hit them and they could move only once in four days.
(Twelve days out of the total journey time of thirty-eight days were
spent in their tent.) When they got going again, Scott's team of dogs
broke into a trot and wouldn't stop. The sledge carrying their tent, one
sleeping bag and much of the food was outpacing them. They ran after
it with increasing desperation through the soft, crusty snow but the
distance between men and sledge was not narrowing. At last, as darkness was falling, Gino caught up with it, dived and held on.

Another near-disaster had occurred earlier when Scott was kneeling
by the primus stove one evening as he was making soup and suffered
carbon monoxide poisoning. He reacted as if having a fit, passed out
and was only revived by Gino dragging him outside. 'Gino's strength
and calmness had saved my life; but you cannot thank a man when he
starts cursing you light-heartedly for making a filthy mess and ruining a
good dinner.'

As they approached the flagged route to the base conditions got
worse, the tent was constantly in danger of blowing away, the shortage
of food became acute for men and dogs, and the dogs were weakened
too by the force of the wind. When one of the storms was at its height
and hurling itself against their tent, and morale was very low, Gino suggested they should read aloud to each other. Some sort of distraction
was badly needed, and Gino started by reading Dickens's *A Christmas
Carol*. At midnight the storm died, and they knew they must move on

at once. The decision was made to dump one sledge and anything that was not essential. Scott remembered seeing Gino consign Trevelyan's *History of England* to the snow.

A couple of days later Gino spotted a wisp of scarlet thread in the snow. It came from one of the marker flags which Scott had driven into the snow on his way up to the ice cap in August and which now would guide them home. The two men then descried tiny black figures against the snowscape, and that remarkable meeting took place with Freddy Chapman's party of six struggling towards the ice-cap station. Chapman observed of Gino and Scott that 'they had given up all hope of getting back and had got morphia tablets ready'. This was probably untrue, but they were in bad shape, with noses and cheekbones flayed raw by the wind. Gino thought one of them should have joined up with Chapman; but they weren't up to it. They were back at base the following night, with one day's food left on the sledge.

It would be nearly four months before Scott went on to the ice cap again. During this time he hunted bears and seals whenever possible, learning from the Eskimos how to live off the country – though not exactly honing his poetic skills:

> Upon the cold wet snow I lay
> And gazed upon the icy water.
> I had to sit there half the day
> And concentrate my mind on slaughter,
> Knowing I would not get a meal
> Unless I shot a bloody seal.

Winter storms continued to batter the base throughout February, and on the only two days when an aeroplane was able to fly to the ice cap, hoping to drop supplies to Courtauld and perhaps to see him, fit and surviving his lonely vigil, the absence of landmarks made it impossible to see anything. On one flight the aeroplane was almost stationary against the wind. Then both planes were wrecked, one by a storm and the other by a forced landing. Courtauld's family were getting anxious and asking why no one had been sent to relieve him. Gino remarked to Scott one day:

> I'm afraid someone will have to go and fetch August while the weather is still bad. I'd like it to be you, for you know far the most

about winter travel. I don't think you'll have to abandon the station, though of course you must use your own judgement about that. We could only afford to have one man there. I don't want you to stay there yourself if the journey home looks difficult. But if it looks easy to get home and the prospect of staying seems unpleasant – well, I'd rather you stayed yourself and sent the others back.

Scott was of course flattered by the compliment Gino was paying him. But he pointed out his limitations: he could find a latitude but lacked the skills of astronomical observation. He had never done longitude, which was a more complicated calculation, and could not be expected to master the necessary skill with a theodolite (which he had never used) within a few days.

This was not a case of travelling hopefully, even doggedly. I *had* to arrive – at a particular point in a featureless desert.... I have often tried to fathom Gino's reasoning in picking on me, with the whole party, bar August, at the base. I might have been the most experienced cold weather traveller but I was only the dogsbody. I was not by a long way the best fitted to find an exact spot.

Gino knew this, he had two surveyors (Rymill and Stephenson) who could navigate with scientific accuracy, using a time-signal set to fix longitude, and yet he didn't send either of them. Nor, in this situation causing mounting anxiety both at the base and among Courtauld's family at home, did Gino apparently consider that he should lead the relief party himself. It was Lindsay who set off with Scott and Riley (after a couple of false starts), and it was he who years later was so critical of Gino's failure to lead the rescue and to choose a surveyor practised in longitude observations to find the ice-cap station. Other members of the expedition must have had similar doubts about Gino's judgement in deciding to rely on Scott to find the place by latitude alone; but none were made publicly or in print. One must assume that Gino was expecting the ice-cap station still to be visible above the snowdrifts, in spite of appalling winter blizzards which had persisted for three months. If this was his thinking, after the conditions he and Scott had had to endure in October – that a precise fixing of the ice-cap station was unnecessary and that he should remain at base, out of touch and with both aeroplanes grounded – then he was surely guilty of a failure of leadership.

Lindsay at least knew how to use a theodolite, so that his observations could be compared with those recorded by Scott's sextant. After more than two weeks' struggling up the ice cap towards Courtauld, Scott reckoned they were on the latitude of the station. He then employed what he called the old sea captains' method – travelling in one direction a few miles either side of Courtauld's believed position, then going north and travelling back a similar distance. They traversed the maximum possible area, stopping every half mile to stand on a sledge and search with binoculars. The cold was intense, up to sixty degrees of frost, the winds furious. Some days they were confined to the tent, dozing and talking, according to Lindsay's recollection, 'of everything from the League of Nations to the price of supper at the Café de Paris'. They conserved as much paraffin as possible for the ice-cap station, and somehow endured the extreme cold. Having dug out the sledges after a storm and made ready to move off, which could take them four hours, the weather might have changed again, making it impossible to see more than a few yards. If the sun briefly appeared, shadows from the snow-drifts restricted visibility. Scott said it was like looking for a man over-board in a rough sea. He recorded that 'we spent twenty-one days in the vicinity of the station and saw nothing. "So lonely 'twas that God himself / Scarce seemed there to be."' He was hoping that Courtauld would have used the eight-foot bamboo poles at the station to mark his position, but this had not occurred to him before he was snowed in.

There were times, after another day spent searching in vain or if the weather had kept them in their tent, when Scott was able to relax and even to pen a few of his verses. These lines were written while the three men were somewhere near the ice-cap station in late March:

> Out of doors the snow had drifted,
> Dogs were buried, traces lost;
> And the boxes that I lifted
> Gripped the ground with bonds of frost.
>
> Now at last the day is over,
> I can get out pipe and book.
> Lying in proverbial clover
> I can watch that bugger [Riley] cook.

I am through with dogs and curses,
I can lie in comfort now,
Read my Oxford Book of Verses
Under, so to speak, the bough.

However, anxiety for Courtauld's wellbeing soon overtook these moments of calm relaxation. When the polar author Gordon Hayes, having studied the meteorological records for this ice-cap journey, commented that 'the conditions approached the limit of human endurance', he was referring to the physical strain imposed on the three men. But for Scott the mental agony was worse – the growing realisation that they were probably not going to find Courtauld. They would either have to go back without him while they still had enough food for themselves and the dogs, or go on looking for him, killing the dogs one by one, then hauling the sledges themselves back to base. In his tent at night, following his analogy with a man overboard in a rough sea, Scott would see in his dreams a man drowning. In another dream he saw Courtauld staggering towards the base, still able to walk but having lost his mind. He came to understand something of the dreadful mental strain imposed on Courtauld by four months' isolation in these conditions. 'My own small tranquillity was further shaken by each new day of unsuccessful search. ... We endured physically. We were young. But the mental strain remains – something you do not usually associate with the Arctic.'

This was a new experience for Scott. He had been able to achieve success in his young life through physical strength and sporting prowess, and now he had this terrible decision to make. Either way someone might die. Undoubtedly, by returning to base with enough dogs and enough time for a further relief attempt, this time properly equipped to find the exact position of Courtauld's tent, Scott did the right thing. But he did have to kill two dogs before they turned back. Lindsay and Riley knew it was the correct decision in the circumstances, but Scott was plagued by doubts, on their hurried, seven-day journey back to base and for long afterwards. For the first time in his life he was unsure of himself, and it showed.

As the three came close to home, after almost six weeks away, Scott began to dread getting back and having to face Gino and the others. Over the last few miles he let the dogs loose and left the sledges.

Darkness had fallen, and Lindsay and Riley went in front to make the trail through deep snow. Scott could no longer lead; he was, in his own words, 'utterly done' and had to lie down twice.

> Alone I should have lain down to wait for the strength which might come back with daylight, for there was none of the old anticipation of pleasure in return... . I was plodding through heavy snow towards a place of inquisition. I did not want to arrive. Gino had trusted me to bring back August: he would ask me why we had returned without him, and I could think of nothing but the unalterable fact. ... I tried to recall the arguments which had led to my decision. I could not remember them clearly but I became doubtful of their soundness; then certain I had done the wrong thing. We should have searched till the last dog was dead and we ourselves were in danger, and I had shirked the issue, had come back with nothing but excuses. ... I had probably condemned one man to death and ruined the reputation of another. I was as low in spirit and body as I ever hope to be.

At midnight, a hundred yards from the sleeping base hut, Scott sat down and asked Riley for a cigarette. The noise of greeting between their dogs and those at the base awakened Chapman, who came outside and asked the question Scott dreaded. No, he shouted angrily and defensively, they had not got Courtauld with them. Gino was understanding, matter-of-fact, asking about the weather and the plan they had followed. He assured Scott that he had done the right thing, that Courtauld would still have food and that another three-man team, led by Gino, would be able to reach him within a couple of weeks. As Gino began to make his preparations he asked Scott's advice on a number of details, which went some way to restoring his confidence and self-respect.

When Courtauld was rescued and returned to the coast, it was he who apologised to Scott for putting him to so much inconvenience. As soon as he had cleaned himself up, shaved and changed his clothes, he and Scott went out together to shoot some ptarmigan for the pot. 'We were alone together for an hour or two, talking away, absolutely at ease.' They had been friends since sharing a cabin on the *Quest* on the way to Greenland, when Courtauld thought him 'quite the most charming person in the ship, but unavoidably large'. There was certainly no question in his mind that Scott might have failed him.

However, when Scott published *The Private Life of Polar Exploration* in 1982, and recalled his feelings as he returned to base without Courtauld, he wrote that 'Memory of that abysmal state of mind and body is painful even after fifty years'. His son Jeremy, in his account of the Arctic expedition, *Dancing on Ice*, published in 2008, concluded that Scott's failure to find Courtauld ruined his confidence and haunted him for the rest of his life. This may or may not be so; but Scott declined Gino's invitation to go back to Greenland the following year, and in fact never went to the polar regions again.

Before going home, however, in the summer of 1931, he did make one more journey on the ice cap, crossing Greenland from east to south-west. It was a distance of about 450 miles, and it took Scott, accompanied by Lindsay and Stephenson, exactly a month. Three months had passed since that nightmare journey when he had failed to find Courtauld and bring him back. Now, once again sledging with Lindsay and buoyed by his cheerful company, Scott's depression lifted for a few weeks as they moved easily across the smooth surface of the ice sheet, blissfully free of stress and hardship. Travelling by night, or by twilight – the sun was below the horizon for only an hour or two – they stopped when the day warmed up. The rations which Scott took proved to be more than ample. When a reporter asked him in Copenhagen, on the way home, what was the worst hardship he had suffered on the trans-Greenland trek, he said that once or twice he had eaten too much.

This journey was in part the conclusion of Gino's and Scott's unfinished business when they had had to turn back the previous October while heading south. This time they went past the line of Nansen's crossing and then turned towards the west coast mountains. Flowers, flies and butterflies began to make their appearance as the Ivigtut glacier and fjord came into view; for Scott his days on the Greenland ice cap were over. The sledge dogs' days were over too: he had to perform the unpleasant task of killing the dogs, which would not be welcome in south-west Greenland. Huskies and domesticated animals cannot live together. He shot them through the head with a .22 rifle. 'Afterwards I sat for a while on the moraine and made my peace before crawling into the tent, where there was no privacy. I read Lycidas and went to sleep.' But he spared one dog, called Nanok, which he took home with him as a souvenir of his Arctic adventures.

Back in England, while Gino gave lectures to pay off the expedition's debts, partied and concentrated the rest of his considerable energies on raising the funds for a new expedition, to cross the Antarctic continent, Scott spent as much time as he could with Pam. While Gino of course included him in his plans to go south in 1932, Scott would soon get engaged to Gino's sister. He had just been away from her for a year, and neither of them relished the prospect of another separation – lasting up to three years if the proposed Antarctic expedition went ahead.

When Gino was compelled to accept the less exciting alternative of returning to Greenland for another year, Scott apparently told his mentor and friend that he couldn't come because he had been offered a job. According to his eldest son Jeremy, this was untrue:

> Scott could not face returning to the place where he had failed. What had happened on the ice cap the year before had shattered his image of himself, but in refusing to accompany Gino now, he created for himself a personal demon who would cling to his back and reproach him for the rest of his life. Until his death at the age of seventy-nine, he believed that if he had said yes and gone with Gino he would have changed the way the story ended.

Scott may well have had his personal demon, but one of the more important reasons for his decision not to go back to Greenland was surely more prosaic, and romantic: he was in love and he didn't want to leave Pam again. He was also engaged in writing his first book, *The Land That God Gave Cain*, about his expedition with Gino to Labrador. Gino wrote, in an introduction to the book shortly before he left for Greenland: 'My greatest regret ... is that in seven days' time I am off to the Arctic again for a year and this time Jimmy Scott cannot come with me.' His last words to Scott before leaving were to say: 'If anything happens to me, look after Pam.'

He did so by marrying her the year after Gino was drowned. In 1933 he was also secretary to the Mount Everest Expedition, one of whose members was Lawrence Wager, geologist on the first Greenland expedition. He then did a similar job, serving as linkman in London, for John Rymill's British Graham Land Expedition to the Antarctic. When Pam and Scott's first son was born in 1934, Rymill celebrated the occasion by naming a promontory on the Antarctic peninsula Cape Jeremy. Scott's principal undertaking for the first three years of his marriage was to write what he called 'the life story of the best friend a man could know' – a detailed, though uncritical and unrevealing, account of Gino's twenty-five years.

At the outbreak of war it was no surprise to find the Watkins boys, somewhat out of place in 1930s Britain, volunteering for the special forces which were being established during the phoney war of 1939–40. Under the nominal command of Martin Lindsay, a regular soldier, Scott, Chapman and Riley joined a battalion which was being formed to fight with the Finns in their struggle against Russia. They were natural irregulars, and their Arctic training and experience of skiing would have been put to good use. But they were too late for 'the winter war', which ended in March 1940, and the battalion was disbanded.

Scott spent most of the war in irregular warfare, first as an instructor at a special training centre at Lochailort, on the west coast of Inverness-shire (where he came across David Stirling, founder of the SAS). After Italy had surrendered in 1943, he commanded a mountain warfare school in the Italian Alps, finishing the war as a lieutenant-colonel, with an OBE. He was then appointed as representative of the British Council in Milan, and afterwards in Belgrade.

Scott had begun writing books in the 1930s – his best-selling biography of Gino was published in 1935 – and also went to work for the *Daily Telegraph*, where he undertook a number of jobs, first as publicity manager and later more agreeably as wine and European travel correspondent. He stayed with the *Telegraph* for nearly thirty years. While continuing to write books with Arctic themes, he appeared to take the decision to loosen, almost to deny, his Greenland connection. In his *Who's Who* entry he described himself as 'author and explorer', mentioning some of his books but without any reference to the British Arctic Air Route Expedition or to his Polar Medal. When he once wrote a mountaineering article for the *Telegraph* he insisted on using the pseudonym of James Maurice (his two Christian names).

It is open to question whether Scott's experiences in Greenland were responsible, at least in part, for his character change after the war. In the view of his son Jeremy, they were. He could not forgive himself for having let Gino and August down, he drank heavily, he became more introspective and in time misanthropic and something of a recluse. His marriage to Pam was, using his son's word and, as anticipated by her father, a disaster: the only thing they had in common was their devotion to Gino's memory. The inevitable divorce was finalised in 1958, and he married an Italian, Adriana Rinaldi, the following year. They lived in Majorca for a while, then bought a thatched cottage in the Cambridgeshire village of Yelling.

From the late 1940s Scott was a full-time writer, turning out at least one book every year for the next two decades, all of them written in longhand. Many were novels, adventure stories of the Boy's Own variety. The most successful, *Seawyf and Biscuit*, told the story of four people on a life raft, the only survivors from a British cargo ship sunk by a Japanese submarine off Singapore, and was made into a successful film, *Sea Wife*, starring Richard Burton and Joan Collins.

Although he had turned his back on Greenland, Scott kept in touch with old friends from those days, and in particular August Courtauld. Before the war they had been walking together in Scotland, and wildfowling in the Hebrides. In 1949 Courtauld decided to sail across the Atlantic to the West Indies and invited Scott, Riley and an Essex banker friend to join him. The purpose of the voyage was to join Courtauld's eldest son, Christopher, for Christmas in Jamaica, where Courtauld's wartime friend Ian Fleming had lent his house, Goldeneye, to Christopher while he was recovering from polio. Courtauld's yacht *Duet*, which he bought on returning from Greenland, closely resembled the ideal design for a boat which he had sketched in his diary on the ice cap. He was an experienced sailor and had taken *Duet* to Scandinavia, the Baltic, round the north coast of Scotland and through the western isles. He was a fearless seaman and looked forward to an Atlantic crossing. But it was a bit foolhardy to set sail for the West Indies in October.

The voyage began with Courtauld's second son, Julien, on board. They sailed across the Channel and through the canal to Caen, damaging the boat and a loch gate on the way. Julien was dropped off in Devon before *Duet* headed south. The weather was bad from the start. They met gale-force headwinds in the Bay of Biscay and couldn't get round Cape Finisterre. A huge wave swamped the engine, putting it out of action, and the topsail yard broke. Having put in to Corunna for repairs, Courtauld learnt that they hadn't enough money to pay for the damage. Without any help from the British Consul, they were obliged to put to sea in the middle of the night while the port official charged with guarding *Duet* was asleep on the quay. The weather got worse, the mizzen boom was smashed, Courtauld was swept out of the cockpit and almost overboard (saved only by a life rail which had just been fitted), and they were soon compelled to turn for home, reaching Dartmouth three weeks after they had set out. Scott recalled that as *Duet* sailed up the Channel and they came in sight of Start Point, they held a thanksgiving service and sang 'Eternal Father, strong to save'. The words meant rather more than usual.

In a subsequent novel, *Heather Mary*, which he dedicated to *Duet*, her skipper and the other two crew members, Scott drew on his experiences with Courtauld on this aborted voyage for the principal character in the book, also skipper of a yacht and a fine seaman. To give one example, both men made their crew drink seawater when they were constipated. Scott's friendship with Courtauld and his family was also confirmed at this time when he dedicated another of his novels, *Cap Across the River*, to Christopher.

In later life Scott continued to walk and climb – in Scotland, in the Pyrenees, which he walked from the Atlantic to the Mediterranean, along the Apennines, which led to a book – but he was usually in debt. He had spent all the money he received from his best-selling novel, *Seawyf and Biscuit*, and the subsequent film before the Inland Revenue came after him. He continued to live a solitary, discontented life; his wife Adriana was with him but he saw his sons only rarely and friends were hardly ever invited to the cottage. It was his love of gardening which did for him in the end. He fell from an apple tree, had a heart attack and died aged seventy-nine.

Scott's hero-worship of Gino never dimmed. In his last book, *The Private Life of Polar Exploration*, published only four years before he died, he wrote again about his unsuccessful journey to find Courtauld at the ice-cap station, but never even suggested that Gino might have made a misjudgement in picking him and sending him off without a surveyor/navigator or a time-signal set. Scott heaped all the blame on himself for having returned without Courtauld. When he declined Gino's invitation to go back to Greenland the following year, was it because he couldn't face it, couldn't bring himself to return to the scene of what he saw as his humiliation? Or did he want to stay at home with the woman he loved? If he was being pulled in two directions it is surprising that her brother Gino's influence did not prevail. Evidence from the family suggests that Scott would never have married Pam had Gino not asked him to 'look after' her in the event of his death. Because of Gino, Scott lost his self-respect, made a marriage which was never happy and took to drink. He had spent more time with Gino in the Arctic than the others, but he was the only one of the Watkins boys who never went polar exploring again.

It continued to prey on his mind that he had not gone back to Greenland with Gino. He would say – rather absurdly – that had he been there he might have saved Gino from his fate. Having ended his Arctic days when he was twenty-five, was his mind really troubled for the next fifty years? Did he never find peace or happiness after Gino? It was not as if he rejected his Arctic experience or his Arctic companions. He wrote books about Greenland and polar exploration, and some of his fiction was based in the Arctic. But he didn't want to keep up with current polar affairs at Cambridge, nor did he interest himself in the doings of the Scott Polar Research Institute. Instead he turned inwards: after his youthful achievements on the rugby field and in company with his hero Gino, he spent much of the rest of his life, in spite of being a successful author, in a state of morose unfulfilment.

6
Frederick Spencer Chapman, DSO and Bar (1907–71)

On 10 November 1930 Freddy Spencer Chapman was leading a party of six from their base on the coast to the weather station in the middle of the Greenland ice cap. Autumn had given way to Arctic winter, the weather was atrocious and they had made only fifteen miles in as many days. Two months earlier, Chapman had had his first experience of sledging with dogs, on a much easier journey to the ice-cap station. For someone who had spent much of his early life walking over the Cumbrian fells, running across country and climbing hills, this new activity was almost too good to be true. 'By Jove I love this sledging. Not too much food and good hard work. I feel as fit as hell. Could go on all day.'

It was this attitude of mind that led August Courtauld to describe him as 'charming but horribly hearty'. Some of Chapman's fellow students at his public school, Sedbergh, would no doubt have found him 'a bit keen'. When the ship taking the expedition to east Greenland called at Reykjavik and they all went to a hotel for the night – the last opportunity to sleep in a comfortable bed for the next twelve months – Chapman preferred to pack a rucksack and head for the hills, where he slept in a tent.

Soon after arriving in Greenland, Courtauld and Chapman had just begun a survey of the coast when their whale-boat capsized during the night while they were camped on shore. Certain articles were retrieved but the theodolite was missing. They waited until low tide, hoping it might be visible in shallow water. Courtauld caught sight of something that did not look like a rock, and they reckoned it must be the theodolite box, lying in about twelve feet of water. The tide was now coming in, and their efforts to reach it with an oar lashed to the boat-hook were in vain. Chapman said he would dive in and get it; having stripped off and despite the freezing water, he swam down and was able to bring the box to the surface.

It was no doubt due to Chapman's keenness, and competence, that Gino Watkins chose him to lead his companions to the ice-cap station to relieve the two who had been there for a month and replace them with two others, who would probably have to spend the winter there. At school and at Cambridge, whether in cross-country races or in academic examinations, Chapman had always fallen short of being number one. Preferring rock-climbing to football and cricket, he was something of an outsider, yet he was almost pathetically anxious to be liked. His feelings of insecurity and rootlessness were understandable in one who from birth had been a virtual orphan. When his mother died of blood poisoning less than a month after he was born, his father, a solicitor, promptly left the country and went to Canada to avoid legal action at the suit of one of his clients. The baby and his elder brother were looked after by an aunt, then given a vicarage upbringing, first in the Lake District and afterwards with another clergyman and his wife at Flookburgh, overlooking Morecambe Bay. Their father was made bankrupt, enlisted with the Canadian Mounted Rifles in British Columbia, returned to England, and was killed at the Somme two years later, when young Freddy was nine.

Rectory life did not turn him towards religion. He could not reconcile himself to 'singing what seemed to me ridiculous hymns and repeating equally nonsensical prayers'. Lacking self-belief as well as a belief in God, he resolved instead to prove himself through taking physical risks and driving himself to the limit. When aged only eight, he persuaded a young ordinand at the vicarage to take him up Helvellyn, a peak of more than 3,000 feet in the Lake District. At his prep school on the Yorkshire moors, he would invite boys to hit him over the head with cricket bats to see how much he could take. Without parents Chapman became of necessity self-reliant. He taught himself to be an ornithologist, spending many happy hours alone, watching and recording birds. But this was an adjunct to the life of adventure and danger which he craved.

Had his parents lived, his life might have proceeded in a more conventional direction. But he was restless as well as rootless, seeking new challenges both mental and physical. He would strive against all the difficulties he could find and overcome them. At Sedbergh he combined his love of climbing with his interest in birds. 'Some of the descents to ravens' or peregrines' nests ... reduced the margin of safety to the slenderest limit. But it was good practice.' He graduated from rock-climbing to mountaineering, in the French Alps, while at Cambridge, enjoying not only the risks involved but the companionship and interdependence of his fellow climbers. The veteran mountaineer Geoffrey Winthrop Young (who climbed the Matterhorn in 1928 with an artificial leg) was one of those with whom he spent many happy hours discussing belays, pitches and cornices.

Chapman relished danger, not for its own sake but in pursuit of some goal which he judged worthwhile. One of these was what at Cambridge was known as night climbing, scaling the roofs and towers of college buildings. There was quite a vogue for this sport at the university in the 1920s; it was not only exciting and dangerous but forbidden, and therefore had to be undertaken after the dons had retired to bed. Two or three would climb together, using ropes, and it was on one such ascent that Chapman first met Gino Watkins. Gino had already achieved some fame at Cambridge, at least in exploring circles, for having led an expedition to Edge Island, Spitzbergen at the age of twenty. What first struck Chapman, as they were introduced in a friend's rooms one evening before a climb, was that Gino was so well dressed. For scaling the heights of St John's (Chapman's college) he was of course suitably attired in dark clothes, but Chapman was at once impressed by the cut of his belted jacket and plus-fours, and the dark green woollen stockings which matched the scarf tied loosely round his neck. His hair was precisely parted and slicked back, and the determined look in his eyes seemed to reach beyond his immediate surroundings.

Chapman longed above all for recognition. After a third-class degree he undertook a trip round Iceland, by boat and on foot, watching birds, eating their eggs and shooting some of them for the pot. He thought he might take up a career as a schoolmaster, but not just yet. He went to Switzerland towards the end of 1929 for a skiing and climbing holiday in Davos, and there he bumped into Gino, whom he already looked up to as an inspirational figure. For the past year Gino had been surveying unmapped territory in Labrador and learning to use dogs for sledging. The following exchange, according to Chapman, took place on the Davos ski slopes:

'Hullo Gino, how was Labrador?'

'Hullo Freddy, how was Iceland? What are you doing here? Come with me to Greenland.'

'Right you are.'

A year had now passed. Chapman was learning the art of dog sledging, which he professed to love, he was feeling 'as fit as hell' and longing for a new challenge. Gino had accorded him the recognition which he craved and had put him in charge. And what a responsibility it was. Starting in the last week of October, Chapman was the only one of the six with any previous dog sledging experience. Three of the dog teams had not been driven since Jimmy Scott had bought them in the Faroe Islands on the way to Greenland, and all the sledge loads were unusually heavy because they were taking a wireless set to the ice-cap station and it required one sledge to itself. Winter was fast approaching, the days were shortening and ferocious winds, which they called 'fornicators', were blowing off the ice cap.

It was the view of Scott, and probably the others, that 'no one could have led this difficult journey better than Chapman did. He had faith and vision. He was a tremendous driver – chiefly of himself. He had reserves of imaginative recreation, and he was an unconquerable optimist.' With his fresh-faced enthusiasm and robustly handsome features, he appeared to be just the man to inspire others. Yet he was having his doubts. 'It seems a very hazardous undertaking …. I hope to God I shall make it.' Two weeks earlier, on his way back to base from the ice cap, he had been delayed for three days by a storm with winds reaching more than 100 mph. As he noted in his diary, he had never been so cold or so miserable.

The party of six – Chapman, Courtauld, Lawrence Wager, Captain Percy Lemon of the Royal Signals, Wilfred Hampton and Alfred Stephenson – were due to set off on 25 October, but gales delayed their start until the following day. The wind was blowing straight down the ice cliff (recorded politely in accounts of the expedition as Bugbear Bank) which they would have to climb to reach the ice plateau, and the dogs were not having it. On the second night the tent shared by Chapman and Lemon blew down, and the others lowered their tent poles so that the canvas lay flat over them. It took them almost a week to get from the base to the top of Buggery Bank, at times using block and tackle to haul the sledges. Then there were the crevasses to contend with: two men roped together went forward, probing every foot of the ground and taking the sledges through in single file. Wager wrote a letter to his father 'suggesting what might be done with my insurance money if I fall irreparably into a crevasse'.

One day the dogs broke into a 25-lb bag of pemmican and ate the lot. On more than one occasion a bitch whelped and her puppies had to be fed to the others. Sledges overturned and the blizzards persisted, making travel impossible on average more than every other day.

> I think this journey is going to be one of the bloodiest ever made – if we make the ice-cap station, that is!…The most fearful night imaginable. The wind increased towards evening and by 10.30 pm had reached hurricane force and the tent roared like sin so that we had to shout to make each other hear. … I really thought no tent could possibly stand against it.… . I wondered how long one could exist in a fur bag before freezing to death.

The dogs might be fighting, or howling in their discomfort, but at least they could not be heard above the noise of the wind. In the morning, after a gale, the sledges and tents had to be dug out of snowdrifts which had become frozen. At 3 am one morning Wager put his head outside and told his leader, who had inquired how light it was, that 'it's light enough to dig'. The shared hardship, and the companionship, gave Chapman the opportunity to learn more about the men he was leading into this hell. 'I was astonished to find that most of them had disliked school chapel as much as I had and that none of them had any more definite philosophy of life than I had myself. … Nothing like a sledging journey for getting to know a man. I don't think Lemon will stand the journey but he has guts.'

Lying up for a day or more in their tents, there were a few things to be enjoyed other than conversation. The primus stove could provide a bowl of porridge, a mug of tea and a sort of stew, which may have been more appealing than it sounds, made from pemmican, peaflour and plasmon (a powder containing casein, the principal protein of milk). Once the primus stove was put out, hoar-frost formed at once on the sides of the tent. A pipe produced more smoke than warmth, but it made reading more enjoyable. Chapman insisted that books should be taken on the journey, and he sometimes read aloud to the others in the evening. '*Tess of the D'Urbervilles* is a most suitable book to read in such circumstances – elemental strife in both cases.'

But reading was not easy, with cold hands and the pages getting wet when the hoar-frost melted and dripped on them. Wager would read poems, and sometimes sing songs, from *The Weekend Book*. Palgrave's *The Golden Treasury* of lyrical poems and songs was one of Chapman's particular favourites. Perhaps surprisingly for a man of action, his love of poetry was nurtured in his schooldays, especially when he was wild-fowling on the shores of Morecambe Bay and would learn and recite Keats's 'Ode to a Nightingale', Coleridge's 'Rime of the Ancient Mariner', and *The Rubáiyát of Omar Khayyám*. Among other books being carried to the ice-cap station were *The Master of Ballantrae*, *Alice's Adventures in Wonderland, Treasure Island*, the works of Shakespeare, Dorothy Osborne's seventeenth-century love letters and *The Manhood of the Master*, by Harry Emerson Fosdick, an American Baptist minister and liberal thinker. No cheap modern trash accompanied these intrepid, and well-educated, explorers. Nor, more surprisingly, did the more contemporary novelists and playwrights: no James Joyce, Franz Kafka, Virginia Woolf, Oscar Wilde or George Bernard Shaw. (Several minor twentieth-century writers appear in the ice-cap station's library list, but no one in his diary mentions having read their books.)

There were some days when they could not move and, because of the howling wind, struggled to make themselves heard over the few yards between tents. 'Your turn to feed the dogs – if you can find them,' Chapman would yell across to Wager. 'Is your primus working?' Or, 'I say, August, will you swap your Shakespeare tragedies for *Kidnapped*? And some paraffin for a candle?'

After the expedition was over, Courtauld recalled, in an introduction to Chapman's book on the second Greenland expedition, 'how, during those dark, fierce days of blizzard, when travel was impossible, he [Chapman] used to read in a clear tenor from one of our books, while the tent shook to the bass of the storm's accompaniment. On such a journey you learn the worth of a man.'

In the tent which they shared, Chapman and Lemon began to discuss the problems they faced due to their lack of progress. It was becoming clear that six people would not be able to reach the ice-cap station and get back to base. They had not enough provisions, either for themselves or for the dogs. Three men would have to turn for home, taking the minimum of food with them, and none for the dogs, some of whom would have to be killed to feed the others. And the wireless set would have to be dumped to lighten their loads. Whether they would have enough food, when they got to the ice-cap station, to leave two men there for the winter (with relief unlikely for another three or four months) was now the most nagging question in Chapman's mind. He decided that Lemon and Hampton should return to base: Hampton was required to keep the aeroplane in working order; it might be needed to resupply the station. And without a wireless at the ice-cap station Lemon would be needed back at base to operate the wireless set there.

For most of the first week of November the wind blew so hard that neither man nor dog could hope to travel in it. When the wind dropped it might take up to seven hours before they were ready to move off. 'Everything was buried under the usual feet of snow and frozen urine.' When at last they were on their way, delays invariably occurred when sledges were overturned by wind ridges and the hollows between them.

The amount of clothing that each man wore must have taken an age to assemble and put on. Chapman recorded that in these conditions he wore 'three pairs of socks and three pairs of blanket shoes and fur boots, pants and vest, sweater, blanket trousers and coat, windproof trousers and coat, canvas leggings to keep the snow out, two pairs of wool mitts and wolfskin mitts, wool helmet and windproof hood'. But his heartiness got the better of him one morning when he dashed out of the tent without windproofs to look for the flags which were guiding them to the ice-cap station. When he returned both his ears were frostbitten. Foolishly he warmed them up quickly in the tent and, in Wager's words, 'almost wept and threw himself about the tent in the agony of ears and hands coming back'. Chapman said it was the worst pain he had known.

The first party on to the ice cap had planted bamboo poles, with a red flag on each one, at every half-mile from the top of the glacier to the place, about 130 miles from the coast and at a height of more than 8,000 feet, where the weather station was established. Now it was vital that Chapman kept on the line of flags. If they lost the flags they would probably never find the station in this featureless white wilderness. Travelling by compass bearing was not reliable enough, and the weather seldom allowed the checking of their position by the sun, which would barely rise above the horizon, or by astronomical observation.

They had left base two weeks ago and were still more than 100 miles from their destination. Yet another blizzard made travel impossible on 9 November, and that night 48 degrees of frost were recorded. 'Things certainly look very black,' Chapman noted. The next morning, 10 November, visibility was poor; the light was diffused and it was snowing. Chapman thought he must be seeing things, or rather seeing nothing through the falling snow, when a few black dots appeared to be moving in the distance. The dots became two men and their dogs, Gino Watkins and Jimmy Scott, returning from a journey which had taken them a hundred miles south, and it was by the merest chance that the two parties met in the white wastes of the ice cap.

Gino and Scott had been travelling for more than a month, having last seen Chapman at the ice-cap station on 4 October. They had encountered terrible weather themselves in the past fortnight, and knew that Chapman's party would have been held up. But as the two drew closer, Gino's first reaction was to congratulate Chapman on being so close to home, having relieved and restocked the ice-cap station in record time. Chapman's sledges were drawn up together and the dogs had turned towards Gino as he approached them, so he was unable to tell in which direction they were going. The awful possibility then occurred to him.

'Which way are you going? Not in to the ice-cap station?'

Chapman nodded.

'But – Good Lord! – you'll never get there.'

'Oh, I know.'

They both laughed. A serious but brief conversation followed, with Gino and Chapman first sitting in the lee of a sledge, then, because of the intense cold, walking up and down. Having put Chapman in charge, it was typical of Gino, and the only realistic option, to leave him to take the decisions in the light of the prevailing conditions. According to Chapman later, 'Gino wouldn't help me at all. He said he didn't know how things stood and gave me carte blanche and hurried on.'

However, Gino did approve Chapman's plan to send three men back and dump the wireless, in order to take a larger quantity of food and make certain of reaching the station and getting back. Eat the dogs if necessary, Gino advised. As for what happened when the two men, Ted Bingham and 'Jimmy' D'Aeth, were relieved, that must be for Chapman to decide; so much would depend on the weather over the next two weeks. Gino briefly considered whether he or Scott should go with Chapman, but rejected it. Both of them were exhausted by their experiences of the past month, and their faces were blackened by frost and whipped raw by the wind. Gino's last words to Chapman before they parted were: 'You'll just have to use your own judgement and do the best you can. You may have to abandon the station. But at all costs you must get the two men out.'

Chapman gave the news to Hampton, Lemon and Stephenson that they would be returning to base the following day. Courtauld and Wager would be the next pair to man the station, possibly for the whole winter. That evening they all enjoyed a full-ration farewell dinner which, described as far as possible as if listed on a menu, consisted of: Soupe à la wild pemmican; Boeuf de chien sauté; Porridge and Plasmon with margarine; Horlicks, chocolate and strong lemon. The next morning the three who were leaving gave up their best dogs, sledges, most of their food, spare clothes and books. They all forgot to observe the two minutes' silence for Armistice Day at eleven o'clock, but agreed to dine together in London on the same day a year hence. The wireless and several ration boxes were left under one of the flags; they were never seen again.

That same morning, Courtauld went into Chapman's tent with an idea. He was volunteering to stay alone at the ice-cap station.

> He stressed what has been worrying me, namely that we shall take so long to reach the station that we shan't have enough supplies to leave for two people. The bad weather, having started so early, may continue until February and even over March, so that no sledge party could come up and the aeroplane could not land. Courtauld says he is used to being alone and is very keen to try the experiment in such conditions. With so many books, a good supply of tobacco and ample food for one man he says he is perfectly happy and is most anxious to do this.... We can't decide anything yet. We've got to find the station first.

It took them another three weeks to get there. Following the flags was now becoming more difficult: several were buried, or obscured by drifts, and the bunting was often torn to shreds. The ice cap was an almost flat plane of snow with a circular horizon as at sea. But they were, of course, constantly walking uphill, now at a height of about 7,000 feet. 20 November was, for Chapman, 'the worst day I've ever had. With the sores in my fork and frost-bitten toes each step is agony. Several times I just couldn't go on and had to sit down for a few minutes.' Progress was distressingly slow for other reasons: sledges were overturning, sledges needed repairing, traces kept breaking. At night, as the blizzards continued, the sleeping bags might be frozen or sodden and, as Chapman put it, 'if the tent goes, we are corpses'. Having advanced no more than two miles in five days, he had to think of their options. 'It looks as if we shall have to go on till the dog food is finished, then kill off the weaker dogs as food for the others, then – if we find the station – collect D'Aeth and Bingham and man-haul back.'

Yet while they were forced to lie up all day in the tents Chapman, amazingly, remained cheerful. He read a lot of Shakespeare – *King John, Cymbeline, Troilus and Cressida* – and so did Courtauld and Wager, either aloud or to themselves. 'Enjoyed today vastly. Though it's irksome not to be able to get on, yet we can't move and there it is. There is a consoling inevitability about it. ... By Jove this is an epic journey for slowness and bloodyness – but Gino was too pessimistic ... it's bloody good fun really.'

'Bloody good fun' it may have been to Chapman, but this was one of the worst Arctic journeys ever recorded – only rivalled, in the estimation of David Howarth, in his *Heroes of Nowadays*, by Apsley Cherry-Garrard's 'worst journey in the world' in 1911, when in the darkness of Antarctic winter he, Bill Wilson and Birdie Bowers were man-hauling without skis for five weeks in search of Emperor penguins and their eggs. One of the most depressing things for Chapman, Courtauld and Wager was that each day was shorter than the previous one, the hours of darkness longer. (Chapman finally got back to base two days before the shortest day of the year.) At the end of the month, the weather and snow conditions suddenly improved, allowing them to travel while sitting on their sledges, for the first time since leaving base. They were doing over ten miles a day and at last, on the evening of 3 December, they spotted the Union Jack and knew they had made it. Chapman, once again in high spirits, shouted 'Evening Standard!' as he burst in on the two amazed and much relieved men, Bingham and

D'Aeth, who were quietly smoking their pipes after supper. They had been at the ice-cap station a month longer than they expected, and it had taken Chapman thirty-nine days to reach them from the coast.

Now Chapman had to decide what to do. Abandon the station and lose valuable winter weather readings? Or let Courtauld have his way and leave him there alone, possibly for four months? Courtauld repeated his arguments, adding that he had no wish to make the journey back as he had frostbite in his toes. He was irritated by Wager and did not want to have to share the ice-cap station with him; but that was now irrelevant as there was not enough food to leave two men there. (He and Wager were getting on well enough a few years later for them to return to Greenland together in 1935.) Both Bingham, a naval doctor, and D'Aeth, an RAF flight-lieutenant, were strongly opposed to Courtauld's idea. Having stayed there together for nine weeks, they thought it highly inadvisable to leave one man alone for what might be twice that length of time. Wager was also against it, partly perhaps because he thought that Courtauld's choice reflected badly on him.

Chapman and Courtauld knew that Gino had anticipated, before the expedition left England, that it might be necessary to leave a man on his own on the ice cap. Gino had said that in Labrador trappers were sometimes alone for nine months without suffering any ill effects. Such a period of solitude, through an Arctic winter, was something that Gino would have accepted for himself; but would Chapman? He had proved himself to have strength of character. He was mentally and physically tough, unsentimental, independent, self-reliant, hugely energetic and generally optimistic. Adopting Gino's favourite quotation, from *Hamlet*, he used to boast that 'there is nothing either good or bad, but thinking makes it so'.

But he had a history of depression, of 'thinking bad'. Only eighteen months ago, having just finished his finals at Cambridge, Chapman had written a revealing letter to the second of his two reverend foster-fathers, 'Uncle' Sam Taylor.

> I really don't think I have ever been quite so utterly miserable in my life. I have just had two three-hour exams today and I know I have failed. ... I shall have to go and plant tea or something abroad, which I really think will be the best thing for me....
>
> I got the most awful fit of melancholy I have ever had. I really

never thought I should last it out.... I simply burst into tears whenever I was by myself – I have had these cheerful attacks before, you may remember – so I had to go out and talk to people.... Also I could not sleep very well, I just moped about; I tried running, and all sorts of things, but no good, my head ached when I worked, and I had to give it up.

One of his previous 'cheerful attacks' had occurred at Cambridge the year before. He recorded this bout of depression in his diary: 'I really am in a very serious condition.... I cannot concentrate on anything or remember anything... . No one realises what an utter rotter and dud I am. ... What a life! I really shall shoot myself soon. If only my father and mother were still alive I might have some hope.' Greenland banished the blues for a while, but they would return.

A few of the members of the expedition thought Chapman, Rymill, Courtauld and Gino were the only ones who could have endured a winter alone on the ice cap. But no psychiatrist, having read what he had written, could have recommended Chapman as a suitable case for a period of solitude in the middle of nowhere. He was a man who needed to keep going, to expend energy and take risks. When during the war he spent three years in the jungle behind Japanese lines and without support, there was constant danger and his survival depended on the action he took. His all-important attitude of mind played a part in influencing the outcome of his ordeal. But on the ice cap there would have been nothing he could do; there was only the unbearable (to him) monotony of taking weather readings, sitting, eating and waiting in the winter darkness, with no one to talk to. (When he spent the best part of a month alone on the second expedition to Greenland, it was mid-summer, he occupied his time in fishing and kayaking, and he had dogs for company.)

Knowing that he himself could not have stayed alone at the ice-cap station, it may be asked why Chapman agreed to leave Courtauld there. Chapman knew that Courtauld was a quite different character: he wasn't hearty or hyperactive, he was 'laid-back', absent-minded, perverse in some ways. He enjoyed his own company, he wanted to stay there by himself, and perhaps by doing so prove something to himself. In the last stages of their journey to relieve Bingham and D'Aeth, Chapman noted one day: 'We tried three in a tent. More cheerful. Bloody for one man alone.' Courtauld would not have agreed.

Chapman judged, correctly, that Courtauld would survive the ordeal and should have his way. The only alternative was to abandon the station and all hope of providing any information on the winter weather to be expected at 8,000 feet on the Greenland ice cap – which was one of the main purposes of the expedition and had never been recorded before. So the decision was taken, and Chapman was anxious to get going. The days shorten more quickly in these latitudes, and they had barely four daylight hours. He allowed himself and the three others fourteen days on half rations for the return journey, leaving Courtauld enough food and fuel to last five months. After two days of gales the weather eased and they had a farewell, early Christmas dinner before departing.

On the trip back to base, which took two weeks, the hardships continued. Now travelling downhill, Chapman went ahead on skis for the first few days to encourage the dogs. But the going soon became heavy, the drifts got bigger, the days got shorter and both men and dogs were exhausted by what they had been through in the past weeks. Diary entries bear witness to their plight: 'We are in a bad way.... Food getting short, ditto candles. Paraffin running out.' They were reduced to eating raw pemmican and margarine. One day they lost the line of flags in poor visibility, but Chapman said they must push on, using compass bearings. The dogs were so hungry they were eating harnesses, snow-shoes and pieces of tent. Chapman had to draw on all his considerable reserves, reminding himself, which was his motto, that almost all difficulties can be overcome. 'Mere cold is a friend, not an enemy; the weather always gets better if you wait long enough; distance is merely relative; man can exist for a long time on very little food; the human body is capable of immense privation; miracles still happen; it is the state of mind that is important.'

In these extreme conditions the morale of one of the party cracked. It was Jimmy D'Aeth: he neglected to dry his gloves at night and his hands became frost-bitten. When it came to making or striking camp, he had to be told what to do and became lethargic. Towards the end of one day D'Aeth was lagging behind, and when the others stopped to unlash the sledges he was nowhere to be seen. Weak and disoriented, he had wandered off in the wrong direction – not exactly doing an Oates, but apparently careless of his wellbeing. In the gathering darkness Chapman walked back along their route, found him eventually after a couple of miles and saved his life.

On 18 December they camped in miserable weather and low spirits. But the following morning the clouds cleared and they could see the coastal mountains. That day they reached one of the food depots and were almost home – with their sledges at last falling to pieces. The aeroplane at the base was able to fly and from the air Gino counted four figures coming down Buggery Bank. He knew that Courtauld must have stayed on the ice cap. Chapman returned with his companions in time for Christmas, he and Wager having been away for eight weeks (fifty-four days) of what to most people would have been almost unremitting hell. Chapman, however, seemed to have thrived on the privations he had endured. 'I was as fit as anything barring toes and fingers,' was his first comment back at base. 'So ended that memorable journey, the first across the ice cap in winter.' Not only had he fully justified Gino's confidence in him, but the experience had given a tremendous boost to his own self-confidence.

One person who was especially glad to see Chapman again, having assumed he must be dead, was Gertrude. She was one of the three Eskimo girls who had arrived at the base hut in September, offering to do some cleaning. Inevitably, they were soon in demand for sexual favours as well. The evidence suggests, however, that only three members of the expedition took Eskimo lovers: Chapman, Gino and Lemon. The others were disapproving, or took the view that it was not the done thing to go to bed with native servants. In the cramped conditions of the hut which they all shared, there were tensions; but it was generally recognised that Gino, as leader, should have the *droit de seigneur* and be able to behave as he liked. He began by taking Gertrude, who was the prettiest of the three, then moved on to Tina, who was commonly known as 'the little slut'. She acquired this name from her habits, of which she was soon cured, of blowing her nose on a sleeping-bag and spitting on the dirty plates before rubbing them with her fingers.

Lemon, who as wireless operator spent much of his time at the base, was the first to have a sexual relationship with an Eskimo girl – Arpika, who was the regular cook and also a good shot. Chapman's affair with Gertrude, described by Martin Lindsay as 'a sex-conscious young woman, highly strung and inclined to be tiresome', may have begun before he set off for the ice-cap station at the end of October. She gave him an embroidered handkerchief and a blanket coat, and got very upset when she understood Chapman to say to her that girls were beautiful in England.

'Actually I said I had no girl in England. She wept all afternoon, bless her. I cheered her up but this lingo is hell.' The tears were of joy when he returned to base in mid-December, and for the next three months Chapman enjoyed 'one of the happiest times of my life. I lived with Gertrude more or less as my mistress and spent my time hunting seals or sledging round about. ... Gino had taken up with Tina now and used to spend most of the evenings with her in the loft. So did I now with Gertrude.'

Chapman was probably a virgin when he came to Greenland. In these harsh surroundings and sharing the carefree attitude of the Eskimos, he now felt more at home than he ever had when living parentless in a Cumbrian rectory; and he may well have felt, too, that he had found love with Gertrude. The opportunities for sexual intercourse, or at least sexual experimentation, may have been rather limited in a narrow bunk in a communal house, but the Arctic winter provided plenty of darkness (about twenty hours of it out of twenty-four) – and there was lots of time for learning each other's language. They were both miserable when Chapman left in mid-March on a sledging journey to the north: 'Felt very weepy all the time, so did G. God knows what the final parting will be like. I shall then become a misogynist again. My temperament can't cope with this sort of thing.' But it seemed to cope pretty well after a few days; 'I feel much happier about Gertrude now, I only hope she is happy.'

This sledging journey achieved little, and the weather drove Chapman and his two companions back to base in time to witness the return of the three men who had set out at the beginning of March to relieve Courtauld. They got back on 17 April having failed to find the ice-cap station. Gino knew he must get back to the ice cap as fast as possible if Courtauld were to be found alive before his food and fuel ran out. And he would take his two best men. Scott was ruled out because he had just got back after six weeks on the ice cap in appalling weather. Gino chose Rymill, who was one of the best surveyors on the expedition, and the indefatigable Chapman, who had demonstrated more than once that no one was better qualified for the job. He and Rymill were the only members of the expedition to make three trips to the ice-cap station and back.

So he had to say goodbye to Gertrude again, but this time there were no tears from him, no sentimentality. It was he who had left Courtauld on the ice cap at the beginning of December, and now he had to go and rescue him. With a load of surveying instruments and a time-signal set, the three men headed inland as fast as they could towards the weather station. For much of the time Gino went in front, his ski tracks leading the dogs. Winter had passed, the days were getting longer, the sun was out for much of the time and sunburn was as painful as frostbite, especially when a freezing wind blew into the cracked and peeling skin on their faces. They made record time to the place where Courtauld in his tent should have been, giving Chapman thirteen days and nights to keep convincing himself they would find Courtauld alive and well. The previous party had no time-signal set and so were unable to pinpoint the exact position of the station by latitude and longitude. But they calculated that they must have got within half a mile of it. They should have seen it, or at least the Union Jack flying above it. Unless, of course, blizzards and drifts had covered the station, in which case Courtauld might be buried inside his tent. And people who are buried are usually dead.

Gino refused to entertain this possibility, and his confidence bolstered the others. On 4 May they believed they were close to the station, but the weather was stormy and they could not fix their position precisely. Towards evening conditions improved and they skied off in different directions to search. They quartered the area for several hours, then returned to camp having seen nothing. Now Chapman was filled with foreboding. He was sure they would find the station, but if Courtauld was dead, he could never forgive himself for having allowed him to stay there. The next morning observations were taken for latitude and longitude, confirming they were within a mile of the station. So they skied off again to find it, each of them with a dog on a lead. Chapman recorded what happened next.

On reaching the summit of a long undulation we made out a black speck in the distance. It was a flag. We went racing down towards it at full speed and as we approached saw a large drift on each side of the flag. It was indeed the station. But as we got near we began to have certain misgivings. The whole place had a most extraordinary air of desolation. The large Union Jack we had last seen in December was now a mere fraction of its former size. Only the tops of the various meteorological instruments and the handle of a spade projected through the vast snowdrift, which submerged the whole tent with its snow-houses and surrounding wall. Was it possible that a man could be alive there?

As we skied up this gently sloping drift a ray of hope appeared when we saw the ventilator of the tent just sticking through the snow. A moment later Watkins knelt down and shouted down the pipe. Imagine our joy and relief when an answering shout came faintly from the depths of the snow. The voice was tremulous, but it was the voice of a normal man.

Courtauld had been alone for 150 days, snowed in for a third of that time. He was living in darkness and the primus stove had just given its last gasp. No wonder Chapman expressed his relief, not to say amazement, that he had heard the voice of a normal man. For he knew he could never have endured such a period of solitude and, perhaps worse, inactivity. Chapman was physically tougher, had more energy, than Courtauld ('horribly hearty' was Courtauld's characterisation of him). But he would not have come through this ordeal 'a normal man' – and would not have survived at all had he the means to end it. The tribute which Chapman paid Courtauld was certainly heartfelt: 'He is the only man I know who could have done it.'

For the last two months of his time in Greenland, Chapman devoted himself to learning how to use a kayak and hunt seals from it, and to observing and photographing the wild flowers and birds of the east coast. Harebells and saxifrages were appearing with the summer weather; so were snow buntings, Lapland buntings and red-necked phalaropes. There were occasional treats such as the sight of a snowy owl or a gyrfalcon. When he carried a gun he might bring back seagulls and guillemots, which the Eskimos taught them to eat, or ptarmigan, which was a real game bird and had no lingering flavour of fish. Action man Chapman was also looking forward to another sledging trip, possibly across the ice cap to the west coast. But he had developed a bronchial cyst and was advised against it by Ted Bingham, the doctor of the party. Gino asked him instead to return to England, deal with expedition business (there were debts to be paid off) and start writing the official account of the expedition. This was a task which would normally have been carried out by the expedition leader; but having already made use of Chapman's remarkable energy and qualities of leadership, Gino was now relying on his literary skills as well.

Chapman and Gertrude were going to miss one another; they had spent much of the summer walking, playing and sleeping together. The initial feelings of being in love with Gertrude had somewhat abated, but he was always happy in her company, and expressed himself delighted, though also slightly apprehensive, when she told him, shortly before he departed, that she was pregnant. The apprehension was due to the fact that Gino had had to agree to indemnify the Danish government against the cost of any illegitimate births resulting from the time spent by the expedition in Greenland. But Chapman was not thinking too much of that when he embraced Gertrude for the last time before the ship left Angmagssalik for Copenhagen and home. Sad as he was to leave her, his mind was filled with thoughts of the future.

Gino's next plan was to head south and cross the Antarctic continent, achieving what Shackleton had set out to do in 1914. He had asked Chapman to go with him, and meanwhile to go along to the Royal Geographical Society in London and discuss the idea. A lot of money would have to be raised, which in the middle of an industrial depression some would judge to be nigh impossible. However, Chapman knew that 'to Gino Watkins the word "impossible" simply did not exist', and he continued to be inspired by his leader's example. His career as a teacher would again be put on the back-burner.

Having returned to London, Chapman embarked on the expedition book, he and Gino lectured on their experiences, and Gino tried in vain to raise the funds required for the Antarctic project. Chapman fell in love again, this time with a schoolmaster's seventeen-year-old daughter called Joss. A more modest expedition was now put together: Gino, together with Chapman, Riley and Rymill, would go back to Greenland for a year, continuing with weather observations and the surveying of the east coast. Chapman was also keen to carry on with his ornithological studies, and to hunt seals with Gino from their kayaks. 'Setting off on an expedition one has a delightful feeling of relaxation and expectancy: behind one, probably a year of disappointed hopes and indecision ... before one, a return to the simple life.'

For the moment, however, he had to finish the book before the four-man party took ship for Greenland in July 1932. He was still writing it on the way to Copenhagen, sending chapters home before they boarded the *Gertrud Rask* (a four-masted steam schooner which would take them to Greenland), then airmailing the final pages from Elsinore. And he found time to write a twelve-page letter to Joss.

When they stopped to coal in Iceland, three of the party went ashore for a short walk. The fourth, Chapman of course, went off alone and, according to Gino, 'came back looking disgustingly healthy, saying he had walked about ten miles over the mountains. Divide by two to get the true distance!' As soon as they reached Angmagssalik, Chapman was greeted by his Eskimo girl-friend Gertrude – and their son. Chapman took it well and seemed paternally proud. 'Hansie is a fine boy and looks just like me. No one is annoyed apparently ... Hansie's presence doesn't spoil her chances of marriage, thank God.' She had in fact recently got engaged.

When told he would have to pay £20 to the Danish government towards supporting and educating the child, Chapman retorted: 'Nonsense – he'll go to Sedbergh.' He spent a few days ashore with Gertrude and Hansie, but after the *Gertrud Rask* took the party north to their new base at Lake Fjord, there is no record of him seeing them again.

Ten days later Chapman and Gino were planning to kayak together, using the new movie camera which Chapman had brought, with the idea of making a film over the next twelve months which would be sold when the expedition got home. But the morning was dull, the sky overcast, and Gino decided to go kayaking alone in the fjord to shoot seals. Chapman and Rymill went in the motor-boat to do some mapping of the fjord, and found his empty kayak a few hours later. 'It seemed incredible. He seemed somehow invulnerable. He dwelt apart and seemed not to be ruled by the ordinary laws.... . I can't grasp the fullness of the tragedy – he might have done so much, and he is dead.'

Chapman walked up the hill that evening after dark and smoked his pipe. The previous year they had been very lucky that no one died. Gino had such confidence in himself and his plans that he felt nothing could go wrong. He had the character of a man much older than his twenty-five years.

> He had his shortcomings but he was a very great man. One could not be really fond of him: he was somehow as cold as ice and quite above the normal bounds of sentiment and emotion... . But I admired him and felt perfectly happy with him; I would follow him anywhere.
> Somehow we felt no grief at his loss... . Although we felt ashamed of ourselves we found ourselves behaving exactly as before. Perhaps it was because we had not yet realised he was really gone.

Chapman continued to sit and watch the fading sunset. The moon rose higher above the sea, and the stars were almost dimmed by the shaking curtain of aurora. 'I saw Auriga and Lyra, the Pleiades and Cygnus, all going round the pole star as if nothing had happened – and Gino is dead in the fjord. How shall we carry on without his inspiration?' But they did, for another year, under Rymill's leadership – sledging on the pack ice, hunting with Eskimos for seals and bears, taking perilous boat journeys to survey the coast, keeping up weather observations. On one occasion Chapman was caught in a storm in his kayak a mile off the coast and had to keep it upright for hours because he was unable to land. He and Rymill made sledging journeys together: mapping, collecting ethnological specimens, trying unsuccessfully to climb Mount Forel. But it was Rymill who did the surveys while Chapman was more interested in hunting, observing and photographing birds and, in summer, collecting plants.

He was laid up for a while with a bad knee, which had given him trouble in England and swelled up after strenuous exercise. The enforced rest gave him time for melancholic thoughts, which tended to haunt him during periods of inactivity. His talent for wildlife photography and for writing were responsible, he said, for what he was slightly embarrassed to call 'an artistic temperament, not good in an Arctic winter ... . I wish I had more in common with the other two ... . The trouble is I am not sure enough about anything. I am far too sensitive to go on an expedition. However it is a good life.' And he felt he was getting over his inferiority complexes.

When he left Greenland Chapman learnt that his son Hansie had died in a 'flu epidemic. 'Poor Gertrude, I adore her still. I shall never find anyone quite like her again.' Back in England, his affair with Joss was not resumed, though they remained close for many years. *Northern Lights*, his book on the first expedition, was well received; he undertook a lucrative lecture tour; and began writing *Watkins' Last Expedition*. He was very tempted by Rymill's offer to join his planned three-year expedition to Graham Land in the Antarctic, but at the age of twenty-six he turned his back on the life of a polar explorer which in Greenland he had resolved to follow. Had Gino still been alive, he might well have decided differently. A few years later, at the beginning of the war, he was moved to write: 'I do not think that any part of my life has been or could be happier than those years in Greenland.'

Chapman accepted a teaching job at a school in north Yorkshire, but it wasn't long before he was lured back to the snows – this time the Himalayas. He had hoped to be chosen for an expedition to climb Mount Everest, but instead was invited to join a government mission to Lhasa, Tibet, which he found riddled with corruption. He subsequently made the first ascent of Mount Chomolhari, on the borders of Tibet and Bhutan, prompting a headline in *The Times*, '24,000 feet for £20' and an article comparing 'this modest ascent of two men with the yak-loads of luxuries which periodically march upon Everest'.

After a spell of teaching under Kurt Hahn at Gordonstoun, and one or two false starts at the beginning of the war, Chapman found himself in Singapore with Special Operations Executive (SOE) in 1941. There followed the extraordinary three and a half years which he spent behind enemy lines in the Malayan jungle, training Chinese communist guerrillas, constantly hunted by the Japanese and not always trusted by the Chinese. It is an almost unbelievable story of survival.* He was once unconscious with malaria for seventeen days, he contracted typhus and blackwater fever, and he lived for months on tapioca and cooked leaves, with the occasional deer or snake to provide some sustenance. He was captured by the Japanese, and escaped. Wavell called him 'the jungle Lawrence' and his remarkable record of endurance and achievement earned him a DSO and Bar. (Mountbatten said he should have got the

---

* For a detailed account of his experiences behind Japanese lines, see *Jungle Soldier* by Brian Moynahan (Quercus, 2009).

VC.) In the highly successful book on his experiences, *The Jungle Is Neutral*, Chapman wrote that 'it is the attitude of mind that determines whether you go under or survive ... the jungle itself is neutral.' He had learnt from Gino's example, that almost all difficulties could be overcome, almost all hardships borne.

When the war was over, Chapman married Faith Townson, a WAAF officer with SOE whom he had met after he came out of Malaya; they had three sons. More teaching jobs followed – firstly as headmaster of a new co-educational school in West Germany for the children of British servicemen engaged in the military occupation. Given a free hand to introduce a number of outdoor activities, he was in his element. But he decided to move on after five years when the British Army of the Rhine began to impose economies and restrict his freedom of action. His next job was as headmaster of St Andrew's College in Grahamstown, South Africa, having first taken his family in an Austin van through much of the southern half of the continent, ending their trip as guests of Stephen and Ginnie Courtauld (he who had largely funded the British Arctic Air Route Expedition) at the house which they had recently built at Umtali, Southern Rhodesia, close to the Mozambique border.

The distinguished post-war career that Chapman and others expected never materialised. After six years at St Andrew's, during which he made known his disapproval of the apartheid regime, he became warden of the Pestalozzi children's village in Sussex, but still felt restless and unfulfilled. He hoped that his application for the vice-chancellorship of Birmingham University would be supported by his old Arctic companion, Martin Lindsay, who was a governor and also MP for Solihull. But when Lindsay said he couldn't, or wouldn't, help, Chapman was annoyed and upset. His spirits were lifted, however, when he was made the subject of a *This Is Your Life* television programme in 1965 – the first one to be spread over two consecutive weeks.

His last post, as warden of a small hall of residence at Reading University, was modest but more satisfying. But he was becoming concerned about his health (a chronic bowel disorder and recurring back trouble) and approaching retirement. He had written years before about fear and of how he lived dangerously, by exploring and climbing in remote places, in order to drive out fear. But he could not conquer his fear of old age and inactivity.

Chapman's periods of depression went back to his years as a student, when he had written in his diary that he might 'incontinently' shoot himself one day. It was hard to equate the enthusiastic, jolly, supremely competent man of action with an introvert tormented by self-doubt and melancholy. But in Greenland his companions observed these tendencies in him. Gino used to warn Chapman, half-jokingly, that his 'weakness of mind' might lead him to shoot himself in a fit of depression; and Quintin Riley wrote presciently of him: 'With his unbalanced mind I should feel most uncomfortable at leaving him alone. The disappointment of not doing anything energetic might play upon him to the very worst degree and tragedy occur.'

Martin Lindsay wrote of Chapman's three most striking qualities: charm, competence, and thirdly, 'a streak of instability'. Another friend described him as having 'no foundation, no destination, no star to steer by, and no anchor meanwhile'. He was a visionary who sometimes needed to invent himself. In his anxiety to please and impress, he was inclined to exaggerate his achievements and experiences. There were even those who doubted his account of escaping from the Japanese in the Malayan jungle.

Chapman was seldom alone in the jungle; when he was, or when he was unable to move around freely, he could use his resourcefulness to remedy the situation. That course would not have been open to him if he had had to spend the winter alone on the ice cap. And there was no way now, he felt, that he could halt the progressive inactivity and, as he saw it, loneliness of old age and failing health. This was the one difficulty he could not overcome. He had had the right attitude of mind on the Greenland ice cap and in the Malayan jungle, but it was failing him now, and when he was informed that his term as warden was not being extended, the optimism of his old self deserted him completely. He had no more adventures, no more challenges to look forward to. Instead he worried about the removal of his prostate and his doctor's advice that he should rest in the afternoons.

His old Arctic friend Quintin Riley went to have tea with him at Reading.

I found him very down in the dumps. I'd heard he hadn't been well and told him we were all slowing down a bit, and things were bound to start going wrong at our age. He protested that he had been so fit all his life, and I told him that the Archbishop of Canterbury [Michael Ramsey], who was older than us, was perfectly fit again after a prostate operation. I tried to reassure him, but he was still pretty gloomy when I left. Then a fortnight later I opened *The Times* and read the obituary of Freddy which I had written ten years before.

He was sixty-four when he shot himself, in his office at the university, on 8 August 1971. His death was attributed to his suffering during the war, his widow Faith was granted a war widow's pension and the estate duty was remitted.

7
H. G. Watkins (1907–32)

Although born in Lincolnshire of middle-class parents, as a boy Jameson Adams ran away to sea and joined the merchant service. He was just short of his sixteenth birthday when he decided, having reached the end of his apprenticeship, to leave his ship at Mollendo, on the coast of Peru, and work his way home. The year was 1896, he found an old tea clipper in Valparaiso, and sailed home before the mast and round Cape Horn, a voyage of some five months during which most of the crew got scurvy. He achieved his ambition of obtaining his master's certificate under sail at the age of twenty-one, then joined the Royal Naval Reserve, and was serving on an armoured cruiser, HMS *Berwick*, in 1906 when he met Ernest Shackleton. A year later, having just been offered a permanent commission in the Royal Navy, Adams was invited by Shackleton to come with him to the Antarctic. The pull of the South Pole proved irresistible.

Adams, known as 'The Mate', was one of the three who accompanied Shackleton on the epic journey which took them 'farthest south', to within ninety-seven miles of the Pole, at the beginning of 1909.* As a former merchant seaman himself, Shackleton had sailed round the Horn several times. Another was Frank Wild, who had also joined the merchant navy as a teenager and later transferred to the Royal Navy. He had already been a member of Captain Scott's *Discovery* expedition and would further distinguish himself on Shackleton's trans-Antarctic expedition. After the *Endurance* had been abandoned, Wild was left as leader of the men who waited for more than four months on Elephant Island before they were rescued. The only member of the Pole party not to have a seafaring background was Eric Marshall. He was also better educated, having been to Cambridge before going on to study medicine, and play rugby, at St Bartholomew's Hospital.

* Descendants of Adams, Shackleton and Frank Worsley, skipper of the *Endurance*, completed what they called 'unfinished family business' when they walked to the South Pole one hundred years later.

Gino Watkins was of a different breed. While he came from a middle-class family, and went to Cambridge, he had no interest in rugby or any other organised ball games. He was also much younger than the Antarctic explorers: twenty-three when he led the British Arctic Air Route Expedition to Greenland, compared with Scott, who was thirty-three when he set off to lead his first expedition in 1901 (and forty-three when he reached the South Pole). Shackleton and his three companions had an average age of thirty-two when they went farthest south. British polar exploration in the nineteenth and early twentieth centuries was dominated by the Royal Navy. Scott looked down on the merchant service – which was one of the reasons he never got on with Shackleton. But at least he was a naval officer. A man without a naval background was almost unheard of among polar leaders, until Gino came along.

There were no British polar expeditions of any importance between Shackleton's return in 1916 from his ill-fated attempt to cross Antarctica and Gino's departure to Greenland in 1930. Gino was only nine years old, and at prep school, when Shackleton made his heroic boat journey to South Georgia, rescued his men from Elephant Island and brought them home. But within ten years, in his determination to become an Arctic explorer and a leader, he had begun to learn from Scott's and Shackleton's mistakes and indeed to revolutionise British attitudes to polar exploration. The so-called Heroic Age had passed; Gino was ushering in the Age of Realism.

Both Scott and Shackleton mistrusted sledge dogs after their experience with them on their 1902–03 Antarctic journey. They never learnt how to handle dogs, and those that Scott had on his last expedition were huskies brought from Siberia – inferior to the Greenland or Esquimaux dogs used by Amundsen. The killing and eating of dogs was always repugnant to Scott, nor would he accept that, as dog will also eat dog, it was the most economical as well as efficient draught animal. So he elected instead to use Manchurian ponies, which were not only unsuited to polar conditions but ate hay which had to be transported by the sledging party. When one had to be killed, it could be fed to the men though not to its companions.

But Scott's favourite means of polar travel was man-hauling. Following the example of his mentor, Sir Clements Markham, an explorer with outmoded ideas (and homosexual inclinations) who was over seventy when Scott first went south, he considered that dragging your own equipment was 'the true British way' of exploring the icy wastes. Markham acknowledged, somewhat patronisingly, that dogs were 'useful to Greenland Eskimos', but neither he nor Scott would entertain the idea of learning from Eskimos who had themselves learnt from experience. The Norwegians were prepared to learn the art of dog-driving from the Eskimos, they were proficient on skis, and so it was hardly surprising that Amundsen should beat Scott to the Pole. The Norwegians were the professionals, the Players, against the British amateur Gentlemen.

Scott was quite happy in this role: man-hauling was in his eyes the superior discipline. He did take dogs as far as the foot of the Beardmore Glacier, then sent them back to base with their dog-driver Meares, who was instructed to bring the dogs to meet them on the last part of their return journey. As Scott and his party struggled back from the Pole towards their deaths, he wrote tellingly in his diary of 'the dogs which would have been our salvation... .'

After the tragic news had been conveyed to England, one of Amundsen's party spoke poignantly of Scott and his companions being 'their own sledge dogs', and Nansen* wrote to Markham regretting that Scott 'would not listen to my advice to take plenty of good well-broken dogs and to trust to them and not to ponies. ... [Had he done so] we should still have had him amongst us.' It was a sorry tale of inexperience, stubbornness and poor leadership. Gino was going to make certain that he did not follow in the footsteps of this heroic figure of failure.

He would become a professional by learning to drive dogs and live off the land, as the Eskimos did. Unlike Scott, who approached Nansen for advice and then ignored it, Gino would listen to and learn from the experience of those, such as Vilhjalmur Stefansson and Knud Rasmussen, who had lived in the Arctic among the Eskimos. He would radically improve the composition of sledging rations – Scott and his party had probably died of hunger and scurvy – by greatly increasing the fat ratio as well as a diet of lemon juice and cod-liver oil. Gino was also much more realistic about the prospect of death. The Watkins boys

* Fridtjof Nansen, doyen of polar explorers, scientist and Nobel prize-winner (see page 23), had a higher opinion of Scott's wife Kathleen, with whom he was having a brief affair while her husband was slogging his way to the Pole and back.

were agreed, at Gino's instigation, that should they get into an extreme situation on the ice cap where one died of cold or hunger, it would be quite acceptable for anyone left alive to eat the flesh of their dead companion in order to survive. Human flesh could also be fed to starving dogs if it gave them the strength to pull the survivors to safety. (A few years later Quintin Riley's father asked members of the Church Assembly for the theological position on the eating of human flesh *in extremis* and was surprised to receive conflicting views on the subject.) They would not, as Scott did, lie down and die like British gentlemen until they had done whatever they could to stay alive. When Gino and Jimmy Scott, travelling together on the ice cap, were delayed for days by storm-force winds towards the end of their journey, with food running out and their dogs getting ever weaker, the question was discussed one night in their tent. Gino made clear that if he was first to die, he would expect his flesh to be eaten. Jimmy Scott, according to his account years later, demurred, but Gino insisted, 'Well, I'd eat you.' The explorer and author Stefansson may have been thinking of Gino when he wrote, in the 1930s in *Unsolved Mysteries of the Arctic*: 'Englishmen are gentlemen still, but few of them confine themselves rigidly nowadays to merely being gentlemen, as the fashion was some years ago.'

Henry George Watkins was born on 29 January 1907. He was always known as Gino, almost from birth, though it is not known for certain where the name came from – possibly from his French-American grandmother Marie-Héloise, who lived for part of each year in Florence. Gino's parents lived modestly in London, but the family were able to spend time at his grandmother's house at Poole in Dorset and at Dumbleton Hall, a Victorian Gothic pile on the Gloucestershire-Worcestershire border where his mother's brother, Bolton Monsell, lived in some style. He married Sybil Eyres, the daughter of a wealthy family, changed his name to Eyres-Monsell and became MP for Evesham before the First World War. He was later made Parliamentary Secretary to the Treasury, then First Lord of the Admiralty in the early 1930s, in which position he was ennobled as Viscount Monsell. He was in his fifties when he retired from public life.

Gino had many happy childhood holidays at Dumbleton, where there were ponies to be ridden, woods to explore and a lake for boating. For almost a year before he was sent away to a boarding school in

Sussex, he shared a governess with his cousin Diana (whose younger sister Joan became the wife of Patrick Leigh Fermor). Captain Scott's trek to the South Pole, which he reached a few days after Gino's fifth birthday, and the tragedy that followed, would have made no impression on the young boy. But he remembered the day, two and a half years later, when his father went off to fight in France. Colonel H. G. Watkins* served for much of the First World War with his regiment, the Coldstream Guards, in France. Shortly after the armistice Gino, then at prep school in Sussex, went to France to visit his father, exploring what was left of the trenches of the Somme. The eleven-year-old boy wrote home to tell his mother he had seen 'a lot of broken-up towns'. The colonel assured her: 'The boy is all right and a great credit to your four years' work on him.'

In ceremonial uniform Colonel Watkins looked every inch the Guards officer, with his sword, row of medals, a moustache and an open, confident face. But things began to go wrong as soon as he left the Army. He became a King's Messenger and managed to lose the diplomatic bag which he was carrying to Cairo and which should have been chained to his wrist; he started an interior decorating business in Chelsea which was never successful; he squandered much of his inheritance and had to ask his mother to send money for school fees and household bills. But he didn't seem to lose the respect and love of his son Gino. Together they went duck shooting in Dorset and Ireland, skiing in Arosa, climbing in Chamonix. On a hunting trip with his father in the Austrian Tyrol, Gino fell from a narrow ledge and was badly hurt, cutting his head open to the skull and his wrist to the bone, though neither injury deterred him from having a shot at a chamois while he was waiting for help. It was about this time that Colonel Watkins was diagnosed with tuberculosis and spent most of the rest of his life in a sanatorium in Davos, Switzerland, leaving his hapless and impoverished wife to bring up their three children in London.

Meanwhile Gino had gone on to Lancing to continue his education. He had tried for the Royal Navy and failed, which may help to explain his less than respectful attitude to service discipline; he would not have lasted long on an expedition led by Captain Scott. Lancing helped to

---

* He had the same given names as his father and grandfather, both of whom were parsons, and passed them on to his first son, Gino.

strengthen him physically – slightly built, he had been a rather delicate child – and though he did his best to avoid all ball games, he liked swimming and cross-country running, and excelled at rifle-shooting, winning a prize at Bisley for the highest total among all competing schools. Both he and Quintin Riley, his contemporary and friend at Lancing, were disdainful of authority; Gino enjoyed climbing the school buildings when the masters were otherwise engaged. Climbing became Gino's passion – in the Lake District and on the island of Sark as well as in France and Switzerland. Three weeks after his fall in the Tyrol, he went up to Cambridge, to read engineering at Trinity College, and from that time, in order to hide the scar on his head, he always parted his hair on the right – and he took care to ensure that his hair was never out of place. A photograph of him skiing in Arosa shows him in tweed jacket, striped tie and V-necked sports sweater, hatless and with 'Brylcreemed' hair firmly smoothed down as he speeds down the slope. His clothes were always smart and well tailored. When he wore a suit, usually single-breasted with a double-breasted waistcoat, his shoes were highly polished and he invariably carried a rolled umbrella. With his strikingly if conventionally handsome, boyish, open face, he gave the impression of a debs' delight, a young man-about-town – which, when he spent any time in London, he was.

For his first two terms at Cambridge Gino had no work to occupy him; he was excused on medical grounds because of the concussion he had suffered after the climbing accident. So he applied to join the university's newly formed air squadron. The committee which reviewed his application was impressed by his 'keenness and a determination of a quality quite different from the other candidates'. He was considered to be too young, but when he was marked top out of ninety applicants, he had to be admitted. The following summer he passed his solo flying test and soon after was involved in a crash with his instructor when the plane's engine failed. He acquired his pilot's licence the year before he went to Greenland.

To stimulate his mind, he and Riley went one evening to hear Raymond Priestley, a veteran of Shackleton's and Scott's Antarctic expeditions, lecture on 'Man in the Polar Regions', which so impressed him that he told Riley afterwards, 'I think we'd better go to the Arctic.' An introduction to James Wordie, who had been on Shackleton's *Endurance* expedition, led to an invitation to go to Greenland in the summer of 1927, which left Gino eighteen months to prepare himself for what he was already beginning to believe would be the future course of his life.

He resolved to toughen himself up for the rigours of the Arctic, by running, climbing college buildings, and always sleeping by an open window with the minimum number of bedclothes. He went climbing in the Lake District to prove to himself that he hadn't lost his nerve in the Alps, he tried unsuccessfully to climb the spire of Salisbury Cathedral, and he spent a week on a trawler in the North Sea. The General Strike provided some amusement for Gino and friends: he was made a special constable in London, as part of the Scotland Yard Flying Squad, to guard food convoys from the docks, an experience which he told his father was 'simply ripping', though he regretted they didn't get into 'a proper fight'. With the approach of the Part I exams at Cambridge, at the end of his first year, Gino realised that he was quite unprepared for them. His tutor told him he would surely fail, which spurred him into doing two weeks of uninterrupted work with his engineering books. During the week of the exams Gino went to Riley's rooms every day for tea after completing papers which he said seemed so easy that he must have missed the point of the questions. But he hadn't, and he got a First. By the end of his third year at Cambridge, however, when Gino was due to take his final exams, he had become so involved in expeditions to the Arctic that he never took his degree.

His rigorous physical regime continued in the summer of 1926 when he and a French trainee guide spent two months climbing in the Alps. He learnt to endure pain and acute discomfort, to sleep anywhere, to keep going on short rations. He was an equable companion, calm in a crisis, unruffled. (Having a father with a quick temper, Gino determined never to lose his.) After spending Christmas with his family in Switzerland, he reckoned Cambridge could do without him for a term while he skied every day on the Parsenn above Davos, sometimes stripped to the waist, before visiting his father in the sanatorium in the evening. Switzerland in winter provided the perfect surroundings for Gino: mountains, snow, the thrill of fear as he tested himself ever further and faster on skis, the company of his father and the relaxation of music, singing and dancing to which he was irresistibly drawn whenever what he considered his day's work was done. He was, in short, a gregarious and attractive twenty-year-old student who was fortunate enough to be able to do what he enjoyed most – spending time in the mountains.

But there was more to him than that, as was shortly to become apparent. Having returned to Cambridge ready to accompany Wordie to Greenland, he learnt that the expedition had been postponed for a year. Most young men would have looked around for another project, another group to join which might be going somewhere interesting. For Gino Plan B was rather different: he would mount his own expedition to the Arctic, and he would lead it himself. He chose an uninhabited island, Edge Island, off Spitzbergen (Svalbard) and some 800 miles north of the Arctic Circle, and he enlisted Wordie's help in organising it. The idea was to survey an island whose interior had never been explored. The Royal Geographical Society gave its approval, made a grant of £100 and lent scientific instruments. Wordie recommended a ship which would take Gino and his party from Tromso in northern Norway, and put him in touch with young men suitably trained or qualified to contribute to the expedition. There was no shortage of applicants, and Gino chose six, principally because he liked them. He also selected two older men – a marine biologist, Ashby Lowndes, who was a master at Marlborough College and a Major Henry Morshead, DSO, aged forty-five and lately a member of the Indian Survey. Here was a distinguished officer of the First World War, now in middle age, who had been a member of two Mount Everest expeditions in the early 1920s, agreeing to join a party to the Arctic under the leadership of someone less than half his age. Undoubtedly Gino had what today is called charisma.

'The smooth course of my life had been changed by the youth I had been talking to,' J. M. Scott wrote of his first meeting with Gino. After half an hour he knew he wanted to go and explore Labrador with him. Even at this early age, leadership came naturally to Gino; it never occurred to him that he might need some training for the job, some probationary period under the guidance of an older man. He assumed leadership without effort because he didn't question whether he would receive the confidence of his fellows. His style of leadership, however, was quite different from what he might have learnt from one of the old Antarctic explorers. Captain Scott never discussed his plans: he took decisions, issued orders, asked if there were any questions, and that was that.

Gino was a modern, postwar leader without military training. He was in command, but he rarely gave an order. His plans were always discussed fully, and he encouraged criticism. He gave himself no special privileges, was indifferent to discomfort and seldom suffered from hunger. He led by example, and by choosing the right men and delegating responsibility to them. As Jimmy Scott wrote of him, 'He was the man who set the pace in action and morale. He led without looking back.' When the Edge Island expedition was over, one of its members said: 'The most extraordinary thing was that Gino gave no orders in the ordinary sense and we all thought we were doing exactly what we wanted to do. But afterwards we realised we had done precisely what he wanted us to do.' Quite an achievement for a young man aged twenty who had known his companions for no more than three or four months.

In spite of bad weather for most of the four weeks that the expedition spent on Edge Island, the majority of the island was mapped and data about its geology, its animal and vegetable life were collected. For much of the time Gino and Morshead trekked together with their plane-table, surveying land and coast which had been inaccurately mapped in the past and almost failing to meet their ship at the north-eastern extremity of the island. Gino expected too much of his 45-year-old companion, who became exhausted and unable to carry his heavy load. 'Things are really looking rather nasty for us at the minute and we have all rather got the wind up,' Gino recorded as, wet and cold, they were held up by fog and struggled through rivers. Paraffin leaked into the third man's rucksack, tainting all their biscuits. The rest of their food – pemmican and chocolate – was running out and there was no sign of the ship. Gino learnt an important lesson for the future: always carry a rifle, because you may have to live off what the land provides. 'If the *Heimen* [their ship] has run aground and can't get to us, if we had rifles we might manage to shoot enough reindeer and freeze them to live through the winter. As it is we shall be bound to starve if she does not come. It is very disappointing as we were expecting to get aboard and have a good meal this evening.'

They had food for only two more days, and Gino was thinking they would have to start eating moss. But the ship turned up the next day and all was well. On the way home he met a man in Tromso who had just returned from a hunting trip to Franz Josef Land, a group of islands

600 miles north of the Russian coast. Gino's interest was at once aroused: perhaps he would take an expedition there next year and explore further east towards Siberia. But for now he had to get back to Cambridge for his final year. He and Major Morshead, who had recovered from his exertions, returned via Lapland and Finland. Morshead then went back to the Himalayas, and on to Burma, where he was killed four years later.

Cambridge didn't see a lot of Gino during 1927–28. He had to collate all the data from Edge Island and give a lecture to the Royal Geographical Society, which was so impressed by his achievement that he was elected its youngest ever Fellow. Gino might have appeared to some elderly RGS members to be a somewhat casual, laid-back expedition leader who, when he got home, spent his time dancing and making merry. But the intensely serious and focused side of his character showed itself not only as he surveyed the island with his chosen team of eight but in his preparation and planning for the expedition, to which the Antarctic veteran James Wordie paid tribute: 'One feels that the party which he took last summer was exceedingly well selected and that they worked together most admirably. All through last winter Mr Watkins spent much time ascertaining what was essential and what was not, with the result that the expedition was very carefully planned and exceedingly well led.'

Gino's mind was already racing with ideas for his next expedition. The Empty Quarter of Saudi Arabia was one possibility, the upper waters of the Blue Nile another. He had been enthusiastic about Franz Josef Land after returning from Edge Island, and Major Morshead had given him the impetus for an attempt on Mount Everest. At the end of 1927, while working at the RGS, he was asked to write a short paper on the disputed boundary of Labrador between Canada and Newfoundland; and he was at once seduced by the remoteness of this undeveloped land. Much of it is thickly forested, and best surveyed from the air, but the funds for an aeroplane were not forthcoming. He would travel by canoe in summer and by sledge with dogs in winter. One of his principal objectives was to map the head waters of Unknown River and its waterfalls, which might be used for generating electricity for a future wood pulp industry. This last point did not weigh very heavily with Gino – his interest was in exploring wild places with Unknown names and testing himself and his equipment for future expeditions – but he thought it would help to raise money and impress the Royal Geographical Society. He had recruited Jimmy Scott as his travelling companion and was well ahead with his plans when the Watkins family suffered a terrible blow. Gino's mother committed suicide.

Part of the problem must have been her husband's absence at a TB sanatorium in Switzerland and his lack of financial support. She suffered from depression, and she could not cope any longer. One morning she left the house in London, took a train to Eastbourne and, it was assumed, either walked into the sea or made her way to Beachy Head and jumped. Her body was never recovered and she left no note. Years later her second son Tony shot himself. Clearly there was a lot of instability in the Watkins family – Gino's sister Pam was also a depressive – and when his mother died he had an agonising decision to make. Should he stay and keep the family together or go ahead with his expedition to Labrador?

Only two months earlier, Gino's mother had attended his lecture to the RGS on the Edge Island expedition. She recorded her trepidation, and her pride, in a letter to her husband:

> I felt in a ghastly condition of nerves, and as the hall got fuller and fuller, I felt iller and iller! ... Gino looking about sixteen, very pale and quiet.... He began very quietly and modestly and rather too quickly, but he gradually settled down to a very easy pleasant style and was quite excellent.... He received an ovation at the end and I can't tell you how many ripping things were said about him.
>
> The President made a humorous speech at the end – about his age, etc., and they were all so good to him, you can see that they think a tremendous lot of him. Old admirals and generals asked him to stay and said they had pretty daughters!
>
> So many people came up and asked me if I was his mother and said they must tell me how wonderful he was.... I've had so many people ringing up this morning. The first said, 'I've rung up to say you are a damned lucky woman.'

Lucky she may have felt to have a son who had already proved himself an outstanding leader before he was twenty-one and had such a promising future as an explorer. But tragically she could not persuade herself that she had any future at all. She would surely have wished

Gino to press ahead with the life of his choice at which he already seemed to excel; and his father was able to convince him that he should go ahead with his trip to Labrador. Gino certainly had misgivings: 'Everything one does now seems so frightfully futile and nothing seems worthwhile. I am going on with the Labrador expedition as I have got the money and the people and it does not seem fair to let them down. However, I don't feel any enthusiasm for it now.'

In the weeks that remained before Gino and Scott left for Labrador, at the end of June, he devoted his energy to meticulous preparation and assembling stores, under the guidance of Mr Reeves, the veteran survey instructor at the RGS. He decided to miss his last term at Cambridge, but instead to go with his siblings and his father to the South of France, for a week of family therapy after their mother's death. There was one other member of the party – Nanny – who had been with the family for almost twenty years and who would remain as its rock through the years of tragedy and unhappiness to come.

Nanny Dennis – no one seemed to know her Christian name – was one of those reliable, unflappable, eminently sensible and to many middle- and upper-class households indispensable figures of British family life in the twentieth century. She had started in domestic service as soon as she left school, joined the Watkins family when Pam was born in 1909 and stayed until she died sixty-four years later. As was the way with nannies, all their love was given to their children, the children they looked after; a physical or emotional relationship with a man was scarcely considered. Nanny Dennis was said to have had one boyfriend in her early years who went off to the trenches in 1914 and never came back.

Gino was two when Nanny arrived: she remembered that 'he was small, but he was forward in other ways. He was never shy, not a bit. He was always very advanced for his age, Gino was.... He was a little monkey, though. He was always up to something; but he never cried if he was scolded – no, nothing like that.'

Nanny was always there for the Watkins children; she was devoted to them and they returned her affection and took her for granted. Gino would have associated himself with the comment of Jeremy Scott, Pam's eldest son: 'It was Nanny who raised me, not my parents, and her I loved.' It was Nanny who effectively ran the house during Gino's boyhood, the more so when Colonel Watkins went off to live in

Switzerland, and then single-handedly after his mother's death. Nanny always packed for Gino – clothes and food – when he went camping or climbing during his teenage years, and she was still putting out a mug of Ovaltine for him every night when he was in London between the Labrador and Greenland expeditions, then bringing him tea and laying out his clothes in the morning.

When Gino arrived in Copenhagen on his way back from Greenland, he was met by Pam, Jimmy Scott, Quintin Riley – and Nanny, who had made the journey from England with them. Nanny was invited to Gino's bedroom where Riley overheard him saying to her, in teasing tones: 'I think I may have got lice, Nanny – can you have a look?' A few weeks later Gino was writing to his father to give an account of their family Christmas in London: 'So far all is going well.... Of course Nanny has already taken over the food supply and the cook decides how many people we may invite in and Nanny decides who these people must be.'

Money was always tight in the Watkins family and remained so after Pam married Jimmy Scott and Nanny went to live with them. She was paid a pittance and died of malnutrition and cancer in her eighties, poorly treated by Pam towards the end. But she had the distinction of being photographed by Jeremy Scott's friend, the fashionable Cockney snapper of the Sixties, Terry Donovan, who caught her looking benign, dependable, alert, with an expression of slightly detached amusement – as much like a favourite grandmother as a favourite nanny.

The death of his mother brought Gino even closer not only to Nanny but to his sister Pam, whom he would often take to the cinema or to a party. They both enjoyed dancing and together won a dancing competition. This is not to say that Gino had no girl friends: whenever he was in London he was seen out with a number of young women, who in turn were attracted by his smooth good looks, his enthusiasm and energy, his extrovert nature. But there were some who thought that, with his dandyish appearance and slightly effeminate air, he must be a 'pansy' (one girl called him 'a bit of a ponce'). The possibility that he had repressed homosexual tendencies was probably not a subject of discussion among his Arctic companions. However, in view of his Adonis looks and the almost godlike status he achieved among his contemporaries, bisexual leanings would not have been surprising. And there was that piece of doggerel penned by Scott in Greenland about Riley's supposed, or fantasy, relationship with his leader ('I'm not a man who often necks / For I go in for homosex: / Tonight's my night with Gino.'). Bisexuality and homosexuality were fashionable tastes at the time among Oxford and Cambridge students, although they – the likes of John Betjeman, Cyril Connolly, Evelyn Waugh (a contemporary of Gino at Lancing) – tended to be aesthetes rather than athletes.

Gino left with Scott from Liverpool, bound for Newfoundland, at the end of June 1928. Once they reached Labrador, an enforced delay of two weeks enabled Gino to spend time meeting trappers, Indians and Eskimos and learning from them how to live, travel and survive in this wilderness. Treating everyone as his social equal, this 'delicate young feller with the fancy parting on the wrong side of his head' soon impressed the locals, with his determination, his enthusiasm – and his gramophone and mouth organ, which he had brought from England. In this outpost of the Hudson's Bay Company, called Northwest River, Gino's musical evenings were a great success. There were dance tunes and the latest hits, mostly from America, mingled with songs which the trappers taught the young Englishmen. When they were travelling with a trapper as companion and guide, they discovered that the Sabbath was observed as a day of rest, and so they sang hymns as well as songs while lying in their tents. In the evenings Gino might sing a song he had learnt in the Swiss Alps, and he would often read poetry – Coleridge's 'Kubla Khan', Clough's 'Say not the struggle naught availeth' and Shakespeare's songs were among his favourites. After a day spent canoeing down the rapids, then carrying canoes and equipment through the branches of rain-soaked fir trees, Gino's thoughts some-times turned to home – and Nanny. 'I am just going to crawl into a soaking wet sleeping-bag. I would give anything to be at home and have Nanny tuck me up in a nice warm bed and bring a cup of Ovaltine.' Was he still a child at heart?

The rations which they carried were sometimes supplemented by porcupines or partridges which the trapper shot. In his appealingly perverse way, Gino looked forward to telling his field-sporting friends at home that the birds could hardly fly, and that he had had some good foxhunting in Labrador, killing the animals in traps. But the reality of their several weeks on the river was often rather grim. They would have to wade up river through rapids, haul the canoe over steep, tree-covered slopes and, when they were able to paddle downstream, use all their strength in rough water to avoid the rocks. 'I have seldom been so frightened,' Gino recorded, 'not so much for ourselves, as we might possibly have reached the shore if the canoe had upset, but I had pictures of all our instruments and papers getting lost.' He then went on to write: 'A fright is the greatest joy in the world and danger, once passed, is worth days of quiet toil. "One crowded hour of glorious life / Is worth an age without a name."'

The glorious life (quoting from Walter Scott) to which Gino referred had to involve danger, and fear. He disconcerted a few of his companions in Greenland by saying that the adrenaline rush of fear through taking risks was to him more thrilling than the achievement of a hard-won objective such as reaching the top of a mountain. He might take unnecessary risks himself – it could be said that his death resulted from one – that he would not allow another man to take. Nor would he seek to persuade anyone against his will that a risk was worth taking. But such was the strength of his personality that his companions followed him willingly because they believed in him and in his luck, when they would have been very reluctant to follow another leader on an equally hazardous enterprise. When Gino decided to set off across Goose Bay, against local advice that the ice was too thin for safety, he and Scott only just made it when the ice began to crack, and it was only by good luck that they did so. Yet Scott wrote that, although not a brave man, he was never afraid when in Gino's company: 'Alone I might be thoroughly uncomfortable, but as soon as Gino appeared danger or difficulty lost its personal menace and became an interesting problem. I watched it fascinated and rather hoped that it would lead to something worse that I might see what he would do about it. So I often felt entirely calm while Gino was alarmed.'

On their first long sledge journey with dogs, Gino, Scott and a trapper got lost in the snowy wastes in December, having followed directions from a family of Algonquin Indians whom they met at what was locally called Big Belly Fish Lake. Gino made the mistake of ignoring a snowshoe track when their food stocks were dangerously low and heading for what he thought was the coast. He was faced with the prospect of killing his first dog, but once again luck was on his side: they found the track again, followed it and reached the Eskimo settlement of Hopedale on Christmas Eve. Goose was on the menu for Christmas lunch, which Gino remembered having eaten, with equal enjoyment and also when desperately hungry, at the end of his trek across Edge Island the previous year.

For the third leg of his Labrador journey, Gino, Scott and their trapper friend spent two months mapping rivers and searching for waterfalls with hydro-electric potential. The going, through snow-covered trees and up steep banks, was hard, the dogs were often of limited use, rations were desperately short. Gino would later admit that 'there is nothing in the world more tiring than slogging on day after day on snowshoes, dragging a heavy weight, with insufficient food'. But he never showed any signs of exhaustion, weakness or hunger. He was not as physically strong as the other two, but he trained himself, by some rigorous exercise of self-control and self-belief, not to feel the effects of tiredness and cold and hunger as others did. It was almost as if he was able to brainwash himself into accepting pain and suffering to the extent that it no longer affected him. The three of them might be cold, depressed and exhausted, but Gino put on a brave face and convinced himself that he didn't feel the cold.

> I was really warm as toast when we arrived ... damned hungry but I am not even eating my full short ration just in case we have to stay up here longer to finish the work.... . I believe in eating as little as possible when one is out on a journey as it prepares one for a situation like this ... of standing great cold, of running all day at about six or seven miles an hour.
>
> I don't care if we have to half-starve and kill every dog we have got. I am not going back until we have finished the work we came to do.

In addition to the self-control, here was a streak of ruthlessness and a single-minded determination which marked Gino as an explorer and a leader to reckon with. He was learning the art of sledging with dogs, and he and Scott were probably the first Englishmen to become proficient at it. He was convinced that it was the only realistic way to travel; having experienced man-hauling of sledges on Edge Island, he saw no point in repeating the exercise when there was a far more efficient alternative. Neither Captain Scott nor Shackleton could handle dogs, nor could they bear to feed dog to dog, or to themselves. To Gino, however, the dogs were there to pull the sledges, and they were expendable. He shocked Quintin Riley when they were driving together to Cambridge one day

and ran over a spaniel. Gino was all for driving on, because they were
late for an appointment and it was 'only a dog', whereas Riley insisted
on stopping the car to see how badly it was hurt. (Gino intended to take
one of the husky bitches home from Labrador to cross with a St Bernard
and breed a larger sledging dog, but having got it as far as New York it
was refused passage on the *Mauretania* and sent to a local zoo instead.)

Gino was absolutely determined not to cut short his surveying of the
Unknown River system (he discovered three new cataracts) because this
would provide the most important data for him to take back to the
Royal Geographical Society. He had sent back a long letter to the secretary of the RGS the previous October; and he knew he had to impress
the RGS in order to get support for his future expedition plans which
were already forming in his mind. But there were times when conditions were so bad, and progress in the last weeks so slow, that, while
not losing his self-control in front of his companions, he recorded his
frustrations in his diary in uncharacteristically emotional terms – then
ripped those pages out and destroyed them. On another occasion he
mused on whether, in a desperate situation when several members of an
expedition might have to be rescued, the leader should put himself first
or last. As the ruthless realist, Gino argued against the old accepted
tradition, yet he knew he would go along with it, against his better
judgement, when and if the time came:

> If they are being rescued one by one, then the members of the
> expedition who are going to give most to the world should be
> taken off first; the members who are going to give least should be
> left to the last. The leader himself should settle the order as he is
> the man most qualified to know the capabilities of his men. If he
> considers that he has most to give to the world and is the best man
> (being leader he certainly ought to be) then he ought to be rescued
> first.
>
> I wonder what I should do under the circumstances? I am
> afraid, even if I knew I was the best man, I should wait till the end.
> Why? I suppose I have got some of the old ideas so born into me.
> But how I should despise myself for waiting till the end. Just pure
> playing to the gallery.

He was not really being serious in saying he would despise himself.
For while logic may have dictated to him that he should be saved first,

he would never abandon his fellows, nor could he be accused of a lack of concern for them. Though he had made mistakes and misjudgements, and would do so again in Greenland, whether through negligence or a lack of foresight, he was always alert to the wellbeing of his companions. He was a true libertarian, in the sense that he would tolerate behaviour in others of which he might disapprove. He did not smoke, yet he made no complaint when he shared a tent with two others who filled their confined space with the fumes and smell of pipe tobacco every evening. However, he would also say that a man should be a slave to nothing. 'There is nothing that he ought not to be able to do without, be it tobacco, drink or women. ... It is only when he loses control of himself that he is damned, or if he is hurting anyone's feelings. The last more important than anything.' Gino would certainly have hurt a few feelings had he left his companions behind because he judged them weak and inferior.

In disdaining, or at least questioning the accepted traditions, Gino was generally critical of Britain for its caution and conservatism – whether in politics, in attitudes or the development of ideas. He never voted in a general election – he was on his way back from Labrador at the time of the 1929 election and from Greenland when the National government was returned in 1931 – but he was certainly not a natural Conservative. He wrote approvingly in his diary of the son of an old Conservative family who voted Labour.

He is looked upon with horror by the rest of the family and called a traitor. Why? It means he has thought for himself and decided that socialism is better for the world. He may be wrong, but anyhow he is a better man than the son who is Conservative because his family is Conservative.

I think that there are two great differences between the younger and the older generation. The younger generation does not blindly accept the old traditions and customs and beliefs, but thinks for itself and it is more broadminded than the older generation.

Gino blamed the older generation for the fact that Britain was behind other countries in the development of commercial flying. Every new idea was opposed, he said, and restrictions put in the way. One such idea began to form in his mind while he was making his way home from Labrador, in the spring of 1929, by way of Ottawa and New

York. He was thinking about an Arctic air route – a North-West passage by commercial aircraft from Britain via Iceland, east Greenland, west Greenland, Baffin Island, Hudson Bay and Edmonton, Alberta to Vancouver on the Pacific coast. Lindbergh had flown the Atlantic non-stop the previous year, from New York to Paris, but he had been carrying nothing but fuel. Passenger-carrying aircraft would have to make refuelling stops every four or five hundred miles. The least-known section of the route was the east coast and central ice plateau of Greenland, and it was here that Gino intended to spend a year, mapping the coast and the mountains and studying the meteorological conditions – all of which would be highly relevant to the flights of the future.

In his plans which he submitted to the Royal Geographical Society, he envisaged finding a suitable base on the east coast which might be used by aircraft needing to put down before crossing the ice cap. The intention was to take two Gipsy Moths* on the expedition which would be used to test flying conditions over the ice cap, then to fly them along the proposed air route as far as Vancouver and back to England. But, after the damage done to the two planes on the ground by severe winter gales, this proved to be a flight too far.

In the small office which the RGS provided in Kensington for Gino to prepare for Greenland, he gave no outward indication of a man about to lead the most important British polar expedition since Shackleton's. A visitor might find him with legs stretched out on the trestle table, singing to himself and possibly waving a Japanese fan which he had looted from a dance – 'so I can give the right impression if anyone very tough and hearty comes to see me'. But the dilettante and rather unmanly exterior masked a single-minded determination that his expedition would be better equipped than any previous one to survive an arduous year in the Arctic. It would also pioneer an air route which – he made the point several times – would be 'all-British', over a country which he described as 'hanging like an enormous tongue of ice and snow' between Europe and North America.

First, there were the men he would take with him. Some were recruited from Cambridge, to which Gino returned in January 1930 in

* Gino was confident he had made the right decision, in opting to take the Gipsy Moths, when Amy Johnson chose one for her award-winning solo flight from England to Australia in April 1930.

Narbrough D'Aeth

Lawrence Wager

Quintin Riley

Gino Watkins

Arthur Stephenson

Percy Lemon

Martin Lindsay

Jimmy Scott

John Rymill

Iliffe Cozens

August Courtauld

Freddy Spencer Chapman

Wilfred Hampton

Ted Bingham

LEFT Vilhjalmur Stefansson, Gino and Admiral Sir William Goodenough the day before the *Quest* sailed for the Arctic RIGHT Mollie Montgomerie, engaged to August Courtauld when he went to Greenland

The *Quest* unloading stores at the base fjord

Gino speaking to Courtauld through the ventilator at the ice-cap station, 5 May 1931

Rymill, Gino, Courtauld and Chapman on arrival at the base, 10 May 1931

Using block and tackle on Buggery Bank

The whale-boat used on the boat journey, August/October 1931

Gino hunting in his kayak

LEFT Gertrude, who had a child by Chapman RIGHT Her married sister

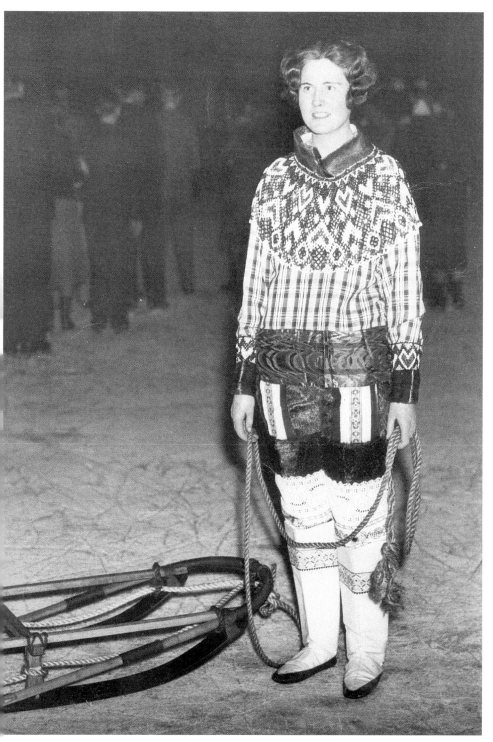

Margy Graham, dressed as an Eskimo at the London Ice Club Carnival, April 1932

The Watkins memorial cross, Lake Fjord (photo Paul Caffyn, 2007)

a vain attempt to complete the number of terms required for him to qualify for a degree. Of course he needed surveyors and meteorologists, but he preferred to choose friends who would acquire the necessary skills rather than experts in their fields who knew the Arctic but might not be such good company. He wrote afterwards: 'I have always deliberately chosen amateurs for such expeditions rather than men who have had Arctic experience on expeditions other than my own. ... I prefer that all members of my expeditions should have gained their knowledge with me, since in that case I always know the exact amount of experience possessed by each member of any sledging party.'

He would also know how each member was likely to behave, whether in an emergency or towards those with whom he might be sharing a tent on the ice cap. Of the thirteen, mostly older, men whom he chose, only Scott had been with Gino before, and only Courtauld had previously been to Greenland. While they were all committed to the purpose of the expedition as described in its title – to gather data which would lead to the establishing of an Arctic air route – they were all determined to have fun together. The conditions might be adverse, but the atmosphere under Gino's leadership was always informal. Captain Scott, imposing a rigid naval hierarchical structure on his expeditions and taking scientific study more seriously, would not have approved.

One man who applied to join the expedition, a mechanic who had been stranded in northern Canada for weeks after his aeroplane crashed, impressed Gino until he learnt that the man had a rifle with him but hadn't bothered to shoot any seals because he would never eat 'those nasty greasy things'. Gino was not taking someone who declined to learn from the Eskimos and live off the land. Having already learnt to drive dogs, he knew this was the only way – the Eskimo way – to travel in Greenland; and he intended to learn everything he could from the Eskimos' experience of living in this harsh land. He won their respect for his handling of a kayak and his skill in hunting seals, and he not only made friends with them but would share his bunk at the base camp with at least one Eskimo girl. It was quite a change from the nice young girls he had been escorting in London.

Whatever the extent of Gino's bisexual inclinations, he was attracted to many desirable young women in London at the various dances he attended during those weeks before the expedition set off in early July

1930. It was the height of the debutante season, Gino was a passionate partygoer and dancer, and it must have been frustrating that he couldn't take a girl home to spend the night at the house he shared with his siblings in Onslow Crescent. It was not that they would have minded, but there was always Nanny waiting to bring him his tea in the morning. So his sexual relationship in Greenland with Tina, his chosen Eskimo lover, must have been liberating – even if it could not be conducted in the privacy of his own room.

When Gino travelled to Copenhagen before the expedition to ask formal permission of the Danish government to spend a year in Greenland, the explorer Lauge Koch arranged for a girl to be sent to Gino's room at the Hafnia hotel. And when the *Quest* put in to Reykjavik for a night as Gino and his party sailed north, he met a girl in the hotel bar whom he invited to share his bed. According to Quintin Riley's account, she declined but said she would come and wake Gino up at 6.30 the next morning. Two hours later, Riley saw the two of them having breakfast together in the hotel dining-room. It was not just the exercise of a *droit de seigneur*: Gino was not only one of the youngest but also the most sexually active member of the expedition he led.

None of his philandering affected the seriousness of his preparations for Greenland. Food was one of Gino's principal concerns. While he intended that they should hunt for food whenever possible, eating fresh meat (seal, bear), fish (salmon, trout) and birds (ptarmigan, guillemot, gull), he spent some time devising the most nutritious rations for long sledging journeys in severe conditions and periods of weeks or longer on the ice cap.

He was the first man to understand that fat was the key to surviving extreme cold and maintaining one's strength. The Antarctic explorers of the Heroic Age subsisted on a ration in which the only fat was in the pemmican; the proportion of biscuit in their diet was far too high and, as Martin Lindsay commented, was 'about as much good for warming one up as a lump of snow'. Accepting that the rations for a sledging party should not exceed about two pounds' weight per man per day, Gino proposed that almost half of it should consist, in equal amounts, of Bovril pemmican and margarine. He had learnt by experience, on the Edge Island and Labrador expeditions, that fat was the most important ingredient, and so he reduced the ratio of biscuit significantly and more than doubled the margarine ration that he had taken to Labrador. This raised the total calorific value, producing a daily diet of 6,000 calories (20 per cent more than in Scott's South Pole ration). Vitamins A, B, C, and D were supplied by small quantities of cod liver oil, dried yeast powder and concentrated lemon juice.

For a scientific opinion, Gino took his intended Arctic ration to the Lister Institute, which endorsed it in theory while doubting whether a man could digest such a high-fat diet. Gino decided to try it out in London for a week, doing his best to create Greenland conditions by sleeping naked next to an open window and skating at the Hammersmith ice rink before a hearty breakfast of pemmican and margarine. Insisting that Jimmy Scott should join him in the experiment, the two men ate the same food in the evening, even if they were at a dinner party and had to produce greasy lumps in front of their bemused fellow guests. Gino said he felt sick most of the time, but he knew they would all be grateful for the fat in really cold weather. Lindsay confirmed this after the expedition: 'Instead of being always ravenously hungry as were our sledging predecessors, we in Greenland never felt more than a little inconvenience when we had to make our week's ration-box last ten and even twelve days.'

Gino also spent some time designing the tent which would house two men on the ice cap, 8,000 feet above sea level, for the best part of a year and would have to withstand unknown extremities of weather in winter. He decided on a double dome-shaped tent, the inner part suspended by tapes from curved bamboo ribs. With a ventilator protruding from the top of the dome, the tent resembled an open umbrella. Despite the blizzards and the weight of snow which buried Courtauld in the tent, it remained standing and enabled him to survive. (He might have been better off if the tent and igloos had been built below the snow level in the first place. The German expedition under Professor Wegener, wintering further north and 250 miles inland, excavated a complex of rooms underground in which three men spent six months – and one of them almost a year. They were better equipped and provisioned, and had the use of motor sledges.)

Moccasins were another item for which Gino was responsible, having been introduced to them by North American Indians in Labrador. For all his concern, however, that his Greenland party should be well insulated against the cold, Gino was less conscientious, or interested, in providing the expedition with tools for building the base hut and repairing the aeroplanes. Percy Lemon, an army officer, wireless operator and the oldest member of the expedition, was heard to complain about the lack of equipment and remark: 'We haven't even got a sixpenny ball of string.'

There were, of course, financial constraints, though commercial sponsorship provided many of their needs, and became easier to obtain after Gino's RGS lecture on his successful year's exploration in Labrador. But the Greenland expedition could not have gone ahead without their benefactor, Stephen Courtauld, agreeing to fund the major part of the £12,000 budget which Gino had calculated. The RGS, having given him £100 for the Edge Island expedition, and £300 for Labrador, now offered a grant of £200, subsequently increased to £300, for this major expedition to Greenland lasting at least a year. In a fulsome letter of thanks, apparently written without irony, Gino described the society's 'great assistance' as 'most awfully encouraging'. For a while he was in discussions with a film company which was offering money in return for assistance in making a romantic comedy set in Greenland. The idea appealed to Gino, because it would shock the elderly Fellows of the RGS, but there were too many problems to be overcome, not least the opposition of the Danish government. *The Times* bought exclusive rights to reports on the expedition's plans and progress which were sent, usually by Gino, at intervals throughout the year.

Apart from August Courtauld's payment for the charter of the *Quest*, no contributions were forthcoming from any of the other relatively impoverished expedition members – none more impecunious than Gino himself. There is a story, possibly apocryphal, that August Courtauld invited Gino to spend the weekend at his family home in Essex so that he could try (he was unsuccessful) to get Courtauld's father to put up money for the expedition. Gino was invited to join the family pheasant shoot, but pleaded an injury to his hand, which was wrapped in a bandage. There was nothing wrong with it, he said afterwards, but he had to find an excuse for not shooting because he couldn't afford to tip the keeper. He could just afford to run an old Lagonda and attend a number of debutante dances every week, and as the time approached for the expedition's departure he longed to get away from the industrial depression of England following the Wall Street crash.

Gino's unconventional style of leadership soon became evident on the voyage from London to Greenland. For those who scarcely knew him, and especially the six men from the armed services, he was almost disconcertingly casual, even indolent. In part this may have been a pose, but he would have said that since there was nothing to do until the ship reached Greenland, there was no point in jumping up and down and issuing orders. He shared his cabin with two others, and his only gesture of authority was at mealtimes to sit on a pile of bedding at the head of the table in the small saloon.

On land he commanded by casual suggestion – 'I say, I wonder if you'd mind....' – and while some initially would have preferred to be given their orders, they all soon got used to and welcomed his easy familiarity, while respecting his undoubted qualities of leadership. In his foreword to the official account of the expedition, the president of the RGS, Admiral Sir William Goodenough, wrote of Gino:

> It is a common saying that in order to command one must first learn to obey, but here was one who appeared to leap fully equipped from the levels of boyhood to the eminence of a man's directive power. At first contact there was little to indicate this to the casual observer. ... Men who looked for some mark in face or speech which would display the commanding personality, which after his first two expeditions they knew existed, were almost startled at his youthful appearance.
>
> It was when one had the advantage of speaking with him, watching his methods and hearing his detailed plans, that one became aware of the deep-seated strength of character that carried him onwards through the busy five years from 1927 to 1932. ... He assumed leadership without effort for the reason that he never considered whether he would or would not receive the confidence of his fellows. He took it naturally.

And his fellows accepted his leadership naturally, because he was so obviously a natural leader. He could assess a situation quickly and act without hesitation (as he did when Scott returned from the ice cap without Courtauld), he listened to the opinions of others before taking a decision (unlike Scott of the Antarctic), and having chosen someone for a particular task, he gave him self-confidence by giving him a free hand. He had a keen sense of humour, told stories against himself, was indifferent to discomfort, joined in with every menial job, and kept everyone happy by his easy familiarity. While several men addressed one another by their surnames, everyone called Gino Gino. He did not wish to be called anything else, though in his correspondence with the RGS he signed himself 'H. George Watkins'.

He was constantly training his companions to be self-sufficient, to show initiative, to be capable of leadership themselves. This was never shown more starkly than when Gino and Scott, returning from their southern journey in November in appalling conditions, met Chapman and his party by chance as they struggled towards the ice-cap station, having covered only fifteen miles in fifteen days. Chapman was grateful for the opportunity to ask his leader what he should do, now that they were so far behind schedule and using up rations intended for the ice-cap station. But Gino said it was up to Chapman to take the decisions, while approving his plan to dump the wireless and send three men back to base in order to conserve food.

Gino had just endured perhaps the worst two weeks in his Arctic experience. He and Scott were returning from a sledging journey southwards from the ice-cap station, with very little objective beyond the urge to explore the featureless interior of Greenland. After nine months in Labrador, they were the experts with dogs, and they would show the others what distances could be covered. But the dogs, with a keener sense than their leader of the dangers of continuing to travel away from base as winter was fast approaching, became lifeless and unwilling to go on. As soon as Gino decided they had to turn back, the dogs seemed to regain their strength, knowing they were on their way home. But the weather was deteriorating and the wind began to blow at storm force.

The day that one team of dogs broke into a trot and refused to stop, running off with the tent and one of the sleeping-bags (see p. 106), was, Gino later admitted to his father, one of the most anxious of his life. He made light of it at the time, and of the weather which he said was bound to get worse. Scott became irritated by Gino's efforts at humorous pessimism, but when rations became dangerously low and an even worse storm struck, they were worried. 'At one point we thought we should never get back,' Gino wrote later. They even considered changing course for the coast in order to find seals for food, but they had no rifle. As they huddled in the tent, waiting for it to be blown away, Gino proposed they should read to each other. The act of reading aloud reminded them of childhood, when they were helpless yet trustful and content. Gino had of course said more than once that what he most enjoyed was the thrill of being frightened, also that he never got tired and could do without food. But when, two days later, the chance meeting took place with Chapman and his team, they saw that both Gino and Scott had had enough. Gino admitted as much when he said to Scott that, had they joined up with the others on their way to the ice-cap station, neither of them would have been much use.

During the winter months Gino learnt how to be an Eskimo. After months of exploration in Labrador, he was already an admirer of the native peoples of the Arctic. He was fascinated by, and in sympathy with, their customs and way of life; and he enjoyed a musical evening with the North American Eskimos just as much as a debutante dance in London. He had learnt to travel with dogs as competently as the locals; now he wanted to be as proficient as they were in hunting for food. By the end of the year fresh meat had become so scarce at the base that he decided to take Chapman, Lindsay and Riley to visit an Eskimo settlement some twenty miles away. To the Eskimos, visiting the house of another family is an important social function. When a hunter returns home with a good haul, usually of seal, he will invite the other families of the settlement to visit. Etiquette requires that the visitors, when asked, will protest that they have no thought of eating, while their host apologises for the miserable carcase he has brought home – which is the cue for them all to tuck in and gorge themselves on the seal meat which is their staple diet. In those days the seal was, quite literally, the Eskimos' lifeline. The meat and blood were essential for food, the blubber for heat and light, the skin to make boots, coats, tents, kayak hulls (stitched with seal sinews) and the traces attaching the dogs to the sledges, the bones to tip their harpoons. It was a hard and hazardous life: many seal hunters would be drowned in their kayaks, and in a bad sealing season a whole settlement might die out. Occasionally a few might survive by eating the corpses of their family and neighbours.

In plentiful times, however, there was no one more hospitable than the Eskimo, as Gino and his party soon found out. When Lindsay first entered an igloo, by crawling through a narrow stone tunnel, he was struck by the muddle and mess. Chapman's powerful first impression was of 'the appalling mixed smell of rotten seal meat, urine, dogs and children'. Gino liked what he saw, was delighted to follow the natives in wearing only a loin-cloth in the warmth of their dwelling, and revelled in their attentions. He and the others had their clothes dried, boots patched, rifles cleaned. One woman made Gino a pair of dogskin socks.

The food they were given was monotonous but full of protein. 'After a week or so of living on seal meat, most of us lost all desire for civilised foods. You do not feel you want anything else,' Gino wrote at the end of the expedition, though his companions would probably have taken issue with that statement. Gino, nevertheless, made a point of saying how delicious was every part of the seal that his hosts fed him, including the eyes and the fermented liver (which a Danish explorer said was so sweet it reminded him of preserved cranberries). Chapman and Riley were quite partial to the brains and even the intestines of a seal, if not as enthusiastic about Eskimo gastronomy as Gino claimed to be (though even he was put off by the sight of Eskimo mothers eating the parasites that they picked out of their children's hair). At a dinner given by their Eskimo hosts before the expedition ended the following summer, and declared by Gino to be one of the best meals he had ever eaten, the menu included raw narwhal skin, walrus brains and putrescent guillemots.

Auks were the birds used for this dish, called *giviak*, in northern Greenland when Knud Rasmussen and Peter Freuchen were living and travelling with Eskimos near Thule during the early years of the century. The birds were stuffed inside a sealskin and left for the blubber to 'cure' the meat during the summer months. When Freuchen attended a *giviak* feast during the winter, the flesh was frozen but, as he described it in *Book of the Eskimos*, memorably delicious: 'You get feathers and bones in your mouth, of course, but you just spit them out. Frozen meat always has an enticing taste, and as it dissolves in the mouth you get the full aroma of the raw fermented bird. … If you happen to come across a fully developed egg inside a bird, it tastes like a dream. Or the liver, which is like green cheese.'

The Eskimos of east Greenland also wished to sample the white man's food – oatmeal, margarine, coffee – which Gino had neglected to bring with him. So he decided to sledge back to the base for some of their provisions and other equipment. It was a round trip of some forty miles, which his Eskimo hosts said would take him two days. Much to their surprise, he got there and back in eight hours. He was using the larger and faster breed of West Greenland dog (which Scott had acquired before the start of the expedition) on a single trace (compared with the Eskimos' fan method of harnessing); and he was hugely pleased with himself. He had always maintained that anything the Eskimos did he could do as well, if not better. They taught him how to hunt seals with a long harpoon, in open leads and at breathing-holes, and when they stalked the creatures with a rifle Gino was a better shot than most. He was impatient to learn the art of kayaking, but had to wait until spring for the kayaks to be specially made for himself and several others. The Eskimos' kayaks were built for men with a smaller and more supple frame, so flexible they could walk along on all fours without bending their knees. Gino's kayak was about eighteen feet long and fitted him 'as exactly as a pair of handmade shoes,' Jimmy Scott commented. And Gino became as skilful in handling it as an Eskimo. 'He could flip it over, roll it, make it get up and dance.'

Before spring came, Gino had to address the matter of relieving the man who was sitting alone in his tent 130 miles away on the ice cap. Courtauld's parents were getting understandably worried that three months had passed without anyone being sent up to relieve him. They were not to know how bad the winter weather had been; but Gino decided that Scott and Riley should leave base on 1 March and that Riley would relieve Courtauld at the ice-cap station. Gino said later that it was a mistake to send a relief party before the winter gales had abated and while the cold was still intense. But he did not admit his mistake in deciding to stay at the base rather than going to relieve Courtauld himself. Nor did he explain his equally bizarre decision to select three men (Lindsay was enlisted when Scott and Riley returned to base with a broken sledge), none of whom was a qualified surveyor/navigator. Yet when Scott's party returned without Courtauld, after six almost unendurable weeks of tramping through the white wilderness with nothing more than the latitude of their objective to guide them, Gino did what he should have done at the beginning of March. He organised a relief party with himself as leader, taking a time-signal set and the surveyor (Rymill) who had fixed the position of the ice-cap station the previous summer.

Having come to the door of the base hut at midnight, in his pyjamas, to hear from Scott that Courtauld was not with him, Gino immediately reassured his friend that he had done the right thing in coming back while there was still time to send another party to find the ice-cap station. Scott was dejected and miserable but Gino calmly asked his advice and restored some of his confidence.

Before leaving with Rymill and Chapman – and with a prayer book thoughtfully provided by Riley in case a funeral service might have to be held – Gino sent a message to the expedition committee in London. He reported the situation and his plans, ending with the words: 'There is always the possibility that Courtauld is not alive, or unwell, in which case the station is probably completely covered.' He must have known this would cause alarm bells to ring and search parties to be organised from England, but at least he would be out of touch on the ice cap. His departure was delayed by bad visibility for three days; they left on 21 April and rescued Courtauld two weeks later, on 5 May. During that time Gino was totally focused: with two of his best men he made good progress in the improving weather conditions, he decreed that the minimum time should be spent in their tent, and he led for most of the way, without looking back. He knew that they had to find the station; it was his responsibility to find Courtauld, alive or dead. Of course he was worried – he had even communicated his fears to the London committee – but he never shared his uncertainties with his two companions. One can only imagine his feelings as he spotted the frayed remains of a Union Jack, then skied over to the buried tent, saw no sign of life, no disturbance of the snow, and the handle of a spade protruding from a drift.

Having returned to England Gino fended off any questions about the length of time that Courtauld had been left alone. He was following the advice of one of his principal mentors, Admiral Sir William Goodenough, president of the RGS. The First World War admiral, now in his mid-sixties, who was described as 'a superb tactician', told Gino: 'If you are criticised, don't justify yourself. Say nothing, except that it was your decision.' In a revealing lecture which he gave to the RGS in December 1931, Gino was concerned rather to gloss over the dangers to Courtauld and go on the defensive. He said he had always known, and had told the members of the expedition, that it would probably be necessary to leave one man alone at the ice-cap station. (He had originally envisaged that only one man, relieved every few weeks, would stay at the station throughout the year.) The trappers in Labrador, he said, are often alone for eight or nine months at a time, 'travelling in a much more difficult kind of country than the Greenland ice cap. Nothing ever goes wrong with these men....' (He said the same thing, using the same words, in a lecture to the Alpine Club the following spring.) Was Gino suggesting that, without dogs or a sledge, Courtauld could have walked back to the coast?

He then went on to talk about Courtauld's five months of solitude in the middle of Greenland. There was never a problem or any cause for alarm: Courtauld had written to him (he must have sent a letter back with Chapman in December) to say that he had ample provisions until May but would like to be relieved before then if possible. Gino acknowledged his 'mistake' in sending Scott on to the ice cap at the beginning of March, but referred more than once to 'the prearranged time' for Courtauld's relief as being 1 May. He reached the ice-cap station, in his words, four days late, and 'walked over to fetch August' – as if he were picking him up at the end of a weekend. Gino found that he had plenty of food left (having been on short rations for two months), though his paraffin had almost run out because two tins had leaked. (In fact he had less than two gallons left by mid-March.) When Gino spoke of Courtauld's imprisonment under the snow, he said this occurred 'four weeks before we had reached him'. It was in fact six weeks and two days. 'Of course he could have cut out through the side of the house, but the snow would blow in, *so he decided to wait inside the house until 1 May when we were due to relieve him*' (my italics).

There was a certain economy with the truth here, and no hint of a crisis or doubt about Courtauld's wellbeing. It had all been prearranged, Gino claimed, and he was only four days late. This hardly squares with Courtauld's understanding of the planned relief schedule. Whether or not there was a letter written to Gino in those terms (Courtauld never mentioned that he had written a letter), his ice-cap diary records on 7 March: 'I reckon, unless something has gone wrong, the relief should arrive between the 15th and the end of the month.' On this assumption, 'I scaled my rations to last till then, leaving a small amount of the less palatable necessities.' Yet Gino wrote, in a dispatch to *The Times* after Courtauld's return to base, that he 'still had food enough left for another two months' – omitting to mention that his fuel had run out – and that everything had gone 'more or less according to plan'. But it had not been planned that Courtauld should stay there until the beginning of May. This was the date by which he had been promised he would be relieved if no one could get there any sooner. Scott recorded that when he returned to base without Courtauld in mid-April, Gino commented: 'Well, he still has food, so he should be all right if we can get there quickly.' There was a great deal of anxiety and it was not, therefore, the whole truth to say that 1 May was 'the prearranged time'.

If Gino's account of this episode, and elements of his leadership, were found wanting, his 'casualness to the point of fecklessness', employing Lindsay's words in relation to Gino's decision not to lead the March relief party, could have cost Courtauld his life again during their summer boat journey down the coast. Several others had said it was a crazy enterprise: the season was far advanced, the weather unpredictable, the boats vulnerable (their outboard motors were, employing Scott's word, 'pensionable') and the 600-mile stretch of coastline largely unknown and uninhabited. However, knowing Gino's luck, it was generally acknowledged that he was the one person who could make it. Percy Lemon made up the party of three for this seventh journey,* the last one undertaken by the expedition.

It was just the sort of journey which appealed to Gino, because they were taking only emergency rations and their lives would depend primarily on his kayaking skills and marksmanship to provide the food – seal meat, birds and fish – which they needed to survive. They had to wait until August for another outboard engine, and the two heavily laden, fifteen-foot open whale boats started out from Angmagssalik on 15 August, the last date on which Gino thought it reasonably safe to set off. Permission from the Danish government also delayed him, and was only granted on his assurance not only that all three could roll their kayaks like the natives (which Courtauld and Lemon certainly couldn't), but that they would not be taking any natives with them.

Before the end of the month they were held up for nine days by gales, a delay described by Lemon as 'very annoying and tedious'. They then spent a week at an Eskimo settlement, not because of bad weather but because Gino was enjoying himself. He wrote afterwards that the time was spent 'mapping the fjord and shooting birds for the

---

* An Australian explorer, Earl de Blonville, made a nearly disastrous attempt in 1986 to take kayaks down the same stretch of the south-east coast of Greenland (with a support ship named after John Rymill's widow) and recorded his experiences in a book entitled *Seventh Journey*.

rest of the journey'; but this could have been done in two days. There was every reason for him to hurry on: autumn storms were expected, the boats' engines were unreliable, and they had 350 miles to go without any habitation until they reached west Greenland. But Gino and Lemon were happy to linger with the Eskimos, while Courtauld became increasingly impatient to get on and get home. Gino had shot four seals in the first two days, then killed a 600-pounder. There was far more seal meat than they could take with them on the boats.

It has to be said that Gino's refusal to leave after two days, despite agreeing with Courtauld that they should push on, showed a culpable disregard for his and his companions' safety. Had they left five days earlier, they would have had a week of good weather before the rains and strong winds hit them and could have covered three-quarters of the distance to their destination. As it was, their journey from Umivik, which might have taken ten days, lasted a month, during which (see p. 40) sea and weather conditions were appalling. They were delayed by fog, wind and rain, the boats leaked, the engines broke down and Courtauld was exasperated by the other two talking of plans for wintering on the coast. 'Gino seems to want any excuse for staying and Lemon backs him up. I have said nothing yet, but my opinion is never consulted … . Why I ever said I would come on this journey I don't know.'

Possibly for the first time on one of his expeditions Gino, though in command, was not in control of the situation. He didn't understand boats or the workings of an engine, and so was helpless as Courtauld and Lemon struggled to repair a damaged hull or unblock a carburettor. Lemon kept losing his temper, Gino lost his temper with Lemon, which was most uncharacteristic, and later told Courtauld that he had never felt so low as when he thought they would be beaten by a stupid piece of machinery. His appearance was ruffled, angry, and Courtauld observed that even his usually sleek hair was unkempt. But they made it, through Prince Christian Sound, close to the southern tip of Greenland at Cape Farewell, with only a gallon of fuel left when they reached Nanortalik on the south-west coast. There they found sheep grazing on pasture, and Knud Rasmussen who had made the coastal journey from Angmagssalik a few days ahead of them, and in a more seaworthy and reliable boat. He said of Gino's trip, admiringly but with a note of criticism: 'A distinguished achievement… . I have seldom seen an expedition with so little equipment and would hardly have believed it possible to make such a journey at that time of year.'

After weeks of misery, uncertainty and acute discomfort, Gino sent a message to *The Times* from Julianehaab (now Qaqortoq) reporting their safe arrival 'after a pleasant journey'. He hoped to have news that Rymill and Hampton had reached Holsteinsborg (Sisimiut), further up the west coast, having crossed the ice cap from Angmagssalik. But there was none, and Gino knew he could not go home without them. So he set off up the coast with Courtauld, having sent two letters back with Lemon, who had to leave by the first boat to rejoin his regiment in England. To his sister Pam Gino wrote: 'I have been absolutely longing to see you. It is wretched, especially as there is absolutely nothing I can do to help Rymill and I am pretty certain he will turn up all right. However, as leader I can't leave.'

He also wrote to his father to ask that 'a complete suit – bowler hat, shoes, umbrella, etc is sent to the Hotel Angleterre, Copenhagen'. So when Gino and Courtauld, now reunited with Rymill and Hampton, reached Copenhagen, the leader could do a quick change from dishevelled explorer to dapper City gent before being welcomed by his Danish hosts, including an audience with the king. He was also welcomed by Pam, Scott, Riley – and Nanny Dennis, who came all the way from London to make sure 'he washed behind the ears'. Mollie wanted to come too, to greet her fiancé who was now something of a hero after his solitary confinement on the ice cap. Courtauld had written to advise her against it, especially as her presence would ensure for them both the publicity which he loathed, followed by what he called 'the dregs of success'. These remarkable young men, returning to 'civilisation' after more than a year, would have been horrified to think they might become celebrities. They were very modest, albeit quixotic, adventurers who preferred to stay in the shadows. Only Gino, with that streak of personal vanity, did not shun the limelight; indeed he told Courtauld to make sure Mollie stayed at home, because he feared that by coming to Copenhagen she might take some of the limelight from him. According to Mollie, Gino resented her and thought she would get in the way.

The chronicling of the Watkins boys' experiences in *The Times* ensured that Gino's return to London in mid-November did not pass unnoticed. Cheering news was in short supply, with the country just forced off the gold standard amid widespread pay cuts and a mutiny in the Royal Navy. Gino had only three weeks to prepare for the lecture he would give, reporting on the work of the expedition, to the RGS. On the same day, 12 December, when he was still only twenty-four, he went to Buckingham Palace, where he was given a glass of port before his audience with King George V, with whom he spent twenty minutes alone. He was much impressed by the king's detailed knowledge of the expedition.

Inevitably, after the various newspaper stories which had followed Courtauld's 'rescue' from his tomb on the ice cap, Gino's lecture was awaited with more than usual interest. It may have been because he was anticipating questions about leaving Courtauld on his own for five months in winter that he gave the not entirely satisfactory explanation of the circumstances. But it seemed to be generally accepted: when Gino sat down, Sir William Goodenough congratulated him on having 'placed yourself in the front rank of polar explorers'. One speaker compared him to Nansen (who had died a few weeks before the start of Gino's expedition), another said his achievements would have won the approval of Scott and Shackleton, and messages of good will were received from Stefansson and Rasmussen. James Wordie, who was present, expressed the wish 'that we may see him setting out again on another expedition as soon as possible'. And the Danish explorer, Lauge Koch, concluded:

> Take care of Mr Watkins and his companions…. Years are pass-
> ing rapidly, and it is only during a short period of one's life that
> one is able to carry on the work they have carried on. Employ
> them while they are young in spite of economic questions and
> other difficulties. Time is short. By this expedition England has
> once more inscribed its name in the history of polar exploration
> and maintained its grand traditions.

This was heady stuff: on that evening Gino's career and reputation reached their apogee. He had to decide whether to go north again, or south to explore the Antarctic. But the cruel truth was that his future was now behind him.

Before making any plans he had to confront a personal tragedy. Captain Percy Lemon, who had been the expedition's wireless opera-tor and had recently completed the coastal journey with Gino and Courtauld, tried to kill himself. He had swallowed hyposulphite (a chemical used for developing film), had been found unconscious at St Pancras Station in London, and was taken to a hospital in Marylebone. When he regained consciousness he asked for Gino. He recovered enough to be taken to his parents' house in Brighton, but died a few months later. At the RGS lecture the absence of three expedition members was noted. Two were abroad, and Lemon was said to be unwell, but it was 'not a very serious business'.

At the age of thirty-two, Lemon had been the old man of the party. He had been interned in Germany in 1914, later joined the Army and took an engineering degree at Cambridge, where he met Gino. Initially critical of Gino's style of leadership, he nevertheless came to admire and like him. He was the first to learn the local language and to take an Eskimo mistress (Arpika), with whom he spent almost a year. At the end of the expedition he was miserable to learn that she had been having an affair with Rasmussen. Having returned to the Army at Catterick, his unhappiness persisted, and he could think only of going back to Arpika in Greenland. Due to the winter weather, this would be impossible for at least six months. Suicide seemed the only solution to his woes. It was a tragedy made the more poignant because of the way Lemon had conducted himself in Greenland. In Scott's judgement, he had the best brain and 'for balanced thinking, general usefulness and stability, he was probably the strongest member of the party'.

Gino's inclination was to go back to the Arctic and travel by sledge round the coasts north of the Arctic Circle. But the Antarctic veterans – Wordie, Debenham, Priestley – advised him that he should go a for a greater prize: the crossing of the Antarctic, from the Weddell Sea to the Ross Sea, which Shackleton had attempted and failed to complete. For Gino the Antarctic option had two distinct drawbacks: there were no natives, and the hunting was not very challenging. But he was persuaded that he should follow in Shackleton's footsteps and solve the Last Riddle, as the press soon called it – whether the Antarctic was a continent or two vast islands.

Having obtained the approval of the RGS, Gino published his plans for a 1,500-mile Antarctic journey, taking a route, not via the South Pole, which had not been travelled before. He intended to take seven men and more than a hundred dogs, leaving England in September 1932 and returning two years later. The *Discovery*, the ship used by Captain Scott thirty years earlier, was available free of charter, but Gino estimated that its running costs would be such that he would need to raise £40,000 to finance the expedition. It was the beginning of 1932: the pound had been devalued by 30 per cent and a National government re-elected. This was not the time to be soliciting funds for a polar expedition, however noble the cause. Gino thought of taking a smaller ship, perhaps the *Quest*, and cutting his party to four men, with half the number of dogs. He could reduce his budget to little more than £10,000, but still no one, and no institutions, responded. While he was approaching people for money for his new expedition, he was also lecturing all over the country to pay off the debts of the last expedition. It was a dispiriting and tiring winter, relieved only slightly by a trip to Copenhagen at the beginning of March to receive the Hans Egede medal (Denmark's highest Arctic award) from Crown Prince Frederik. When he got back to England he knew that time was running out if he was to leave for the Antarctic, as he planned to do, in six months. If only he could get a commitment of, say, £5,000 from the Colonial Office (via the Discovery Committee, which was primarily concerned with the Falklands Islands Dependencies), there were one or two firms which had promised to help, either with a few hundred pounds or free equipment. But the weeks passed and no offers were forthcoming; the uncertainty and frustration continued. Fortunately, he did have something more positive to occupy his mind: he had fallen in love.

Margaret Graham and Gino had been seated next to one another at the dinner given by Stephen Courtauld in London to welcome the expedition home. A week later, on the last day of November, he wrote to her – 'Dear Miss Graham', 'Yours sincerely Gino Watkins' – to ask her out to lunch, and love was soon in the air. Margy, as he came to call her after their first date, was a member of the port family and two years older than Gino. Having been brought up in Scotland, she had spent a bit of time in Kenya, where she was one of those who could claim to have danced with the Prince of Wales; she was energetic and she enjoyed physical activity. Gino appreciated the fact that she had learnt to fly a Tiger Moth and drove a Lancia, which was a lot faster than his old Morris. (He soon exchanged it for a Lagonda.) As spring approached, Gino and Margy were spending as much time together as his efforts at fundraising and his lecturing engagements would allow. At weekends they might lunch at the Guards Boat Club at Maidenhead, go canoeing on the river, and then on to the Café de Paris at Bray.

At Easter they went walking in the Lake District, together with Gino's sister Pam and Jimmy Scott. They attended the London Ice Club Carnival (the club had been built by Stephen Courtauld in 1926), with Margy dressed colourfully as an Eskimo and pulling a sledge. Gino's heart was apparently still in the Arctic.

It was now the beginning of May, and Gino was being urged by Wordie to modify his Antarctic plans and undertake a survey of Graham Land (where Rymill would lead an expedition in two years' time). The Discovery Committee at last came up with the offer of a grant of around £3,500, but it was too little too late. Gino was turning his thoughts northwards again; his enthusiasm for going south had been little more than half-hearted for the past two months. Professor Debenham wrote a letter to *The Times*, in which he lauded Gino's plan to cross the Antarctic continent 'from one British possession to the other', while regretting that Americans would make the journey first unless the funds were made available for a British expedition. 'In another week or so it will be too late to secure a ship for the expedition, and their plans will have to be given up, their personnel dispersed and the chance lost for ever. ... In the past [Britain] has managed to send off its Franklins and Scotts, its Shackletons and Mawsons. It seems a thousand pities that for lack of a timely £10,000 their successors should be forced to give up their brave project.'

Debenham may have hoped that his letter would bring in the core funding, but nothing came of it, except for a few cheques of £5 and £10 and letters of moral encouragement. However, three days before the letter was published on 16 May, Gino had written to Margy to say that he was abandoning his Antarctic venture. He was aware of Debenham's letter and wished he hadn't written it. Debenham had also arranged what Gino described to Margy as 'a big conference of RGS people and Colonial Office people' to see Gino in Cambridge. It was a last-ditch attempt to raise the financial support which Gino needed to go south. But Gino had already decided he was not going to the Antarctic, and told Margy that the meeting in Cambridge was 'going to be a bit awkward but rather funny and it can't be helped'. He ended his letter by asking her, when they met later in the week for lunch: 'Could you possibly bring my umbrella with you?'

The question, already discussed in connection with John Rymill, presents itself again. How did Gino fail to obtain the funds for his

Antarctic expedition when, little more than eighteen months later, Rymill was able to raise twice the amount that Gino had set himself as a target? 'Private finance was more surely frozen than the ice of the Antarctic,' Jimmy Scott wrote in relation to Gino's project. But to say it was frustrated by the economic crisis is an insufficient answer. There was no sign of a thaw towards the end of 1933, when Rymill was putting forward his plans: the Great Depression was as deep as ever, and unemployment in Britain had increased to almost three million. When Gino was persuaded that Graham Land was a better option than a crossing of the continent, the offer of £3,500 emanating from the Discovery Committee, which was a branch of the Colonial Office, was only a third of the sum that Rymill got from the Colonial Office.

Gino had formed an Antarctic committee which included James Wordie, Frank Debenham and the president of the RGS, Sir William Goodenough, but one wonders whether he had the full backing of all of them. In writing to *The Times*, Debenham clearly supported Gino's cause, but was he an unqualified supporter of Gino? Debenham thought him unreliable, and a woman who worked for Debenham in Cambridge at this time recalled that 'when serious questions were asked about Gino, shadows would come over people's faces and the conversation would cease'. Was she referring, perhaps, to committee meetings with prospective sponsors? After Gino had died and Rymill had replaced him as leader for a year in Greenland, then put himself forward as a future leader of an Antarctic expedition, one is driven to the conclusion that he was considered, not least by his fellow Australian Debenham, to be a safer pair of hands.

Having dropped the Antarctic idea, Gino moved quickly to find a sponsor to send him back to Greenland in order to continue research to establish an Arctic air route. He was in touch with Imperial Airways, and at the end of May (as he told Margy in a letter on writing-paper headed British Antarctic Expedition 1932–33), he accepted an offer from Vilhjalmur Stefansson, acting for Pan-American Airways, of £500 to spend another year in Greenland.

It wasn't much, but Gino jumped at it, knowing that he could live like an Eskimo and was happy to do so: hunting for food, building an Eskimo house, travelling by sledge and kayak, using animal skins for their boats and clothes. Of the members of the previous expedition, several were kicking their heels in England, waiting for Gino's next move and willing to follow him anywhere he chose to go. Few of them were inclined to look for a job or stay in a country where there was 20 per cent unemployment. So Gino booked four places on the *Gertrud Rask*,* sailing from Copenhagen to east Greenland in mid-July, and chose three of his friends, Rymill, Chapman and Riley, to accompany him.

It was an impulsive decision, as if he felt he had to get away from the England of mass demonstrations, hunger marches, factories closing down and general economic misery. He and his family had very little money, prompting Gino to suggest, perhaps only half joking, that they should all move to the Arctic, plus Nanny, where he could house and feed them for free – on seal meat, blubber and berries which, he said, was 'one of the most satisfactory and pleasant diets I know'. It must have been bitterly disappointing, not to say wounding to his ego, that while he was being fêted as the greatest explorer/leader since Shackleton (the RGS awarded him its Founders Medal, the youngest man ever to receive it), he was now having to accept second best as leader of what was no more than a minor expedition. Five months' work towards his Antarctic venture had come to nothing. He never showed his disappointment – Chapman described him as 'cold as ice' – though Nanny, who had known him all his life, noticed that he became more introspective, which worried her.

But his affair with Margy was flourishing, to such an extent that in early June he asked her to marry him, and she accepted. It was not exactly a whirlwind romance, but they had known each other for little more than six months, and in another four weeks they would be parting for at least a year. One person who was less than pleased with the turn of events was Margy's mother. She had asked Gino about his prospects when the engaged couple went to stay with her for the weekend and was unimpressed by his lack of income and lack of any salaried job to support her daughter. As soon as he got back to London, Gino wrote to his future mother-in-law (her husband had been killed in the First World War) to put the best possible gloss on his financial future. He had, he admitted, only £50 a year of his own, but his father had promised him £150 a year when he married – 'provided everyone has

---

* Gertrud Rask was the wife of the eighteenth-century Greenland missionary, Hans Egede.

not gone bust, in which case he would not have it to give!' He estimated that on his return from Greenland he should be able to get a job paying £400–450 per year, possibly more if Pan-American were to offer him another job in connection with the Arctic air route. (He had had an offer from the Hudson's Bay Company to be an inspector, based in Winnipeg, for their northern stations, but he and Margy decided they would rather not live in Canada.) In addition he anticipated being able to sell a film of Greenland life to America and to earn a four-figure sum from lecturing. With his characteristic optimism, he reckoned he might make about £18,000 from his year in Greenland. 'On the other hand everything might go wrong. In that case I shall be left with my £50 a year plus £150 from my father plus £400 or £450 (which I ought to get for a job in England).'

'As you know,' he continued, 'I love Margy more than anyone in the world and I only want to do what is best for her. ... I do not want to do anything against your wishes or anything which would be bad for Margy, so that I leave it to you and Margy to decide what you think would be best.' It is, one might think, a rather endearing, if naïve and unrealistic letter from a young man with no money and not many prospects beyond being a hugely acclaimed Arctic explorer. Mrs Graham was so exasperated by what she read that she tore up the letter.* A formal announcement of Gino's and Margy's engagement soon followed, to the surprise of his friends who knew he was about to leave his fiancée for at least twelve months and of his siblings who didn't believe he would ever get married and settle down.

Gino now had about three weeks to prepare for his year-long absence on the remote east Greenland coast. Survey and meteorological instruments were lent by the Air Ministry and the RGS, some food and equipment was donated by a few companies, the RGS put up £200 and *The Times* £100 for press rights. The meagre total, with a few small donations, was less than £900 (£45,000 today). That sum had to cover the cost of getting to and from Greenland, the purchase of essential stores, petrol, dogs, sledges and at least some provisions for four men and the dogs for a year. They would have to do a lot of hunting and fishing, and build their house with earth and stones encasing a domed

* Margy rescued it, taped the torn pages together, and kept it, together with the letters which Gino wrote to her. They are now at the Scott Polar Research Institute in Cambridge.

tent. Fortunately Riley was able to save the expedition a lot of money by agreeing to lend his motor-boat *Stella Polaris*.

It is doubtful if Gino had many second thoughts about this expedition. He had discussed it at length with his father, who wrote: 'I do hope Gino has made a wise decision… . Even if we have decided wrongly, Graham Land is an appalling place and not the expedition he wanted, and he loves Greenland.' But would it be challenging enough for him this time? The seal-hunting would be fun, and he would develop his harpooning and kayaking skills. He planned to cross the ice cap the following spring to Godthaab (now Nuuk) on the west coast, and he intended to do the 500-mile sledge journey alone. It might be dangerous and frightening, which made it all the more appealing to him – so he wouldn't mention it to Margy. There was so little time to spend with her in London before the expedition left in early July.

During the past months one might have expected Gino to write the official account of the British Arctic Air Route Expedition. It is the customary practice for the leader to do this. He should have written the book, as he acknowledged in a brief introduction, but he hadn't found the time while he was making plans to go to the Antarctic. Martin Lindsay did not accept this explanation when he wrote years later that Gino 'couldn't be bothered' to do it. So the task fell to Chapman, who was working on the book (*Northern Lights*) until after they left to sail north again. (Scott, who was staying behind, made final corrections and read the proofs.) Gino always claimed that he found it very difficult to express himself on paper, and was surprised to receive an offer at the end of June, from a large publishing house, of £500 for a book on this second Greenland expedition.

So reluctant was he to say goodbye to Margy that he persuaded her to come as far as Copenhagen with him. The two young lovers met at Harwich on 11 July, together with Rymill, Chapman, Riley and Riley's father, and reached Copenhagen two days later. Chapman was completing his manuscript of *Northern Lights* during the voyage while Gino read it; then he and Margy had a last day to themselves in the Danish capital. That evening, after they had dined and danced, Gino returned alone to his hotel and wrote her two letters. The first one was posted the following day to Margy's mother's address in Buckinghamshire.

'You are absolutely the only thing in the world that matters to me. It is simply terrible to be going off like this, but it is obviously better to carry on the work I have been doing for the last five years (but with money as the object rather than scientific work as it has been up till now) rather than take the first job that offers itself in England. I feel certain I can make money out of this expedition, and then I can get the job on my return.' (Surprisingly, Gino left £979 when he died, worth more than £50,000 today.)

Was he trying to persuade himself, or Margy, that he was only in Greenland to make money for their married life together? And would she have believed him? She surely knew that he was there because he loved the self-sufficient, challenging life of the Arctic and would never be able to adapt to life in England. Pan-American Airways might not have been particularly pleased to know that he had no real interest in the 'scientific work' for which the company was sponsoring his year in Greenland. But the science had always taken second place with Gino to the exploration and the testing of himself and his physical skills.

He ended his letter by telling Margy: 'I don't know how I shall get on, as I hate being away from you even for a day. Look after yourself, my angel, and don't forget me!' Later that night, at 2.30 am, he wrote her another letter to wish her many happy returns (her birthday was on 5 August) and sent it to Oban care of Stephen Courtauld and his wife with whom she would be sailing in the Hebrides on their yacht *Virginia*. 'My darling, I don't believe I shall ever go through a complete hour during the whole year without thinking of you.... I hope you won't fall in love again with any of your former boy friends! .... All my love to you my precious, from your loving Gino.'

The next morning, 14 July, the expedition set sail in the *Gertrud Rask*, taking Margy and Riley's father as far as Elsinore. For three hours she and Gino sat together holding hands in the bows, until Margy had to leave in a pilot boat. 'She was wonderful but it was hell. I watched her boat glide away across the water until it was a speck in the distance and eventually was hidden by a pier.' The ship steamed on northwards, past Gothenburg, through the Skagerrak, round the southern coast of Norway and into the North Sea. Gino had always hated the sea, it was a rough voyage and the captain decided to shelter in the lee of the Shetlands. For the first time in three days it was not too rough for Gino to put pen to paper and write to Margy again:

It was simply awful saying goodbye to you. I really never thought
it was going to be half so bad. I simply could not speak at all to
say goodbye.... I sat up in the bows where you had been sitting
and read your letter. It was simply wonderful my darling and I
should think I have read it a hundred times since then....

My darling it was simply too sweet of you to come to Copenhagen – it made all the difference. It would have been horrible
saying goodbye on the platform in London. I have been thinking
of you ever since we left. Of your journey home, arriving in
London, seeing Nanny etc. Oh darling I wish I could be with you.

Two days later Gino wrote to Margy from Iceland, telling her his
feelings about going back to the Arctic. 'Normally I would be frightfully excited about it ... [but] I realise the only thing in the world that
matters is you and I am not looking forward to it a bit.'

The language of the time ('simply awful', 'simply too sweet') might
have come more naturally from a woman, but the letters reveal more
interestingly a man who is vulnerable, uncertain, in need of love as well
as conventionally and deeply in love himself. These were traits in Gino
– the man of decision, resilience and icy self-control – which had never
been shown before. In his next letter, written from Greenland – and still
using writing-paper headed British Antarctic Expedition 1932–33 – he
was telling Margy that he had been re-reading her last letter to him
'again and again, I think I know it absolutely by heart!'

For all his protestations to Margy, saying that he would much rather
be with her than spend another ten or twelve months in the Arctic, he
was also writing in his diary about 'the call of the North'. 'This is the
fourth time I have come to the Arctic. It is queer how it gets hold of
one... . In the last five years I have only spent about a total of two out of
the Arctic... . I suppose this is the last time that I shall be coming to the
Arctic.'

Why, one wonders, did he think it would his last expedition to the
Arctic? Was he still planning a major expedition to the Antarctic; or
was he really intent on settling down, with Margy as his wife, in
England or North America and earning his living? Or did he perhaps
envisage that he might keep answering 'the call of the North' by
remaining where he was, in the Arctic? He was clearly aware of the
financial imperatives for his future and wanted to reassure Margy – and

no doubt his future mother-in-law – of his determination to make money after the expedition was over. Having discussed with Margy the idea of her coming out to west Greenland the following summer to meet him (he was planning to sledge across the ice cap), Gino was now advising her, in more than one letter, not to come. He gave differing reasons – the discomfort of the journey in rough seas, the risk that they might fail to meet up, the expense ('it would be much better to have the money when I get back') – but then left the decision to her, saying he intended to reach Godthaab towards the end of May. To maintain her interest in the Arctic, whether or not she came out to meet him, he suggested she read *Hunters of the Great North* by Vilhjalmur Stefansson. In a subsequent letter he reiterated that it would be 'best if you did not come out'.

His reasons may have been those that he stated, but having thought about his plans he probably did not want to commit himself to be at a certain place by a certain date. He wrote to Scott to ask him to send his kayak (which had been lent to Margy) to Godthaab so that he could get to another port further down the west coast. He would be carrying meteorological records of the nine months spent at Lake Fjord which he wanted to send by ship as soon as possible to the expedition's sponsors, Pan-American Airways. Whether he would take them back to Europe himself, or whether he planned to continue in his kayak up or down the west coast, was not known.

The *Gertrud Rask* reached an almost ice-free Scoresby Sound, some 500 miles north of Gino's 1930–31 base, in the last week of July and, having unloaded stores for the settlement, arrived at Angmagssalik on 1 August. While Chapman, Riley and Rymill went to the old base to leave some equipment and stores that Gino would need for his crossing of the ice cap in spring, he chose to stay in Angmagssalik to renew old Eskimo friendships – and show off a photograph of his bride-to-be. The *Gertrud Rask* left Angmagssalik on 8 August and the next day dropped off the four men, together with the motor-boat *Stella Polaris*, at Lake Fjord, which would be their base for a year. The ship's captain was entrusted with a letter and a telegram from Gino to Margy, also a despatch to *The Times*, which would be sent from Copenhagen. The telegram – Gino's last communication to Margy – read, 'Just starting north all well heaps love darling Gino.' His article was published in *The Times* two weeks later, on 23 August, three days after his death.

Having discovered Lake Fjord (Tugtilik) two years earlier, Gino realised it would be an ideal place for a base on a trans-Greenland air route. Seaplanes could land on the lake in summer, and aeroplanes fitted with skis in winter. Unlike the previous base, Lake Fjord experienced very few gales, even in winter. A wind speed above 15 mph proved exceptional during the winter of 1932–33, and the absence of gales allowed the lake to freeze quickly. It was estimated that there were only ten days, during October 1932, from the time that the lake was suitable for seaplanes until the ice was strong enough to support heavy aircraft. During that time, and again during the spring thaw, a lake at Angmagssalik might make a suitable landing-ground. If one place were fog-bound, the chances were that the other, a hundred miles away, would be clear.

Gino's idea for two working airbases on the east coast was set out in his article for *The Times*. He also explained that, due to their lack of preserved food, they would have to start hunting and fishing at once. 'We shall hunt every day in our kayaks and hope to get a large quantity of seals and bears. ... It should take us about a month to lay in a supply of food sufficient to last for the year.' He went on to say that 'we shall be entirely cut off ... since we have no Eskimos with us and the nearest Eskimo encampment is about sixty miles north of here'. The picture he painted of isolation and self-sufficiency was not entirely true. The base was frequently visited by Eskimos, and the Danish explorer Captain Ejnar Mikkelsen brought supplies of food to Lake Fjord and built a wooden house in September to replace the tent in which Gino's party lived for the first few weeks.

Gino was keen to go hunting. In the past year he had been practising his kayaking skills on the Thames (often with Margy) and the Cam. He was now as expert as an Eskimo, both in manoeuvring and rolling his kayak and in harpooning and retrieving a seal. He also knew that a very high proportion of Angmagssalik Eskimos died while seal-hunting – drowned in rough seas, or as a result of a wave from a calving glacier or an attack by seal or walrus. The death rate among young male Eskimos was said to be the highest in the world; and a man lost while out hunting in his kayak was considered to have died a natural death. The Eskimos hunted in pairs, which was safer than going alone, but Gino reckoned that none of his companions could match his skill and that two kayaks would therefore reduce the chance of a successful stalk. In any event the other three men had their own tasks: surveying, photography and meteorological observation. So Gino hunted alone, confident in his abilities while at the same time aware of the risks he was taking and enjoying the sensation of being frightened by what he considered the most exciting sport in the world. His first fright came on the third day out in his kayak. He had already brought home a couple of fjord seals, straining his right wrist in the process, and on 14 August he harpooned a seal very close to a glacier which he knew was in danger of calving.

> Luckily it was almost dead and I towed it out of the danger zone. Then I had a very narrow escape. I got out on an ice floe with my kayak and started to blow up the seal [to make it float when being towed behind the kayak]. I was about twenty yards from the cliffs and half a mile from the glacier. Suddenly a large piece broke off the glacier. I knew what would happen and seized a piece of line and fastened it to my kayak. Suddenly the wave reached me and the floe was carried against the cliffs and broken up. I clung on to a ledge. My kayak was turned over and all the hunting gear carried away. Luckily I managed to collect everything. On the way home the ice started to close in but I got through all right.

Even from his understated description, one can imagine it must have been a pretty terrifying experience. But Gino was not deterred. Over the next five days he went hunting again three times but had no luck. There was too much ice in the fjord, and when he shot one seal he then missed it with his harpoon and it sank. On the evening of 19 August the four men were joined for supper in their tent by two Eskimos who were hunting in the fjord. Records were played on the gramophone and Gino talked of his next expedition – to the Antarctic, by way of Mount Everest, which they would attempt to climb first. Then all of them tried to persuade Gino not to continue hunting alone in his kayak. Chapman and Riley may have recalled the letters they had written to Margy a month earlier, as the *Gertrud Rask* was heading towards the Greenland coast. 'We will look after Gino – not that he needs it very much – and see that he doesn't go through the ice or anything,' Chapman wrote. Riley assured her, 'We will do our best to send him safe back to you.'

As Gino put another record on the gramophone, the two Eskimos told him they never hunted without a companion; one of them had been kayaking for twenty-five years. Gino listened but said that food was needed and that he must go after it. When they advised him at least to avoid going under the face of the glacier, which ended abruptly in a ragged perpendicular wall of blue ice a hundred feet high, he replied that it was the best place to find seals.

The next morning Chapman was due to go with Gino and from his own kayak film him while he stalked and harpooned a seal. But the day was overcast, the light was poor, and Gino said he would go alone while Rymill and Chapman did some surveying in the fjord from the motor-boat. At about eight o'clock Gino began paddling swiftly and smoothly the mile and a half to that part of the fjord, beneath the tongue of the glacier, where he had had a narrow escape a few days before. He was never seen again. In the early afternoon Rymill and Chapman saw from the boat what appeared to be an empty kayak floating half a mile from the northern shore. Having confirmed this, and recovered the paddle a hundred yards from the kayak, they shouted for Gino and searched the area for an hour, to no avail. They found a pair of trousers and a kayak belt lying on a small ice floe, less than two hundred yards from the wall of the glacier. They became increasingly, then desperately, worried, but told themselves that he must have got ashore and walked back to the base. They returned to the base camp, with Gino's kayak on board, to find only Riley and an Eskimo there. Further searches were made on foot until midnight, when the northern lights appeared, filling the sky with an awesome green light, quivering and waving in vertical ribbons, as if announcing Gino's entry into Valhalla. His companions continued to look for him the next day; it took some time for the awful tragedy to sink in. 'Gino was dead. We could not believe it. He seemed somehow invulnerable,' Chapman wrote. Gino used to say that a man should have achieved everything he wanted in life by the time he was twenty-five. He lived a little less than seven months beyond his twenty-fifth birthday.

From what Rymill and Chapman had found in the fjord, it was possible to guess what might have happened, though no further evidence emerged. Many Eskimo hunting accidents result from an attack by a bladder-nosed seal, particularly dangerous when wounded, which can even take a chunk out of a kayak's skin. Gino's kayak was undamaged and his harpoon was still in place. His rifle was missing, suggesting that he may have overturned while in the act of shooting and lost his paddle. Clearly he must, for whatever reason, have got himself out of his kayak and on to the floe – perhaps in order to get a better shot or because his rifle had jammed or because the white cotton screen (which imitated a piece of ice and which he hid behind when stalking a seal) had become dislodged. The glacier may then have dumped another huge piece of ice into the water, as had happened the week before, but this time Gino failed to attach a line to the kayak before the wave created by the calving glacier had reached his floe and taken the kayak out of his reach.

Since his trousers and kayak belt were wet when found, it is reasonable to assume either that he was thrown into the water by the force of the wave or that he jumped in after the kayak, failed to reach it and so removed the encumbrances of his baggy trousers and belt before swimming desperately after it. The kayak was almost full of water when Rymill and Chapman retrieved it, indicating that Gino may have reached it and was struggling to heave himself into the cockpit when, overcome by exhaustion, cramp and hypothermia in the icy water – it was a few degrees below freezing-point – he could do no more. He was wearing only a shirt, an anorak and a pair of socks. His fingers, numbed by the cold, released his hold on the kayak and he slid down into the dark waters of the fjord.

He could never have swum from the floe to the shore, which was half a mile away. He could have stayed on the floe until the motor-boat found him – the arrangement was that Rymill and Chapman would come to collect him and his kayak in the afternoon. But that may have been a no less dangerous option because he was so close to the ice cliff that he could have been thrown into the water by the wave effect of more ice falling into the water. In his subsequent report to *The Times*, published in early October, Chapman wrote, 'we knew he expected us there and were surprised he had not waited', but added, no doubt correctly, that Gino was not the sort of person to sit and wait to be rescued. 'We rather think that natural pride made him try to recover his kayak, since it would be so ignominious to be found stranded on a lump of ice.' In an earlier article, published ten days after the event on 1 September and carrying the sub-heading 'Warning Disregarded', Chapman entered a more direct criticism of his leader: 'As usual, disregarding the expedition's and Eskimos' urgent advice, Watkins hunted alone.' By this time the obituaries and tributes had already been written and published.

A message was received by the RGS from King George V: 'It is with sincere regret that the King has heard of the tragic death of Mr Watkins ... the loss of one who at such an early age had already attained such a distinguished position among the explorers of this country.' Stanley Baldwin wrote of Gino as 'a man – a boy, I was going to say – whom I had the pleasure of knowing. If he had lived he might have ranked, and in the opinion of men qualified to judge would have ranked, among the greatest of polar explorers.'

Gino's loss was felt even more keenly in Denmark. The Danish Minister in London wrote that the whole country was mourning his death. 'Why should such a brilliant youth be recalled in the bloom of his years? He stood for me as a representative of the best that there exists in English youth: energy, strong will and sportsmanship.' Knud Rasmussen, who was in Julianehaab when the news reached him, sent a telegram to the RGS: 'England has lost a prominent explorer who still had many big tasks waiting for him and Denmark has lost a good friend who always pleaded the cause of the Greenlanders with the greatest understanding.'

The Times's obituary referred to a career 'already as full of achievement as it was of promise', and was followed by a remarkable appreciation from Dr H. R. Mill, vice-president of the RGS, a friend of Captain Scott and both mentor and biographer of Shackleton. Wishing he had the power to express the emotion which inspired Milton's poem 'Lycidas' and Tennyson's 'In Memoriam', Mill wrote:

> I have known, I may say, all the polar explorers of the last half-century, but no one can stand beside young Watkins, save the young Fridtjof Nansen as I met him first on his return from the first crossing of Greenland 44 years ago. Both had the charm of a winning personality; both had the clearness of vision to plan great and new ventures and the firmness of mind to carry them through despite all the buffeting of fate... . Watkins was loved by his comrades, with whom he generously shared the credit for their joint achievements, and he drew the affection of older men in a way I had never seen equalled.

One of those men, Ashby Lowndes, who was twice Gino's age and was with him on the Edge Island expedition in 1927, paid tribute to Gino's 'remarkable qualities of leadership'. August Courtauld also added his appreciation of Gino in *The Times*.

> We who knew Watkins have lost a leader whom we would have followed anywhere. Those who have travelled with him and watched his work will know that England has lost a man who should rank among the great masters of his craft. He could plan with care and execute with audacity, and could not only lead men by the force of his personality but with his charm inspire them to do more than ever they knew was in them.

Gino's mentor, Admiral Sir William Goodenough, president of the RGS, not only wrote to *The Times* of 'his spirit of adventure, his indomitable resolution, his sincerity of mind, his directness of purpose, his originality of ideas', but also corresponded with Margy over the next three months, in one letter advising her of the therapeutic value of voluntary work. He was concerned to set her mind at rest over criticism of Gino: that he should not have let Courtauld stay alone at the ice-cap station, and that he should not have endangered his life by hunting alone for seals. Margy was particularly upset at Chapman having implied in *The Times* that Gino's death resulted from his having ignored warnings and advice from his companions and from Eskimos. Having asked Rymill about the dangers of hunting alone when he returned from Greenland in 1933, the secretary of the RGS, Arthur Hinks, wrote to Margy: 'Rymill admits that it is a thing you condemn in theory and carry out in practice. After the accident he and Chapman felt for a time that they ought to keep together, but very soon found it impossible... .' (having lost a quarter of their manpower). 'I have received a very firm impression from Rymill that the experience of the year confirms the soundness of Gino's plans.' Gino's death, he said, 'was a lamentable accident, but a pure accident, and due to no error of judgement'. Not everyone would have agreed with his comment, but Margy may have been reassured.

Over the weeks and months after Gino's death Margy must have wondered whether they would ever have married had he lived. She had his letters, and all the memories of their intense eight-month relationship, but she knew that neither Gino's family nor his fellow explorers really believed he would marry – and certainly not in the foreseeable future. Margy had been very hurt when Chapman told her, just before the start of the expedition, that Gino did not take his engagement seriously. Chapman apologised in a letter to her, saying, 'I didn't mean it that way at all,' but it would have given her pause. She took on the responsibility of organising a memorial service for Gino in London, held at St Michael's in Chester Square (the Watkins family address when he left for Greenland) on 7 November. A trust fund in Gino's name to help young explorers was set up at the end of 1932, to which £1,600 (£85,000 now) was contributed in the first year, £320 (£17,000) of it from members of his Greenland expeditions. Another, much smaller, fund with similar objectives was established at Gino's old school, Lancing College. As Cambridge University Air Squadron's first applicant when it was formed in 1925, a memorial to Gino was unveiled in 1933. And it was fitting that after the war a British European Airways Viscount aircraft, which once flew the Queen and the Duke of Edinburgh home from a state visit, was named 'Gino Watkins'.

It was many years later that visitors to east Greenland heard rumours about Gino's death from Eskimos at Angmagssalik. Some of those who remembered Gino and his companions and their two expeditions told not only of the baby sired by Chapman but of another baby, born to Gino's mistress Tina, who had his blond hair. During the week that he spent at Angmagssalik at the beginning of August 1932, Gino 'stayed with the Eskimos all the time', as he wrote in his diary. What he did not record, according to the local Eskimos' account, was that while Gino was playing with his baby in the near darkness of Tina's hut he inadvertently trod on it. The baby was so badly injured that it died shortly afterwards. So devastated was Gino, the story went, that he took his own life two weeks later by throwing himself into the icy waters of Lake Fjord.

In those days suicide among the Eskimos was not uncommon. It often resulted from depression brought on by a bad season's hunting and a failure to provide for the family, or sickness or some great sorrow. There was understanding rather than disgrace if you ended your own life. During his years in Greenland Peter Freuchen, writing in his *Book of the Eskimos*, learnt that 'when, as they express it, "life is heavier than death", then no man hesitates to make an end of his torment and cross into the distant land'. Many Eskimos of the east coast believed that Gino must have found life heavier than death after what happened to his child and had decided 'to make an end of his torment'.

The possibility is worth considering, if only because of the mental instability in Gino's family. His sister Pam suffered from depression for most of her life, his mother had committed suicide four years earlier, and his younger brother killed himself in the 1960s. However, even if the story about his child is true, the idea that Gino took his own life by drowning does not really make sense. He was clearly in love with Margy, he thought of her every day, he said he wanted to make money for their future together, and he was as leader of the expedition responsible for his three companions. But it is hard to reconcile this responsibility with his recklessness, his irresponsibility not only in hunting alone, which at times may have been unavoidable, but in going to what he knew to be the most dangerous part of the fjord. After the fright he had given himself a few days before, under the face of the calving glacier, he seemed to be drawn irresistibly back to the danger zone, almost as if he had a death wish.

His self-confidence helped to make him a brilliant leader of men, who were inspired by him and said they would follow him anywhere. But he was too confident of himself, believing himself to be invulnerable. Two nights before his death, according to Chapman, Gino said that a man can get and do anything he wants provided he sets about it in the right way. He went on to say that he had no morals or scruples about anything. It may be that he believed in the first half of that statement and then made the second comment in order to shock his friends. Several of his fellow explorers said that no one ever really knew him; he always kept his feelings under tight control. Scott said that after spending nine months with Gino in Labrador he knew him only to a limited extent, and that when they came back to England 'he was more or less a stranger'. In Chapman's words, 'he dwelt apart and seemed not to be ruled by the ordinary laws'.

His charm seemed to seduce almost everyone, but perhaps only Margy and Nanny Dennis were able to see below the handsome, confident surface. Margy knew that he had a vulnerable side, that he needed love and affection, while Nanny, who had known him and the Watkins family better than anyone, and had kept the family together through difficult times, must have been aware of a depressive trait in his personality. In the spring of 1932 Gino successfully hid his bitter disappointment at failing to raise funds for his Antarctic venture from everyone except these two women. He had the consolation of Margy's love and understanding, but Nanny knew how it was affecting him. She saw him when she brought his cup of Ovaltine at night and tea in the morning, and he confided in her. So when he went back to Greenland, only two months after he had been compelled to give up on the Antarctic, Nanny's opinion that he would never come back was probably a more informed view of Gino's intentions than anyone else's. It was shared by Scott and thus probably also by Gino's sister Pam.

If this was correct one can only guess at what Gino intended. If he was going to end his life, it was surely more likely that he would complete the year's work at Lake Fjord, sledge across the ice cap with the meteorological information and survey reports which he would despatch to Pan-American Airways – and then? He might have kayaked down the south-west coast and back to the east coast, following his boat journey of 1931 in reverse. He might have gone back to Angmagssalik and continued to hunt and live as an Eskimo. And he might have left his bones in the sea or on the ice cap. Whatever might have been, and however tragic his death at such a young age, he was not the sort of person who was going to make old bones. He had largely fulfilled the extraordinary promise he had showed when he led his first expedition to Edge Island at the age of twenty. And he had in effect achieved his stated ambition, to have done everything he wanted in life by the age of twenty-five – but for a crossing of the Antarctic, which did not call him with the same sense of urgency as did the North.

With the exception of Scott, the Watkins boys who were left behind followed their leader's example and went back to the ice and the mountains. Lindsay led one of the longest self-supported sledge journeys ever undertaken; Courtauld was the first to climb the highest mountain in Greenland, which Gino had found and photographed from the air; Chapman made the first ascent of one of the highest mountains of the Himalayas; Rymill led a three-year expedition in the Antarctic, together with Riley and three other old Greenland hands, one of whom (Stephenson) said that he went because Gino couldn't. Scott married Gino's sister and put his polar experiences into print.

Margy travelled widely after Gino's death, to Florence, Austria, Egypt, Lebanon, then married an airman, Flight-Lieutenant (later Air

Marshal Sir Humphrey) Edwardes-Jones in 1935. They lived in Sussex after the war, where she became somewhat reclusive, also anorexic. She had lost the energy of her youth, was dominated by her husband and was never really happy again. She didn't want to talk about her eight months with Gino, nor about the circumstances of his death. But she kept the press cuttings, and his revealing letters.

Three months after Gino had drowned, Rymill made a cross with some beams left over from the hut which they had built. Chapman carved an inscription on it – 'Gino Watkins aged 25, drowned in this fjord 20th August 1932. RIP' – and they towed it to the headland between the two branches of Lake Fjord, looking out to sea past the pyramid rock which they called Ailsa. While Riley read the burial service, some lines from Shakespeare came into Chapman's mind:

> Fear no more the heat o' the sun,
> Nor the furious winter's rages;
> Thou thy worldly task hast done,
> Home art gone and ta'en thy wages.
> Golden lads and girls all must,
> As chimney-sweepers, come to dust.

Almost eighty years on, Lake Fjord remains a place of pilgrimage for kayakers, from Europe and as far away as Australia and New Zealand. In 2004 three Englishmen kayaked up the coast from Angmagssalik and described their 'very strange feeling' as they paddled into the fjord.

We had all read so much about it; to be there now was a very emotional experience. We paddle under the glacier in the northern branch to the place we estimate Gino died and sit for a while contemplating the events which brought us here.

After a while we leave the glacier and retrace our route a little to look for the memorial cross on the headland. The cross had come down over years of winter storms, so we found a good spot to wedge it into and built a cairn round its base. It should now be good for many years to come.

This was a metal cross, erected to replace the deteriorating wooden one by a British Schools Exploring Society Expedition in 1982, fifty years after Gino's death. A brief ceremony was held, attended by two surviving members of Gino's 1930 expedition. A New Zealand kayaker, Paul Caffyn, visited the site in 2007 to pay homage to the man who, he said, 'was largely responsible for introducing the skill of rolling skinny kayaks to the Western world'. He and his companion paddled their kayaks to the foot of the glacier which had probably caused Gino's death and, with plastic glasses of New Zealand whisky and bits of ice taken from a small floe, drank a toast to his memory.

Select Bibliography

Apollonio, Spencer: *Lands That Hold One Spellbound* (Calgary University Press, 2008)

Barker, Ralph: *One Man's Jungle* (Chatto & Windus, 1975)

Bechervaise, John: *Arctic and Antarctic* (Bluntisham, 1995)

Butler, Mollie: *August and Rab* (Weidenfeld & Nicolson, 1987)

Chapman, F. Spencer: *Northern Lights* (Chatto & Windus, 1932)
  Watkins' Last Expedition (Chatto & Windus, 1934)
  Living Dangerously (Chatto & Windus, 1953)

Courtauld, Augustine: *From the Ends of the Earth* (Oxford University Press, 1958)
  Man the Ropes (Hodder & Stoughton, 1957)

Croft, Andrew: *A Talent for Adventure* (SPA, 1991)

Francis, Gavin: *True North* (Polygon, 2008)

Freuchen, Peter: *Book of the Eskimos* (Fawcett, 1961)

Howarth, David: *Heroes of Nowadays* (Collins, 1957)

Kirwan, L.P.: *The White Road* (Hollis & Carter, 1959)

Lindsay, Martin: *Those Greenland Days* (William Blackwood, 1932)
  Three Got Through (Falcon Press, 1946)
  The Epic of Captain Scott (Heinemann, 1933, 1980)

Ridgway, John: *Gino Watkins* (Oxford University Press, 1974)

Riley, J. P.: *From Pole to Pole* (1989)

Scott, J. M.: *Gino Watkins* (Hodder & Stoughton, 1935)
  Portrait of an Ice Cap (Chatto & Windus, 1953)
  The Private Life of Polar Exploration (William Blackwood, 1982)

Scott, Jeremy: *Dancing on Ice* (Old Street, 2008)

Wollaston, Nicholas: *The Man on the Ice Cap* (Constable, 1980)

Index

The summarised narrative of the expeditions included in pp. 11–14
is not indexed

151; Labrador to be next destination, Jimmy Scott to be companion, 151–2, 153; mother and, later, brother Tony commit suicide, 152–3; and Nanny Dennis, 153–4; and sister Pam, 154; speculation over bisexuality, 154–5; and Labrador with Scott, 155–8; meeting trappers, Indians and Eskimos, 155; two months mapping rivers, 157; dogs expendable, 157–8; ruthless realism,158–9; political views, 159; and commercial flying, 159–60; first expedition to Greenland, 160–74; hunting for food, and diet, 162–3; design of tents, 163; and Stephen Courtauld's financial backing, 164; and kayaking, 169,172; and questions about August Courtauld's isolation, 170–2; unnecessary risks on three-man boat journey down unmapped coast, 172–4; return to London and audience with King George V, 174–5; lecture at RGS, 175; congratulations from Goodenough, Wordie and Koch, goodwill messages from Stefansson and Rasmussen, 175; and Lemon's attempted suicide, 175–6; advised to try a crossing of the Antarctic, 176; publishes his plans, 176–7; difficulty in obtaining finance, 177, 179; awarded Denmark's Hans Egede medal, 177; increasingly involved with Margy Graham, 177–85; abandons Antarctic venture, 178; appeal of living like an Eskimo, 179; RGS Founders Medal, 180; second Greenland expedition sets sail, 183; keen to go hunting in kayak, 186–7; narrow escape, 187; advice from Eskimos, 187–8; his disappearance, 188–9; King George V's regret, 190; testimonials, 190–1; trust funds in his name to help young explorers, 192; local rumours about Tina's child and Gino, 192; a death wish?, 193–4; Scott and Chapman on, 193; the Watkins Boys' subsequent adventures, 194; memorial cross, 195–6

Watkins, Pam, later Scott, sister of preceding, 9, 75, marries Jimmy Scott, subsequent divorce, 113–15; 117, and Nanny Dennis, 153 –4; 174, 178; depressive, 193

Watkins memorial cross, 10, 76, 195–6

Watkins Mountains, 13, 28, 43

Wegener, Professor Alfred, 27, 163

Wild, Frank, accompanies Shackleton on 'farthest south' expedition of 1908–09, 142

Wilkins, Sir Hubert, 96

Wingate, Orde, 29

Wordie, Sir James, with Shackleton on *Endurance* expedition 1914–16, two expeditions to East Greenland coast in the 1920s, 16; 29, 30, 59, 65, 147, 149; praise for Gino's conduct of Edge Island expedition, 151; and first Greenland expedition, 175; urges Gino to modify Antarctic plans in favour of a survey of Graham Land, 178; 179

Worsley, Frank, skipper of Shackleton's *Endurance*, 142n

Young, Geoffrey Winthrop, 120